LOOKING FOR LAFORGUE

Looking for Laforgue

an informal biography
by DAVID ARKELL

CARCANET PRESS
MANCHESTER

1979

SBN 85635 285 3

First published in 1979 by
Carcanet New Press Limited
330 Corn Exchange Buildings
Manchester M4 3BG

The publisher acknowledges the financial assistance of
the Arts Council of Great Britain.

Printed in Great Britain by offset lithography by
Billing & Sons Ltd, Guildford, London and Worcester

PREFACE

MY first introduction to Laforgue was at the Atelier Theatre, Paris, in April 1939. With my friend Vera Volkova, a Russian dancer who was studying with Mme Egorova in the rue La Rochefoucauld, I had gone to see a performance of Laforgue's *Hamlet* with Jean-Louis Barrault in the title role. I remember that Vera was especially impressed with the way Barrault looked and moved, but I think it fair to say that the words washed over us both, leaving little trace. *Hamlet* is difficult enough to absorb from the printed page; spoken at speed, it was too much for our concentration and our French. But afterwards we sat next to Barrault and his friends at a café in the Place Dancourt, and shamelessly eavesdropped on all they said.

The next time I met Laforgue was the following year in a house by the sea in Brittany. Gauguin's monkey was reputed to be buried in one of the garden urns, but I didn't bother to investigate. With a friend I had fled Paris by bicycle, and we were just congratulating ourselves on having outwitted the stupid Germans when a row of green helmets flashed by the other side of the hedge, followed by another and another. In the library I happened on a book of poems by Laforgue and found solace in what then seemed the light-hearted philosophy of Ariel himself. Only later did I discover what Ezra Pound has called the 'deeps in him'.

My third encounter with Laforgue was after the war when I became involved in a controversy about his English wife, the mysterious Leah Lee. At that time her identity was unknown, but various things were being conjectured about her which I instinctively felt to be untrue. Gallantly I entered the lists on her behalf and was able to establish her true identity (with photograph) in the *Times Literary Supplement* of 10 June 1965.

This article drew interesting letters from Mr Peter Quennell and Mrs Valerie Eliot—it turned out that Laforgue and Eliot had been married, at an interval of seventy years, in the same London church —and eventually led to my most conclusive encounter of all.

For then it was that I met the noble quatuor of Frenchmen who are engaged, against all the odds, in the brave venture of publishing everything that Laforgue ever wrote. They are: Pierre-Olivier Walzer, Daniel Grojnowski, Pascal Pia and Jean-Louis Debauve.

With these four musketeers of French criticism I have exchanged several hundred letters and passed many enjoyable evenings. They were my true introduction to Laforgue.

I have particular pleasure in thanking Jean-Louis Debauve for his great generosity in placing at my disposal valuable unpublished material discovered only recently. In many cases his finds are linked with the names of Mme Elisabeth van Rysselberghe and Mme de Mazières (the former the daughter of a most Laforguian family, the latter a niece of Laforgue himself) and to these two ladies I would also express my gratitude.

My thanks, also, to Mmes: Paule Jean-Aubry, Isabelle de Wyzewa, Clara Candiani, Charlotte Countess von Klinckowstroem, Marie-Jeanne Durry, Margot Fuss, Anne Holmes, Joanne L'Heureux and Anneliese Botond; and to MM: François Chapon, of the Bibliothèque Littéraire Jacques Doucet, Paris; Rodney G. Dennis, Curator of Manuscripts, The Houghton Library, Harvard; William Jay Smith; Warren Ramsey; Marc Loliée; Michael Collie; Pierre Reboul; Léon Guichard; James Hiddleston; Martin Turnell; Denys Sutton; Anthony Atmore; the Rev. Clive Warwick Lee; the Library of Congress, Washington; the Bibliothèque Nationale, Paris; the British Library, London; as well as (not least) the West and East German Archives.

DAVID ARKELL

CONTENTS

Acknowledgements to Mme Elisabeth van Rysselberghe and M. Jean-Louis Debauve for the remarkable unpublished drawings by Jules Laforgue on the cover (both front and back) as well as on pages 76-7.

We thank the Bibliothèque Littéraire Jacques Doucet, Mme van Rysselberghe, William Jay Smith and Jean-Louis Debauve for further unpublished drawings by Laforgue.

For permission to print the hitherto unpublished family portraits on Plate 1 (b and c) and Plate 2 (a and b) we are indebted to Mme de Mazières and Jean-Louis Debauve.

Acknowledgements are also due to the following: Anthony Atmore, Plate 16 (a); *Apollo* Magazine, Plate 11 (a); Bibliothèque Nationale, Paris, p. 137; Marvyn Carton, p. 190; Jean-Louis Debauve, Plate 1 (a), Plate 2 (c), Plate 11 (b), pp. 157, 159, 161, 224 (a); Mme Elgar Duval, Plate 14 (a); Mary Evans Picture Library, endpapers; Marc Loliée, p. 175; Radio Times Hulton Picture Library, Plate 5 (a and b), Plate 6, Plate 8, Plate 13 (a and b); Bertram Ratcliffe, Plate 10; Roger-Viollet, Plate 12; Ullstein Bilderdienst, Plate 7, Plate 9, Plate 11 (c), p. 166.

PHOTOGRAPHIC SECTION

Part 1:
GROWING UP

CHAPTER 1
Montevideo and Tarbes
(1860-1876)

JULES LAFORGUE was born in a flat overlooking the main square of Montevideo on 16 August 1860, the second son of a young French couple, Charles and Pauline, who had come separately to Uruguay as children.

Charles had set up as a freelance teacher and Pauline had been one of his first pupils. Immediately after the marriage he started a proper school in the calle Rinçon, but it failed and he became a clerk in the Duplessis Bank, calle Cerrito, where he prospered exceedingly. He was a serious young man who read Latin for relaxation and had an inordinate admiration for Jean-Jacques Rousseau. It was natural, therefore, that his first son should be called Emile after Rousseau, and the second one Jules in homage to Caesar. He wore an artificial hand following a hunting accident, and this is perhaps the most mysterious thing about him, since hunting in his case seems so out of character.

For some time there was doubt about the exact date of Jules Laforgue's birthday, and only recently the reason came to light in his father's newly discovered diary.[1] Under the heading of 24 August 1860 he wrote:

> I took my child, whom we are calling Jules, to the consul for registration. I lied when declaring he was born the day before yesterday. We'd been told they wouldn't register him if we hadn't applied within the regulation three days. I think it was all nonsense. But it's done now.

So Laforgue's birthdate is often given, even in articles by his intimate friends, as the 22nd instead of the 16th August. But the father's diary is interesting for other reasons. To Jules in later life his father seemed unbending and harsh and, because of his timidity, difficult to communicate with. Yet, reading the father's diary, one notes many resemblances to the son, such as transparent honesty and a naive spontaneity. Indeed, if Jules ever saw this diary it must have been a revelation to him. The comedy of the generation-gap is so much in evidence here that the diary is worth quoting fairly fully. Charles was twenty-three at the time and his Pauline eighteen.

He had no prospects and hardly even a job. He was giving private lessons to three pupils including his wife-to-be; but his prospective father-in-law M. Lacolley seems to have taken a fancy to him, seeing him as a serious young man, which he certainly was. Mme Lacolley, on the other hand—she was Pauline's stepmother, M. Lacolley's second wife—is distinctly less enthusiastic. As for Pauline herself, she is absolutely determined to have him. An irony of the later pages is that the first cloud on the horizon is the arrival of Jules himself. But when the diary begins, just before Carnival Week 1857, Charles is still starry-eyed:

19 Feb: Pauline reproaches me for not answering yesterday's letter.

20 Feb: I slip a note to Pauline which says, 'Will you be mine?' Her mother invites me to dine with them on Monday, second day of the Carnival. I accept.

21 Feb: I threaten Pauline not to come to the dinner. She says, 'If you don't come, I won't love you.' I try to make her jealous by talking of my other two pupils. It isn't difficult. I do it for the pleasure of being able to say, 'Never fear, Pauline, it's you I love.'

23 Feb: Today is the happiest day of my life. I spend the afternoon with Pauline. I dine at the same table with her, opposite her. How lovely, natural, innocent and kind she is! I do my best to make a good impression.

24 Feb: I try to go out but get soaked. Everything happens at Carnival-time; on Sunday a woman fell off a roof.

5 March: As I leave their house, the Lacolleys seem cool. *Nom d'un chien*, have they noticed something? Pauline says no but I'm scared. My situation is critical. I love this young lady and am ready to make her my wife. All would be well if I had a decent job. Either I must come out into the open and declare myself— or stop giving her lessons.

6 March: I was wrong yesterday about the Lacolleys being cool. Pauline gives me a little bunch of immortelles. She sends the maid out to get them. When I tell her how worried I am that her parents may not consent, she says she is fairly certain they will. What will you do (I ask) if they don't? 'If they do that to me,' she replies, 'I shan't do anything mad and crazy. I'll just say to them: "All right then, if I can't have *him*, I won't have anyone." '

7 March: Delicious evening with Pauline. I promise to pass under her window tomorrow, so that she can see me.

They were married not long afterwards, in 1858. Two years later Charles is a sadder and wiser man but still relatively happy. Jules has arrived but he is making a nuisance of himself:

27 Aug: The excellent M. Lacolley came to see how his daughter and new grandson were doing. How different he is from his wife!
28 Aug: Little Jules was baptized this evening. My brother and sister held him over the font. This morning I bought a quarter of a lottery ticket and now I've lost it. These things upset me.
29 Aug: Am reading Goethe's *Werther*. I liked his *Faust* better.
30 Aug: There's always something somewhere to stop one being completely happy.
31 Aug: Baby-trouble inside. Baby-trouble outside. Never a moment's peace!
1 Sept: Double-trouble from Baby. I think we'll have to put this child out to nurse, Pauline can't cope. How sad life is!
2 Sept: Have finished *Werther*. Splendid but pernicious.
8 Sept: It's impossible—Pauline can't feed the child but I've found a wet-nurse. Tonight we handed over little Jules. I've only known him for a month but it was painful.
11 Sept: We've just been to see the little one. Emile still at home.
A few lines further on, the diary ends. Presumably the harassed M. Laforgue senior no longer has time for such frivolities.

For the first three years of his life Jules Laforgue lived in the flat where he was born. It was in a rather grand building (since demolished) called La Sirena, bearing the number 1373 calle Juncal, and situated on the corner of that street and Independence Plaza. His first explorations were in the great square itself, bordered with arcades, where the band played in a setting of palm trees. People who lived in Montevideo at that particular time often looked back on it as a lost paradise; it was especially popular with Frenchmen from the south-west who wished to try their luck in the New World. The writers Lautréamont and Jules Supervielle were both born there, and the latter, in his poem 'Montevideo', wrote nostalgically:

Dans l'Uruguay sur l'Atlantique
L'air était si liant, facile,
Que les couleurs de l'horizon
S'approchaient pour voir les maisons.

[In Uruguay on the Atlantic, the air was so free and easy that the colours of the horizon came to look at the houses.]

Jules's favourite relation was his grandfather Louis Lacolley (Pauline's father) who had a magnificent bootmaker's shop in the main street of Montevideo, the calle 25-de-Mayo. 'El gran botero', as he was known, was a swashbuckling character who had fought for Uruguay in the war against Argentina. By contrast, his least favourite relative was Pascal Darré, a baker cousin of his father's who owned the Panaderia del Sol. By bad luck the one he was to see in later life was M. Darré, whom he hated not only for his alleged meanness but just for being a baker.

When he was three years old, Jules and the family left Independence Square and went to live in a farmhouse on the outskirts of Montevideo, between Soriano and Canelones. At this point we get his first recorded memory:

The windy weeks came round again, with the buffeted silhouettes along the street. Sundays, with Grandmother Laforgue, we set off for long jaunts, all got up and peeling bananas. To eat a galette maybe with some distant cousin who was a baker. There were rats behind the sacks. Next Sunday it would be to an uncle who had a factory. Here it was all very posh: the boys were always out riding but there were two little girl-cousins. Then there was that fine shop of Grandfather Lacolley's. Mornings we went bathing in the sea . . . and when I was six there was that meal that went on for ever. (J:33)

A year younger than Jules, his sister Marie had been born in 1861. She was to become his confidante and the recipient of some famous letters. In fact, although the family was to grow eventually to eleven, the three older children—Emile, Jules and Marie—remained a little group by themselves. And Jules, although the younger of the boys, was always the bigger and the more responsible. As they got older the difference became more marked. In portraits of them as grown men Emile is the lazy, placid, easy-going one. There is in existence one remarkable unpublished letter in which Jules lectures Emile on his morals, career and general well-being. It could easily have been written by a concerned father to his son.

In the Montevidean farmhouse the Laforgue family increased by two more children and life continued peacefully until about 1865, when Uruguay once again found itself at war, this time with Paraguay. Towards the end of 1866 Charles decided to pack the family off to France, so mother and five children set sail in an extremely slow boat—so slow that, becalmed in mid-Atlantic, it took seventy-five days to reach Bordeaux, instead of the normal thirty-five. These were traumatic times for the six-year-old Jules:

not only had he left paradise but the crossing gave him his first experience of the famous Ennui, that peculiarly nineteenth century paralysis of boredom that was to dog him all his life. It also began his love-hate relationship with sunsets.

Having at last succeeded in crossing the Atlantic, Mme Laforgue and her brood made their way south from Bordeaux to their final destination, the dismal little town of Tarbes on the fringes of the Pyrenees. It was a far cry from the gentle Montevideo. Near the Pyrenees but having nothing of their glamour, Tarbes today cannot have changed much since the days of Laforgue. It is perfectly in character, for instance, for the local bookshops not to stock his books. True, there is an avenue Jules Laforgue (ending in the pleasantly named place de la Courte Boule), but when it was first inaugurated the nameplate was wrongly spelt. There is also a bust of him in the Jardin Massey, where reverent Laforguians, passing through, occasionally remove the moss from the pate.

Laforgue was never very fond of Tarbes but towards the end of his life his feelings mellowed slightly and the town makes a fairly relaxed appearance in the last poem he ever wrote (number twelve of *Derniers Vers*):

> Un couvent dans ma ville natale
> Douce de vingt mille âmes â peine,
> Entre le lycée et la préfecture
> Et vis-à-vis la cathédrale (A:311)

[A convent in my native town boasting hardly 20,000 souls, between the lycée and the préfecture and facing the cathedral]

It was quite near the convent in question that the Laforgue family took up lodgings: in the rue Abbé Torné (now rue Saint-Louis). At this time Laforgue still had his mother with him, but a further traumatic moment came two years later when she and the three youngest children (including his beloved confidante Marie) returned on the slow boat to Montevideo. Emile and Jules were left behind to enter the lycée as boarders at the ages of nine and eight respectively: an ordeal more common in England than in France. Anyone who has suffered it will feel special sympathy when reading these lines from the poem 'L'Hiver Qui Vient' ('Winter Coming On') which is number one of *Derniers Vers*:

> C'est la toux dans les dortoirs du lycée qui rentre,
> C'est la tisane sans le foyer (A:281)

[The coughing in lycée dormitories as term begins, and lime-tea without the sweetness of home]

Even during the holidays they had no escape, for they were placed in the care of the hated Pascal Darré, who in the meantime had retired to Tarbes and bought a house in the rue Massey. But M.

Darré may not have been all bad. Someone arranged for the Laforgue boys to have drawing lessons during the holidays and they were given by François Lataste, art master at the lycée. One would like to think that the idea came from M. Darré himself, or perhaps from his sister. In any case it was a good idea because Jules proved a most talented pupil, while the less brilliant Emile was at least able to earn a living from it.

In a recently discovered and hitherto unpublished document[2] —the rough draft of a letter to someone unknown—Emile has provided valuable biographical details, from which we shall quote at various times in the course of this book. Emile's notes begin with the first days at school:

We could just about read and that's all. Of those first years in junior school the main thing I remember is chilblains. Everyone knew us because of this: the Laforgues were those two poor little kids who spent the breaks in a corner of the playground, crying over their chilblains. For two years we were everyone's butt: we'd only just left home and were very shy, and then we just looked absurd because we were always smothered in iodine. But almost overnight we changed. My brother (since it's him you're interested in) became the classic bad pupil, so lazy that the phrase 'incorrigibly lazy' became a permanent feature of his end-of-term reports. The sad fact is he took part in every school disturbance. He had an amazing gift for guying the masters and also a complete lack of guile, which meant that it was always he who was caught in the act, while the others got off. So he was continually getting detentions and being kept in—or even locked up in the punishment room. And this went on for years. Once I remember he was locked up the first day of the school year and again on the eve of prize-giving. It was as if he'd never been out. He was never the kind to choose a friend and walk soberly round the courtyard during recess. Though clumsy at games he used to hurl himself wildly into everything that was happening. He was the craziest of us all.

Laforgue himself had an amusing memory of being locked up:

One day in the punishment room, I just happened to raise my eyes from the lines I was writing. There was a window in the middle of the door and in it I saw the face of the headmaster's daughter looking tenderly, passionately sorry for me. She'd been standing on tip-toe in her little boots, and immediately dashed away. What if they'd spotted her there! She must have planned the visit with great care in the loneliness of her heart, her good heart. Imagine taking such a risk at such a time in that corner of the tower which contained nothing except the lamp-room and the punishment room! Ah, whatever became of that one? (J:34)

But to return to Emile's notes:

My brother's first verses were written when he was in the sixth form [aged eleven] though as far as literature goes it was more poking fun at the teacher [M. Menginou] than anything else. All the same the whole class was grateful and their admiration for my brother was immense. Next year, in the fifth, we had a master so weak [M. Senmartin] that nothing so subtle as verses was called for. Instead it was one big riot. But the fourth form master [M. Douyau] avenged his colleague of the year before and made us all tremble—Jules was now thirteen—without a single outing of any kind, to the country or anywhere else. And so to the third form [under M. Dalléas] where my brother became a little more serious at last. In fact, the way he walked round the yard during recess, you might almost have taken him for one of the senior boys. [For the names of the Tarbes school-masters we are indebted to J-L. Debauve (L:16-17).]

Between November 1870 and March 1873 one of the junior assistants at the Tarbes lycée was a certain Théophile Delcassé, who was later destined to become Foreign Minister of France and the architect of the Entente Cordiale. It was the first example of Laforgue's knack for meeting exceptional people and making an impression on them. Though he was not more than twelve at the time Delcassé never forgot him. The first time they met Laforgue knocked off his glasses but Delcassé was never one to bear a grudge. Indeed it was one of his most famous traits. There is a story that when he was coaching the children of M. Roman, a civil servant at the Quai d'Orsay, it became known to M. Roman (an Orléaniste) that Delcassé spent his nights working on Gambetta's paper *La République Française*. So he sacked him. Years later, when Delcassé became Foreign Minister, and found M. Roman still working at the Quai d'Orsay, he immediately sent for him and . . . gave him the Legion of Honour. And so with Laforgue: the incident of the glasses quickly forgotten, he helped him with his exams, while later in Paris he took him out to dinner, encouraged him to start writing plays and finally arranged for his paper to publish a review of Laforgue's first book—a review written by Laforgue himself!

The writer Laurent Tailhade (six years older than Laforgue) has given some idea of the gruelling pace of the boarder's day at the Tarbes lycée about this time. (There were three hundred pupils in all, nearly half of them boarders.) It is contained in a letter to his mother in 1874, when he was finishing his 'philo' in the top form:

> We get up at 5.30. At six we go down to the prep room and stay there till 7.15. Then fifteen minutes for breakfast, fifteen minutes for recess and another short period of prep till eight o'clock. From eight to ten we have lessons. Then prep, lunch, recess and more prep passes the time till two o'clock, when another period of lessons begins, lasting till four. One last recess and three hours of prep fill the rest of the day. At eight we have supper, followed immediately by bed. But on Monday, Wednesday and Friday we are allowed to stay up till nine.

Emile in the notes now speaks of another side of Laforgue: his love of the countryside:

> I've not spoken yet of our best moments of all: the holidays. It was only then that I was really with my brother in a real sense. When I look back they seem wonderful days. We lived exactly like wild creatures, in love with the sun and air. We trekked for miles and then went to sleep among the vines. We spent hours watching the cray-fish and the woodland animals that to most people are invisible. We filled our pockets with stolen fruit and installed ourselves, each in his own tree, by the side of a lake, very high over the water. Steeping ourselves in sun, we hung suspended there for hours and hours. At moments like that my brother found tremendous pleasure in giving life to everything around him, making up the most astonishing stories, building castles in Spain and asking huge hypothetical questions beginning with the words: 'What if . . . ?' In those hours of fantasy there was no question of writing poetry. To force himself to write anything it seemed he needed the boredom of a classroom; and there'd been no developments of that sort since those sixth-form satires when he was eleven.

Laforgue wrote two short stories about Tarbes. In both of them the dates tally with his own life and the basic details seem to be true. The first is 'Stéphane Vassiliew', which tells of a strange Russian boy—strangely like Laforgue—who arrives at a lycée (clearly Tarbes) and finally dies in a way very much like Laforgue himself. There is a distinct flavour here of *Le Grand Meaulnes* by Alain-Fournier, who could not possibly have read 'Stéphane' since it was not published till years after his death. But Fournier had always identified himself with Laforgue. As evidence we have his long correspondence (or argument) with Jacques Rivière, and his use of certain lines from Laforgue's *Derniers Vers* as epigraphs for

his own poems. At one point Fournier quite unequivocally stated: 'I
intend to write a novel that springs from Laforgue.' And this he did.

In 'Stéphane' famous Laforguian motifs make their first dif-
fident entrance, for example sunsets and the Unconscious. Already
there, too, is Shakespeare's Melancholy Jaques, claimed by Gustave
Kahn to be Laforgue's 'favourite role in his favourite play by his
favourite author'. (M:235) 'Suffering nature,' says the narrator, 'is
the kind that most touches our hearts today.' (H:52) And there is
that chilling prophecy: 'Often he came home drenched to the skin,
and that was how he contracted a small dry cough that never left
him.' (H:52) Stéphane has Laforgue's own chilblains, though they
are less plausible in a Russian gypsy than in a boy just arrived from
the tropics. And Stéphane in his misery thinks of Philoctetes, that
other victim of fate, just as Jules did. The story of 'Stéphane
Vassiliew' begins in 1870:

> I was in the junior form of a little school buried deep in the
> provinces. One June afternoon when the whole class, including
> the master, were dozing to the monotonous purr of a word-for-
> word translation of *De Viris*, we heard a well-known noise. It
> was the deputy headmaster importantly clearing his throat. We
> all woke up. He had a new boy with him.
>
> When a pupil enters a lycée in June, one month before the
> prize-giving, it can only mean he's going to spend the holidays
> there and settle in: that's to say he's an orphan, or his parents
> are nobody knows where.
>
> The new arrival was a pallid boy of eleven, with a delicate and
> resigned air. The master showed him where to sit.
>
> —Your name?
> —Stéphane Vassiliew.
> The master, straining to hear, asked him to spell it.
> —And you come from . . . ?
> —The station.
> We all tittered but the boy didn't seem to hear.
> —No, I mean your previous lycée.
> —There wasn't one.
> —Come now, where did you have your first lessons?
> —Nowhere. We moved about.
> That was as much as could be got out of him. He must have
> been very tired because he propped his elbows on the desk as if
> to resume a little nap which his interrogation had interrupted.
>
> —Now then, my friend, this isn't the dormitory. Follow care-
> fully in your neighbour's book while we construe.
> The neighbour was me. I pushed my *De Viris* in front of him
> and, as the margins were full of comic drawings, he raised his

eyes with a gentle sad smile towards the book's owner. I smiled too, more openly, but with pity for all the pain I could feel in him. I think he must have liked me because from that day on I became his friend, the only one he could suffer during his five years at the lycée. (H:27-9)

Many, many times I watched him day-dreaming and lost to us during those long evening preps: the silence and scratching of pens on paper interrupted at times by the shuffling of feet, the crash of a ruler falling to the floor, the crumpling of a sheet of paper or a sudden burst of laughter held back by a serious fit of coughing. (H:31-2)

How desperately long those five years must have seemed to him as day followed day inside those same grey walls, the same barred windows of that small-town lycée; five years of days all alike, cut into appointed portions by the rolling of the drum. Who ever forgets the bell of his lycée: that bell, the very soul of the prison, with its special sound of being deadened by the sadness of so many years, of letting the slow hours drop one by one in a world without interest or love. (H:35)

First there was the sad winter, two long leaden months during which we were shut up far from the sky, far from the fields, and which Stéphane spent almost continuously in the infirmary on account of the chilblains which made two open wounds of his poor delicate feet. It was during that first winter that the junior assistant wrote these lines in a report to the Head: 'Monsieur Vassiliew, for reasons I have not been able fully to ascertain, disturbs the dormitory nightly with his exaggerated sighs.'

In the hard cold life of the lycée the infirmary struck a maternal note with its atmosphere of idleness and small attentions. Under the supervision of the sisters, in an atmosphere of calm made languid by the good smell of the linen-room, far from books and boys and the schoolyard with its frozen puddles, Stéphane passed those winter days gently, monotonously: days that were so short between the late sunrise and the lighting of the gas at four o'clock.

Of course, in the mornings, there was that terrible hour when his feet were being dressed and the warm water wasn't quite enough to bring away the bandages—and at night again when they burned in the warmth of the bed and made him cry out with pain. But how quiet and melancholy were the afternoons and how cosy to hear at certain hours the vague drum-rolls below, the steady sing-song murmur of the sisters at their devotions, the bugle-calls from the cavalry barracks opposite, and the cries of the boys at recess, followed by the great silence of the lycée.

Stéphane, day-dreaming over a book, let it fall from his hands and wandered from his bed to the white faience stove which stood in the middle of the room, soberly snoring, and then from there to the window. He was always happiest there, as he drew back the yellow serge curtain and looked far down into the street where a few passers-by hurried through the mud and snow. Before him, as far as the horizon, the huge sky was swept with a dirty mist, an immense swirling mass of ashen-grey clouds. No longer daring to move he stood there for hours, alone, gently withdrawing from things, lost in that everlasting silent swirl of snowflakes, descending endlessly. And night was already falling when the sister arrived, and scolded him for having dirtied the windows again by writing on them in the vapour from his breath. But Stéphane was still dreaming, lost to the world. (H:37-9)

Visitors to Tarbes today will not find it impossible to visualize that 'maze of dirty little lanes at the back of the lycée, from which one sometimes heard, in the dormitory at night, cries of Murder, or the laughs of artillerymen dragging their swords'. They were centred round the rue Bramabuque (now the rue Portier).

March passed by, carried quickly away by blustering showers, and it was April. The plane trees burgeoned in the courtyard and day-boys brought cockchafers to school in paper cones . . . and there was a sudden need to wander aimlessly about . . . but Stéphane, his feet still painful from the winter sufferings, often couldn't get his shoes on. . . . In those sad hours one book consoled him: [Fénelon's] *Télémaque* and above all the twelfth chapter, those pages where Philoctetes tells how he was abandoned on the isle of Lemnos because of the putrid smell that spread throughout the Greek camp from the wound devouring his foot. Stéphane felt infinite pity as he read and re-read the passage: 'I remained, almost throughout the siege of Troy, alone, without help, without hope, without solace.' And in his copy he underlined these special phrases: 'That wild and deserted isle where I heard nothing but the waves of the sea breaking on the rocks' . . . 'For it was during my sleep that the Greeks departed. Judge of my surprise, then, and the tears I shed on waking, when I beheld their ships cleaving the waves' . . . 'O shores and promontories of this isle, it is to you I make my lament, for there is none but you to hear me, and you are used to my sorrow.' (H:39-41)

But soon the days lengthened and a happy relaxation spread through the school at the thought of the approaching holidays. Work came to a standstill, there was discussion about prizes and the masters read us amusing snippets. . . . In prep, to keep the

air fresh, the junior assistant, in shirt-sleeves, ordered constant
sprinklings of the floor. We dozed or made fly-cages with a cork
and pins. . . . At last came the awaited day; the prize-giving was
soon over . . . and the abandoning of school began. . . . Alone,
seated on a bench in a corner of the schoolyard, Stéphane
watched his comrades leave one by one. By twilight it was all
over. Stéphane walked through the silent school. . . . Nobody
loved him. (H:43-4)

Nul ne l'aimait is a recurring theme of Laforgue's. But Stéphane,
left at school for the holidays, finds (like Laforgue) infinite
resources in the surrounding countryside. He goes for long walks
by himself:

It was usually striking seven when he passed the toll-house.
The peasant women in their best bonnets were just arriving for
market in a flurry of baskets brimming with eggs and vegetables,
cans full of milk, and chickens lying in the dust, tethered by the
feet. (H:45)

Stéphane proceeded at random: jumping, taking short steps,
sometimes running, sitting down and at once getting up again
for no reason, stopping in front of everything, his every pore
tingling with liberty, safe at last from the stares. . . . But soon he
made for places that he knew . . . where a pond lay sleeping. . . .
The midday sun streamed down from on high. Little by little
Stéphane felt a torpor spread through him as he gazed without
thought, his eyes half closed, at the stricken landscape in the
distance, the motionless maize with its long hanging leaves, the
flowering lucerne, the acres of golden wheat undulating at times
as the hot wind touched it. And Stéphane, himself burning in
the torrid sun, absorbed in the deep *unconscious* fixity of all
things, felt his head begin to spin. Without the will or strength
to resist he slid into a state of delicious enervation, enjoying the
vague sensation of his mind dissolving into a thousand kinds of
floating reverie, of his whole identity being atomized and
scattered throughout nature in the scorching air, along with the
cri-cri of cicadas, the drunken sap of the plants and all hidden
life. He closed his eyes and when the breeze moved across the
foliage, he imagined that he was a part of the limitless rustling
of the leaves. And he remained there, it seemed, for hours.

This passage and the one following are interesting for their use
of the word 'unconscious' (which I have italicized)—still without
a capital letter. Later he was to deify the Unconscious. But it is
important to note that his use of the word never had Freudian or
even Jungian connotations. As Warren Ramsey has said, 'Nineteenth-
century philosophies of the Unconscious are only restatements

of Romantic doctrines of enthusiasm. Man is absorbed by a god that is virtually nature.'³

Sometimes, from the four corners of the sky, there arrived bundles of black clouds. The atmosphere grew heavy and stifling. Soon the tops of the trees began to bend under sudden squalls and great tepid drops began to patter on the leaves. When the downpour came at last it filled the countryside with its great noise. And Stéphane, sheltering in the deepest part of the wood, listened to the rain and watched the scurrying clouds. But now the sun reappeared between vague wisps of white scud to drink up the showers. Life returned fresher than before, the greenery smelt more green, the snails came out and even the birds: after moping like feathered balls on the branches they preened their ruffled plumage and flew off with a light heart. Then twilight descended, bringing peace to everything. Far over there the sun went down, spreading across the fields a fan-pattern of pale rays which here and there lit up the green dome of a wood, the red tiles of a little house, distant threads of rising smoke. The hills lengthened their shadows across the plain, and the golden orb sank behind the horizon in a magnificent conflagration, softening itself little by little into a bloom of rosy clouds. Then came the gentle hour, consoling sometimes; sometimes infinitely sad. On the surface of the pond swarms of dancing midges were suddenly cut through by flashing swallows as they drank on the wing. A cool breeze sprang up over the meadows, bringing the healthy smell of new-mown hay. The curtain of poplars rustled its silvery leaves. Far off the flocks of sheep were returning home in a powdery mist. Carts passed by with a groan of axles. Stéphane rose, intoxicated, staggering almost, from this day entirely absorbed without will or strength in the *unconscious* life of nature. And as he slowly walked back to town along a road lined with trees he was seized with a sweet pain at hearing behind him, in the peace of the fields, the melancholy sobbing of the toads. (H:46-51)

Five years have passed. It is now April 1875. Stéphane is fifteen (and coincidentally Laforgue himself will be fifteen in four months' time). They are both in the third form. News comes one day that the circus has come to town. On Sunday the boys are taken there, wearing not only their brass-buttoned tunics but white gloves as well. The great attractions are a gypsy orchestra and a Magyar bareback rider. It is all too much for Russian Stéphane who faints with excitement. Back at the lycée he decides to escape and join the gypsies and Wilma:

He loved her. He loved her as one can only love at the lycée—

with that special kind of love that's made up of a lot of head, a little heart, and where the senses play scarcely any part at all. (H:63)

So one day he slips away from the lycée and plunges into the countryside, bound for Toulouse where the circus has last been reported. On and on he walks, hungry and tired and soaked 'while his comrades in prep were reading by lamplight those amusing books that were allowed on Sundays'. Finally he collapses and is found next morning by a peasant on his way to market. The ending is of unrelenting gloom: a slice of reality which Laforgue, after writing about it, was going to experience very fully himself.

He lay very pale, with a slight flush around the cheekbones. . . . Standing near the bed the headmaster, looking grave, spoke to the doctor. It was a case of galloping consumption. The boy was going to die. . . . Resigned and without regrets Stéphane felt himself dying a little every day. . . . They had cleared his night-table now of all the medicine bottles. They still watched him but they were watching only for the end. . . . The doctor, the headmaster, the nursing sister, the junior assistant were all talking, commiserating; but Stéphane didn't look at them. Did he even know them? Not one of them had shed a tear. Nobody loved him. As for the doctor, he'd seen it all before. . . . The nursing sister? Stéphane remembered that at first when she had tended him, he had hoped for a sort of healing touch . . . but nothing happened. The headmaster was congratulating himself on the poor boy not having a mother: she would have uttered such anguished cries. It would have led to talk and frightened other mothers. . . . Heavens, what trouble a headmaster had! As for the junior assistant, he was just waiting to be released so that he could go and have his absinthe at the Brasserie de la Gare. . . . No, he had nobody. He was alone. He could now say goodbye to the sweetness of this spring day which announced that everything was going to flower again, and that for many long months it would be good to be in the sun, under the trees, out in the fields, with the cicadas, the harvest, the vintage, and the flaming sunsets; and at evening, in the twilight, coming from a great distance, the sad sobbing of the toads. Everywhere life was to be renewed and enjoyed. Through the window came a ray of sunlight in which danced golden particles of dust. It was on these that Stéphane kept his eyes as he felt himself slowly descend into the night. (H:74-8)

MONTEVIDEO AND TARBES / 27

'At the end of 1875,' says Emile in the unpublished notes,

> our father brought the family back from Montevideo to settle in
> Tarbes, and he was determined to take control of our education.
> A few days after his arrival he pushed a Horace under our noses
> and subsequently announced that we were completely ignorant.
> It was as day-boys that we now entered the second form [under
> M. Abadie], and my brother [now fifteen] became in the eyes
> of the lycée a model pupil. He was also bitten anew by the writing
> bug—to the point of starting a pocket-sized school magazine
> which turned up daily in morning classes. Having a wide reader-
> ship, it was the direct cause of many detentions, many pages of
> Demosthenes laboriously translated.

What Emile does not say is that Jules's new status of day-boy—and
the greater independence it allowed—enabled him now to embark on
his first love-affair. This is recorded in the second of his early stories:
'Amours de la Quinzième Année' ('Loves of the Fifteenth Year').
Once again Laforguians will recognize some familiar motifs making
their first appearance, for example the girls in their white dresses.

> I was fifteen at the time, a time of strange awakenings as they
> say. I attended the lycée of my little town as a day-boy. But alas,
> Greek and Latin largely escaped me, history bored me, and
> geography appealed only to the extent that one could talk more
> conveniently behind an atlas. As for arithmetic, the principles
> of division were so clearly determined to be my stumbling block
> that I didn't like to insist. The only thing that amused me was
> drawing. Not only was I good at it but the master in charge had
> the richly comic and unusual habit—when utterly exasperated—
> of picking up a boy and hurling him bodily through the door. I
> remember that once when it happened to me I was tickled
> irresistibly by his beard and sneezed in his face. But enough of
> that. Let's talk about love.
>
> Up till then, as everyone would agree, I had been incredibly
> lazy. But at about fifteen how one changes! It was spring. I used
> to cut school, it's true, but only to wander into the countryside,
> roll in the grass and burst into tears for no reason. Regularly on
> Sunday mornings I found myself, as if by chance, waiting outside
> church: it was to see the girls wing their way out of mass in their
> white dresses. A critical time, yes, but precisely the time when a
> Balzac novel, *Un grand homme de province à Paris*, chose to fall
> into my hands. I devoured it, dreamed of it and had a sudden
> vision of Paris. That distant hell excited me. Lucien de Rubempré
> had been a poet. I would be a painter.
>
> At once I broke with my comrades, considering them hence-
> forth as but the common stock of grocers and notaries. I spent

all my leisure drawing, either at the library or at the museum. Then I began to paint. Who will ever sing the impossible joys of squeezing out one's first tube of colour on a new palette! At night I stayed up late copying the busts of Roman emperors, and on Sundays from eight till six I spent the day with a little moulder of plaster casts who lived at the other end of town. While he was pouring plaster into the moulds he'd strung together, I'd be copying the Dancing Faun and other antiques. It was a real crisis of work and ambition. You could be sure love wouldn't be long making its appearance. Very soon, in fact, I found my Dulcinea. At a certain window of a certain street—if I close my eyes I can see it still—I discovered her. It was she. (I didn't know her but I recognized her.)

She must have been at least three years older than me, but she was exquisite: there in the frame of her window hung with wistaria, with her delicate colouring, her big clear eyes, the eternal blue ribbons tied to her pigtails and the wide embroidered collar hugging her shoulders. That's all I could see from the street, but one day I saw her close up. I almost collapsed when I saw the soft rosy dimple in her chin, a real nest for kisses. But it was that look of a wounded antelope that finally finished me. I returned home completely in the clouds. The whole night I spent planning. It was all arranged: I'd love her from afar, kill myself with work, go to Paris, become famous. I imagined the triumph of my return when I would place at her feet both my heart and my renown.

It's true I could have wished her a bit more elegiac; and her crazy manner and great gusts of laughter scared me terribly; but I adored her, oh yes, so much so that sometimes I'd cry out with rage, at night, before going to sleep.

I got more and more ambitious, more and more in love, but soon I began to feel dejected. Paris was still far away, and progress so slow it exasperated me. And then Marguerite—her name was Marguerite—didn't seem to be noticing me much. Indeed (though I tried to persuade myself it wasn't true) she even began to flirt with one of her cousins. The day actually arrived—oh Othello, how well I understood you at that hour!— when I was almost sure I'd seen him taking diabolical liberties with her!

Well, one Sunday in November, feeling sad and cold, i.e. my usual suffering self, I called at eight on my friend the moulder. Till nightfall I stayed there, seated before the Gladiator of Ephesus, working badly, my heart bursting with bitterness, thinking of her and her cousin, my ambitions and Paris. At six o'clock I left, portfolio under arm. I was worn out. I hadn't eaten since eight that morning and, at the other end of town a wretched cold room awaited me. I crept along the walls, through the crush of noisy townsfolk, all dressed up and returning from their outings. And there was I, without money, without love and without Sunday clothes. But even now something still sang in my heart at the thought of seeing her as I passed her window. Perhaps she'd smile at me. God knows, I needed it! I quickened my pace.

But what was this? They were giving a party. The windows were lit up and you could hear the sound of a waltz playing on the piano. Shadows of people dancing crossed behind the curtains, and at one moment I recognized her shadow and his interlocked.

With dry throat and aching heart, unable to cry but blinded with tears, I picked up a stone—a cobble-stone to be precise—and threw it at one of the windows. With the crash of glass breaking on the pavement the dance stopped, windows opened and a crowd began to gather in the street. Since I just stood there gaping, a policeman came up and hauled me off, under a barrage of insults, to the police station near the town hall. And all the time I was struggling, sobbing, pleading: 'Let me go, I may have hurt her. Marguerite, Marguerite, oh brute that I am.'

After a night in jail our hero is set free in the morning; and the story ends with these words:

I got over my love. As for *them*, they were married and will probably have lots of children. Amen.[4]

Though Laforgue tells the story in a jokey way, he is in dead earnest and it is largely true. He may not have thrown the rock but he did go to Paris and become famous—for he never lacked either talent or ambition—and he never forgot Marguerite, who in some ways remained the most important influence in his life. The last words should therefore be taken with a pinch of salt: he did not give the couple his blessing and he did not get over his love. Consider the facts:

In July he sent to the Toulouse paper *La Guêpe* (*The Wasp*) a poem called 'Excuse Macabre' in which he remembers her with fury. After imagining that he sometimes drinks from her skull, he asks if he may sell it:

Ton crâne, je puis bien le vendre, n'est-ce pas,
Margaretha, ma bien-aimée?

[Your skull, you'll let me sell it, won't you, Marguerite, my beloved?]

On 30 December 1881 he wrote to his friend Charles Henry:

'The fiancée of my fifteenth year in the provinces was called Marguerite. I wrote lines for her which were extremely advanced for my age, like this one: "Marguerite, if only you knew how much I love you!" ' (D:76)

In September 1882 he wrote to a woman friend Mme Mültzer: 'Here I am in the depths of the provinces, in the little town where I lived . . . and also loved with that sublime passion we have in our schooldays, and which makes us shed genuine tears and no fooling.' (D:195-6)

In June 1883 he visited a dive in Berlin and noted in his diary: 'The girl who made me get her a pineapple salad looked just like Marguerite.' (F:237)

Later that same year (21 August) he was on holiday at Tarbes and saw her in the crowd round a bandstand: 'In the general bustle, a brief view of Marguerite, looking pale and distracted, head held high, talking to a fat vulgar gentleman.' (F:254)

An unpublished fragment suggests that the fat man was her husband: 'There was that adorable little childhood friend whom he had loved. He knew that she'd become a schoolteacher and a writer of uniquely bad verse before finally marrying a provincial tradesman (whom he had seen). Sometimes he imagined her being taken for the first time by that man and it cut his appetite for the rest of the day.'[5]

As Laforgue once said, 'The way our puberty happens: that's everything, and everything stems from there. An hour of our fifteenth year decides our character and gives us our own personal view of the universe.' (J:101)

But scholars will also have noted a literary influence in the story just told, showing that Jules had already begun his life-long love-affair with Heine. The source seems to be poem sixty of *Die Heimkehr* (*The Return*):

> Sie haben heut abend Gesellschaft,
> Und das Haus ist lichterfüllt.
> Dort oben am hellen Fenster
> Bewegt sich ein Schattenbild . . .

[This evening you have a brilliant reception, and the house is full of lights. Up there at that lighted window I see a shadow move.] He was living his romance with Marguerite in the shadow of Heine's with Amalie.

The identity of Marguerite-Amalie has not yet been discovered. Even Jean-Louis Debauve, the Paris judge who knows more about Laforgue's life and times than anybody, had to admit defeat on this score when, after a recent visit to Tarbes, he reported to us: 'Dossier remains open: case unsolved.'

CHAPTER 2
Paris (1876-1881)

IN the autumn of 1876 the whole family moved to the Batignolles quarter of Paris, where the father's mother and sister had preceded them. They found a cottage and garden at 66 rue des Moines and stayed there for three years. The father had done well at the Duplessis Bank and had saved a fair amount of money. Some say he had bought an apartment-house and was now living on the rents; others that he had made lucky investments which suffered subsequently from fluctuating exchange rates but nonetheless left him technically a *rentier*. The short answer seems to be that he was well off but had too many children, the eleventh having been born in Tarbes in November 1875, shortly after the return from Montevideo. Now another was on the way, and they had hardly settled in when the mother had a miscarriage in January, leading directly to her death from pneumonia on 6 April 1877. Exactly how close to his mother Laforgue ever was is a matter for conjecture; he said later that he had hardly known her, yet he still wrote poems about her. What is certain is that the manner of her death left him with a permanent revulsion from the whole reproductive process.

On arriving in Paris in October, Laforgue (aged sixteen) had enrolled for his year of *rhétorique* at the smart and easy-going Lycée Condorcet (then called Fontanes) near the Gare Saint-Lazare. This was the school of Marcel Proust and a number of other writers. One of Laforgue's own comrades was 'Willy', the future husband and slave-driver of Colette. Meanwhile Emile, as the official artist of the family, had been directed towards the Ecole des Beaux-Arts on the other side of the Seine.

'I hardly saw Jules at this time,' says Emile in the notes.

He was at the Lycée and I was at the Ecole, so I only caught a glimpse of him in the distance. He never told me about his plans or anything; we never had time. Occasionally, on my way back from the Ecole, I'd see him outside the Comédie-Française: two or three times a week he used to queue hours for a seat. At that time he was planning to write novels, and was a great

admirer of Zola and Co. Then one day he met a former junior
assistant from the Tarbes lycée [Delcassé]. This man had had
three plays refused by the Comédie, but nevertheless his example
spurred on Jules to try his own luck, and for a time after that
he thought of nothing else but writing plays.

This must have been the psychological moment when Delcassé was
moving reluctantly from the stage to politics. But the effect on
Jules was to make him sit right down and write *Tessa*, a play we
only recently discovered—if it is possible to discover something
that has been lying for all to see in one of the world's great libraries,
the Houghton Library at Harvard, for twenty years. Let's say that,
if anyone knew about it, they were keeping it dark, aided by the
fact that the manuscript is almost too fragile to examine.

Tessa is a very odd affair indeed. Dated 'Batignolles, 1877', it is
decorated with the usual sprinkling of girls' heads, which Laforgue
doodled everywhere—they were his
special trademark. It is written on
orange-coloured foolscap paper
of which there are nineteen sheets
written on both sides, but it has been
folded in two to push into a pocket
and has suffered in consequence.
Laforgue's writing is in brown ink
but there are comments or corrections in red ink by a second hand
whose owner is unknown. Oddest of
all, *Tessa* takes place in a Renaissance
Italy where they read Schopenhauer!
But the particular lines of Schopenhauer quoted by Laforgue come
from an article in the *Revue des
Deux Mondes* of 15 March 1870,
which suggests that this is all that

Laforgue then knew about the philosopher who was to become one
of the great influences of his life. The lines in question are these:

> Life is an evil. The end of the world will mean the salvation,
> the deliverance of humanity. The value of continence is that it
> leads to this deliverance. Love is the enemy. Women are its
> accomplices. The ascetic cancels the life of whole generations.
> He sets an example which has almost saved humanity on two or
> three occasions. But women didn't want it and that's why I
> hate them.

It is the message of a sermon which Laforgue later preached himself in his role of melancholy Jaques (or melancholy Dane). But at

the time of *Tessa* he is actually laughing at it, as was the custom of
the time in plays by Pailleron and others. His misanthropic hero is
saved only in the nick of time by Tessa, a little beggar-girl whom
he has found in the streets and adopted. And it is Tessa who suggests that they should burn Schopenhauer and read Dante instead:

Ah la femme, la femme. Eh bien, la femme en somme?
La femme est faite pour emparadiser l'homme.
C'est Dante qui l'a dit. Eh bien nous le lirons
Ensemble, et celui-ci . . . Quoi? . . . Nous le brûlerons.
[Ah woman, woman. Well, what about woman? Woman is made
for the delight of man. Dante said it. So let's read him together
—and this one we'll burn.]

All through the play Laforgue is mocking the sort of person he
was often to resemble in later years. He calls his hero a misanthropic
hedgehog and a grumpy porcupine, who is saved at last by little
Tessa . . . just as Laforgue himself was often a grumpy hedgehog
before he met Leah. In this, his first known work, he seems to
see himself and his future with great clarity. He is the man who is
melancholy by nature but laughs at himself for being so. The
melancholy Jaques, too, it will be remembered, was the most
genial of melancholy men.

There has been some discussion about whether the word 'emparadiser' is Laforgue's first neologism. He eventually became
famous for the many words he invented and this would seem a very
attractive one: a verb meaning to delight someone or send him to
paradise. But apart from its use by Dante it was probably used by
Petrarch, and Littré even gives an obscure early use in French, so
it seems the delightful word was only adapted.

Laforgue puts his signature on this play with another mention
of those golden particles of dust dancing in a ray of sunlight,
which were Stéphane's last vision of the world. This time it's
'gold dust drifting up from the floor', of which he says: 'On
dirait un ami qui me viendrait chercher' ('Almost like a friend
coming to fetch me').

In *Tessa*, too, we meet the Heine allusion noticed in 'Amours
de la Quinzième Année' (and which he seems to use almost as a
mascot):

Heureux si, même après toute une nuit d'attente,
J'emportais sous mon toit cette pensée ardente
D'avoir cru deviner aux lueurs des flambeaux
Votre ombre qui passait derrière vos rideaux.
[Happy, even after a whole night's waiting, if I carried back to
my room the ardent thought that I'd actually seen in the
torchlight your shadow passing behind the curtains.]

It reinforces the feeling that what Laforgue really borrowed from
Heine was not so much the Heinean irony but rather spontaneity,
romanticism, lyricism—something that Laforgue calls 'le goût
allemand' ('the German manner') (L:165)—just as it is another
very different German manner that he appreciates in Schopenhauer:
circumspection, scepticism, cynicism. In other words it was Heine's
naturalness and simplicity that Laforgue loved; he loved the man
who 'obeyed his own moods, kept a light rein on himself and never
postured'. (J:144) As for irony, Laforgue came to it much later.
In *Tessa*, when he talks of his hero 'protected by irony' (*cuirassé
d'ironie*) it is still a dirty word.

Even the hero's melancholy is mocked in *Tessa*:

J'aime bien mieux l'hiver, on est d'humeur plus triste.

Mais en plein mois de mai, jouer le pessimiste . . . !

[I much prefer winter when one can feel nicely sad. The middle
of May is no time for pessimists!]

We meet the eternal girls in white:

Et là-bas cet essaim de joyeuses fillettes

Qui s'en vont trottinant et vives et proprettes.

[And look at that swarm of happy girls who come trotting
along so neatly alive.]

It is a foretaste of 'Dimanche', one of the *Derniers Vers*: 'Comme
tout se fait propre autour d'elles!' ('How clean and tidy they make
everything seem!') (A:287) We even find one of the characters in
the act of composing a poem: 'Il fuyait par la plaine' ('He fled
across the plain') which Laforgue will echo in a later poem of his
own: 'Elle fuyait par l'avenue' ('She fled down the avenue'). (A:49)
These are all reminders that it is a Laforguian work, but not yet
a very good one; interesting mainly for its lightheartedness, showing
none of the cosmic despair that will descend on him around the
twentieth year.

The most intriguing thing about it remains: who was the mysterious corrector? Who was it who remarked in the margins that
some things were 'très joli' while others were 'pas joli'? Could it
have been the father? Sometimes the corrections do seem to fit
the rather rigid temperament of a retired schoolmaster with a
turn for the pedantic. We also know that M. Laforgue always
encouraged his son in the career of literature, a calling that he
himself had wished to follow in his youth. 'In this very nice mono-
logue,' says the corrector, 'you have used the word "but" eight
times. Don't you think this is too much?' And further on he
repeats: 'Look out for your "buts"—they are scattered wholesale
through the play from beginning to end, most of them superfluous.'
Upon which Laforgue conscientiously tries to eliminate them—but

the 'buts' are hard to part with. True, the corrector's handwriting does not resemble the father's as it was in the diary of 1860, but Charles Laforgue subsequently lost his right hand in that hunting accident: it is not impossible that the *Tessa* corrections were written with his left.

During the course of this year (1877) Laforgue had the traumatic experience of twice failing his baccalaureate examination. According to Emile's notes he twice passed the written part and twice failed the oral, largely because he ran into some freakishly difficult questions. But this may just be brotherly loyalty. Whatever the reason, Laforgue's school career was now drawing to its close. He joined the *philosophie* class for one term and then called it a day.

After leaving Condorcet at the end of 1877, Jules seems to have joined Emile at the Beaux-Arts as an unregistered student in the class of Henri Lehmann. It was always known that he had followed Taine's Beaux-Arts lectures on the history of art, but notes have recently come to light which seem to suggest much more. It would seem that he positively threw himself into the art-student life, becoming a fully paid-up bohemian with all that that entails. What now follows is an attempt to make sense of a mass of incoherent jottings:[6]

Once a week Lehmann's students have to bring a drawing for him to see. 'It could, for instance, be Daphnis and Chloë—which might show Chloë with a mauve stomach sitting on a bit of jagged column, while Daphnis on bended knee and grimacing horribly pushes a big yellow flower towards her. Chloë meanwhile is showing the whites of her eyes to suggest deep satisfaction.'

Lehmann: Now then, Laforgue, let's see your drawing. You weren't here last week.

Laforgue: I was sick, sir.

Lehmann: I can well believe it. That's a sick drawing if ever I saw one.

Painting expeditions are described: to Charenton, for instance— they go along the quays and make echo-noises under the bridges; and to Clamart, where they shake sweet chestnuts off the trees and eat them. They bring back their sketches done in the open air, but Lehmann says, 'I know it's the fashion but I still don't like it.'

He goes through the routine initiation ceremony of having to strip, after which the whole studio cries, 'Allons, salope, rhabille-toi!' ('Put your clothes on, dirty devil!') He sings all the corny old songs, for example,

> Ils n'ont pu rattraper
> L'ouvrier caléchier

in which 'caléchier' puns with 'qu'allait chier', as pitman might

with shitman. He even goes singing in the courtyards for a dare
and to earn money for paints. He keeps tubes in his back pocket
and sits on them with odd results. He becomes a mock newspaper-
seller: 'Drame de la rue Berthollet, horribles détails, 5 centimes.'
('Terrible murder in the rue Berthollet. Read all about it.') When
they are copying in the Louvre (Salle Lacaze) and wish to get rid
of over-curious tourists, they have a simple routine: one of them
puts a finger to his nose and looks slowly round, remarking, 'I
think one of you gentlemen has forgotten himself.' The tourists
quickly disperse. Then Lehmann makes his appearance, urging
the more pallid copyists to look at Rubens. One of the students
imitates one of the tourists who have just left: 'Ch'aime pas les
Rupens, ce n'est pas tes femmes, c'est tes vaches. C'était un
salicaud ce Rupens.' ('That man painted women like cows. Him
no good.') One day a horse-cab is very slowly climbing the rue des
Martyrs, so a group of them line up behind it, hat in hand and
looking suitably miserable. 'Bare-headed and with trembling legs,
he had to be supported on both sides, his hair falling mournfully
over his face.' Another time they were walking, on the boulevard
Saint-Michel, behind a pastry cook who carries on his back a hodfull
of ice. 'So he loped after the man, licking greedily at the ice, and
as they passed "La Source" the whole café exploded with laughter.'
It is an unusual Laforgue (if Laforgue it is)—perhaps the last
appearance of the little boy who knocked off Delcassé's spectacles.
    At about this time (says Emile in the notes) Jules began to haunt
the Bibliothèque Nationale. But this is not quite true. Jules was
going only to a small branch of that great library. Situated in the
rue Colbert, it contained a fair supply of books, mainly novels, but
before long Jules decided it was not enough. On 6 July 1878 he
made an application[7] for a full ticket to the Bibliothèque Nationale
itself. His demand was later supported by the director of the
Beaux-Arts but was turned down flat with the comment: 'Refused.
He is not a graduate.' One of Laforgue's early poems is dated:
'After leaving rue Colbert' and it was assumed at one time to refer
to a famous brothel in that street, which might have made a good
footnote but is untrue.
    While still going to the rue Colbert Laforgue met another of his
school friends from Tarbes. For several months he and Victor
Riemer were inseparable, until the latter left to become a German
teacher in a provincial lycée. It was about this time, too, Emile
tells us, that he took his first small step into journalism.
    It was one of those rags with coloured cartoons which invited
    people to contribute and to keep it short and sweet. My brother
    sent them a ten-line poem, which was short enough, and one

must suppose that it filled the other condition too, since it got printed. Which poem was it? I can't remember. All I know is it was signed with some strange pseudonym concocted from surname and first name combined, and that the paper only lasted three or four weeks and was called *Le Pétard* (*The Fire-Cracker*).

Sad to say, Laforgue's first published poem has not been traced. There was indeed a famous *Pétard* but it ran for at least two years and contains nothing recognizably by Laforgue.

Having once broken into journalism, however minimally, Laforgue's appetite was now whetted, and Emile recalls meeting him one day on the stairs of the newly-founded *La Vie Moderne*. Emile (coming down) had just had some pen-and-ink drawings refused after a cursory glance; but Jules (going up) had better luck. Emile says that his brother's 'slight offering' was accepted but never published. Could it have been the manuscript of 'Amours de la Quinzième Année', to be printed at last one week after his death?

More productive was the suggestion of Hyacinthe Soula—another Tarbes schoolfriend—that he and Laforgue should found a new Toulouse weekly *La Guêpe* (*The Wasp*). This was the classic way to get published and one that Laforgue consistently followed: the wasp in one's pocket is worth a dozen of somebody else's fire-crackers. This Soula, who later became a doctor, seems to have been an enterprising character; his student thesis on the influence of music on medicine got a flatteringly long write-up in *Le Temps* of 23 August 1883 (but the British Museum copy was unluckily destroyed in one of the intervening wars).

Laforgue's contributions to *La Guêpe* run through 1879 from May to November and include poems, articles and drawings. The latter can be dismissed as hardly up to Laforgue's high standard. Neither can it be claimed that he was ever much of a columnist, either in *La Guêpe* or later in the *Revue Indépendante* of 1887. In journalism he waters himself down into insipidity; he is really only interesting when he dares to be his eccentric self. Some of the articles, however, have documentary value, for example his review on 21 August 1879 of *Le Coffret de Santal* (*The Sandalwood Box*), second edition of Charles Cros's famous book of poems. This suggests that Cros might well have been his stepping-stone to Heine. Also of documentary value are the poems of *La Guêpe* and none more so than the contented 'Epicureanism' in which he expresses his simple pleasure in the life he is leading in the Paris of 1879. Notably it shows a still light-hearted and indeed almost jubilant Laforgue. Beginning with the words 'Je suis heureux gratis' ('I'm happy for nothing'), it goes on:

Je ne suis pas obèse, et je vois à merveille
Je ne quitte mon lit que lorsque je m'éveille
[I'm not fat and my eyesight is good, I stay in bed till I wake up.]
'I breakfast and go out,' continues Laforgue,
idly look at drawings, books and newspapers in the arcades of the
Odéon. Then I cross the Seine and, on my stroll, see a blind man
with a nasal voice and a dog. I stop still and find a new pleasure in
water splashing round the arch of a bridge; or in the meanderings,
swept about in space, of the smoke from a passing tug. I have my
gardens, too, like the Luxembourg, where, if my heart desires it, I
go for a walk. I have a museum that's unique in the world; where I
can follow my every mood, from Memling to Rubens, Phidias to
Watteau: a museum where you can find both good and bad—the
naive, artificial, pagan or mystic; Renaissance arms on Antique
torsos. Then to the library I make my way, the finest in the
world. I sit down and select Sainte-Beuve, Théo [phile Gautier],
Banville, Baudelaire, Leconte [de Lisle] and finally Heine, whom
I prefer to all the rest: 'That clown of genius,' as Schopenhauer
calls him, who sighs and smiles, but the smile is bitter. Then on
I stroll past the shop-windows, while soon night falls and Paris
lights up. And my happiness is complete at last—if I can go and
sit in your pit, Oh Comédie-Française! (L:92-3)
This happy 'day in the life of' is of special interest for the link
between Schopenhauer and Heine:
'Ce bouffon de génie,' a dit Schopenhauer
Qui sanglote et sourit, mais d'un sourire amer.
It also indicates that on 18 September 1879, the date of publication, Laforgue was living on the Left Bank in the Latin Quarter.
When exactly did the family move from the Batignolles district,
up by Montmartre? Certainly before 21 July 1879, because that
is the date of his second application (this time successful) for a
Bibliothèque Nationale library ticket.[8] On this occasion he was
more artful. 'My sole aim is to become a writer,' he told the director,
'though that honourable word is in such disproportion to my present
worth that I hardly dare aspire to it. Yet I do not altogether despair
of getting the card, Monsieur, persuaded as I am of my own sincere
intention to use it seriously.' It worked—and the letter is headed 5
rue Berthollet, which is to be the family's address for the next two
years. Like all Laforgue's addresses it has been painted in colours of
sentimental gloom. On the contrary, it was a brand new house in a
pleasant street, only a short walk from the boulevard Saint-Michel
and the Luxembourg Garden. The Laforgues, however,—and this
was the snag—were crushed together in a first-floor flat, all twelve
of them, with the brave Marie now playing the role of mother.

In a sense Laforgue opted out, which was not untypical, burying himself for the next two years in libraries. He was away from home for most of the day—and also in the evening, for in the nearby Bibliothèque Sainte-Geneviève, which remained open till ten at night, he had a heaven-sent excuse. It is fairly obvious that one of the objects of the exercise was to escape the din of family life: there were three boys and three girls under the age of ten at 5 rue Berthollet. But, more importantly, he was now setting forth on an adventure of self-instruction, an extraordinarily intense period of acquiring knowledge outside the formal structures of education, during which he would spend thousands of hours on a self-inflicted cramming course which would leave him one of the most knowledgeable poets of his time—but also a mental and physical wreck. His mind absorbed the widest possible range of interests, from biology and medicine to religion and philosophy. And, as we know, he tried to introduce them all into poetry—not always with success but with lasting results for the art. In the process he had, as one would expect, a major nervous breakdown, brought on partly by physical privations and partly by the obsessive drive of his over-heated mind. It was complicated by the loss of his Christian faith and a lurch towards Buddhism, under the aegis of Schopenhauer. This is how he described it after the event, writing to his friend Mme Mültzer in March 1882: 'Only three or four people know a little about the life I led in Paris two years ago. But that's not quite right; only I know. When I read my diary of that period I ask myself with a shudder how it was I survived.' (D:127)

Indeed, in his 'diary' of the time his self-pity is such that he almost reproduces[9] the rhythms of Philoctetes on Lemnos: 'Deux ans de solitude dans les bibliothèques, sans amour, sans amis, la peur de la mort.' ('Two years of solitude in libraries, without love, without friends, fearing death.') (K:7) His letter to Mme Mültzer continues:

I was nineteen, and so without experience in my craft. Otherwise what a black and bitter book I would now have to my name. . . . But I have no inclination to gossip about those two years which will probably be the most acute phase of my whole bleak destiny. It's the sort of thing that comes out in fits and starts at odd times when it seizes you by the throat. . . . For five months I played at being an ascetic. I acted the little Buddha on two eggs and a glass of water per day, plus six hours in the library. . . . Understand, Madam, that at nineteen I dreamed of going out into the world bare-foot and preaching the word. (D:127-8)

It seems likely that the five months in question were the winter of 1879-80, after which he slowly returned to normal. One of the

legacies of his illness—for such it was—is the mass of turgid poems
called *Le Sanglot de la Terre* (*The Sobbing Earth*), whose accent,
too emphatic to be effective, is unlike anything Laforgue struck
before or after. Though they do express in a crude form his fundamental beliefs, his compassion and pity for humanity, they are
practically unreadable today: the agonized cries of an angry but
artless young man. If the manuscripts are still in demand on the
autographs market, it is more for the doodles that decorate them
than for anything else, for his drawing had improved if nothing
else had. Laforgue did not recover his form as a writer until he
went to Germany, and that was still some months away. But
meanwhile he did not waste his time. 1880 turned out to be one
of the most important years of his life, not for anything he wrote
but for the people he met: the three key figures, in fact, of his
life. For once again Laforgue exercised the talent for making an
impression on exceptional people. It was perhaps this talent,
hardly less than his talent as a writer, that saved him from his
'bleak destiny' and enabled him to make his existence something
that is remembered.

At this point Emile was called up for his military service, from
which Jules as junior brother was excused, the result being that
Emile's observations are now interrupted; but one of the last things
he records is Jules going to a meeting of the *Hydropathes* (a non-
sense name) and returning in a high state of excitement to cover
page after page with enthusiastic notes. The Hydropaths did not
necessarily believe in the virtue of water taken either internally or
externally. They were just an off-beat literary society, a fore-
runner of the Chat Noir (Black Cat) fraternity, who held riotous
meetings twice a week (Wednesdays and Saturdays) in a small
hall in the Latin Quarter.

One day in March 1880 Jules went along to one of these meetings.
He found the place only with some difficulty: a wine shop called
Chez Cosson at 29 rue de Jussieu. But this was only a front; when
you had arrived in the wine shop you squeezed behind the counter
and along a passage until you found yourself in a long narrow room
with a high ceiling and lit, of course, by gas. Despite the fire risk it
was normally let for local dances and wedding feasts, but at the
moment was occupied by rows of benches, a platform at the far end
and some three hundred Hydropaths in an atmosphere resembling
a Turkish bath.

As he stood there, listening to the poets declaiming, Jules had
a rapt expression on his face and his mouth partly open, no
doubt with awe. Without knowing it he was being observed by
his neighbour, who later introduced himself without any fuss:

Gustave Kahn

Gustave Kahn. They made a date to meet at two the next afternoon at the Luxembourg Garden, in the famous Allée des Veuves, among statues representing all the queens of France and other illustrious ladies. Gustave Kahn was a small bubbling man with red hair and a pronounced Jewish nose. A year older than Jules, he had prominent cheekbones, bright little eyes and bounced about like a pea on a drum. More important, this ebullient and confident young man was already an habitué of Mallarmé's Tuesdays in the rue de Rome, and these were early days when the poet was still at number 87 (he later moved next door to 89) and few people had heard of him anyway. Laforgue was suitably dazzled. From the Luxembourg they strolled past the Odéon to the rue Racine hotel where Kahn was then living. In the diminutive bedroom they went on talking and by the end of the afternoon Jules was already beginning to drop the name of Mallarmé as casually as his new friend.

Next time, they met at the Café du Palais in the place Saint-Michel (where Hemingway was later to do so much of his early work). The talk now took in philosophy and religion, and Kahn noted that Jules was already totally detached from all forms of belief, or at least claimed to be. But the black winter of 1879-80 had only just passed and perhaps the vehemence was partly to convince himself. They strolled back up the boulevard Saint-Michel and along the rue Gay-Lussac to the rue Berthollet. The flat (Kahn remembered) was very bourgeois and also very quiet, which suggests that Jules must have picked his time very carefully indeed. Jules's room (Kahn noted) was small and bare, a twin of his own.

After that day they met frequently, and when Kahn was called up at the end of the year to go to Algeria, it became one of Laforgue's self-imposed duties to keep his friend informed of art and life in Europe, a service he performed conscientiously, except when Kahn neglected to send him a change of address.

It is impossible to overestimate what Kahn did for Laforgue, both then and later, but one of his main services was to introduce him to the extraordinary Charles Henry, whom Kahn himself had only met a few months before on the pavement outside the Bibliothèque Nationale. The same age and almost neighbours in the Latin Quarter, Kahn and Henry had nothing else at all in

common. Henry was a tall, languid man with fair hair, loose
limbs and long delicate hands. Laforgue later depicted him as
the heron in a pastiche of La Fontaine's fable:

> Un soir sur ses longs pieds allait à la Sorbonne,
>> Sa serviette ventrue au bras . . .   (A:467)

> [One evening, on his long legs, bound for the Sorbonne, with
> fat briefcase under his arm . . .]

Like Kahn he was a precocious character who had already made
his mark on Paris, tossing off brilliant papers, both literary and
scientific with equal ease. As far
as formal honours were concerned
he was hardly more qualified than
Laforgue, his attitude being that
he had so many interesting things
to do, he grudged the time wasted
in sitting for exams. But not since
Leonardo had so many different
disciplines been so effortlessly
mastered by one man. More than
that, he cross-fertilized them,
applying the principles of art to
science and vice-versa. If Kahn
could quote Mallarmé's latest

Charles Henry

poems, then Henry could explain them by means of equations on
a blackboard. Later he would do the same for Seurat. He is said to
have been the model (or one of them) for *Monsieur Teste*, and
curiously enough he even looked like that character's creator,
Paul Valéry himself.

Perhaps not the least impressive thing about Henry was that he
had a regular mistress. Not just girlfriends like Kahn, but a genuine
mistress, who indeed had given him a son two years previously.
Léonie Duhaut was a delightful blonde who was also Henry's
brilliant collaborator in more scholarly fields. They had been
childhood friends and now were lovers, but Léonie's passion was
to prove too much for Henry's cool and careful temperament.
They were to part early in 1883 and it is sad to report that her
subsequent husband made her destroy twenty letters written to
her by Laforgue. It would seem that the man need not have been
so jealous: although Henry, for his part, might not have been
averse to a Laforgue-Léonie affair (to take some of the heat off
himself) it is extremely doubtful whether Léonie would have been
interested. She loved Henry too much to be unfaithful.

Nothing gives a better contrasting picture of Gustave Kahn and
Charles Henry than the respective interviews they gave in 1891 to

Jules Huret's massive enquiry into the state of literature in France.
Kahn was interviewed in the Taverne Anglaise, rue d'Amsterdam,
in the course of a hilarious Sunday lunch which ended with him
only just catching the 6:20 train to Brussels. In a sustained fire-
work display he demolished every literary name in Paris. Henry,
on the other hand, gave a cool appraisal of the state of France and
the western world which even today is remarkable for its prophetic
overtones. It is a tour de force to which we shall have to return.

Both Kahn and Henry were indispensable to Laforgue. Of two
hundred and fifty of Laforgue's extant letters, these two received
fifty each. In his absurdly short life one can truly say they were
his oldest friends.

No less remarkable was the third of the trio of 1880 friendships.
It was an important day in Laforgue's life when he made contact
with Paul Bourget (not yet, of course, the society lap-dog of later
years). How the meeting happened we cannot be sure. Bourget
was a Hydropath (though an extremely elegant one) and lived only
a couple of hundred yards from the infamous little hall at 19 rue
de Jussieu. Jules would certainly have seen him there but, being
shy, would not have talked to him. He would never have met Kahn if
that ebullient gentleman had not broken the ice. It seems more likely
that Laforgue wrote Bourget a letter, enclosing a poem. It happens
that one of the poems dating from those days—'Apothéose'—is
indeed dedicated to Bourget. Was this the one that served for
introduction? In any case we soon find Laforgue visiting Bourget
regularly every Sunday morning for a series of friendly tutorials
that changed his life.

By the time of these Sunday visits, however, Bourget had left
his tiny top-floor room near the Hydropaths (9 rue Guy de la
Brosse). Somewhat older, at twenty-eight, than Laforgue and his
friends, he had moved farther along the road to success. Perhaps he
felt that he now owed it to himself to move into more appropriate
surroundings. Apart from his reputation as young poet, his newspaper column and dramatic criticisms already had a large following.
He could probably afford a change of air.

Number 7 rue Monsieur, his new abode, was a fascinating building
that still stands: a pleasantly rambling eighteenth-century mansion.
Nancy Mitford later had a ground-floor apartment there and used
to translate the rue Monsieur to her friends as Mister Street. In
another wing, Bourget's flat was reached by steep steps and occupied
the two top floors which were joined by a spiral staircase. Below
were the salon and dining-room and two small bedrooms. Upstairs
was the library (a spacious room looking down on a jumble of
peaceful gardens) with a tiny adjacent round-windowed cell where

he worked. Laforgue himself described it thus in one of the
autumn 1886 (undated) issues of *Les Hommes d'Aujourd'hui*:

> Seven rue Monsieur. The district is correct and provincial. A
> steep flight of steps. A bell that is both shrill and uncom-
> promising. And then, to welcome you, a smile—a smile that
> seems always about to set off on some new journey. The
> gentleman is French, solid and distinguished. His features have
> seen life but are still firm: a fine nose, a brow tortured with
> care, eyes as enigmatic as his latest book, an impressive mous-
> tache, sensual lips and the strong chin you would expect of a
> Balzac hero. In dress: the elegant correctness of a truly wise
> man, light years away from both Bohemian disarray and the
> doubtful Romantic tastes of the Dandy. Bourget began to study
> his appearance and the background of his life under the influence
> of the Balzac heroes . . . his is the correctness of the free man,
> who needs to glide gracefully through life, to take all daily
> surprises in his stride, thanks to the reassuring effect, on himself
> and others, of being dressed for the part. Similarly, if there do
> exist writers who can only be inspired to write in a lumber-room,
> Bourget belongs to the other kind, who need high windows,
> white curtains, spotless linen, ice-cold water, white porcelain,
> books bound in cool cloth . . . and never, never a stain or a
> grain of dust anywhere. (H:86-7)

This was the man and the setting which Laforgue began to visit on
Sundays towards the end of 1880. Besides poems Laforgue also
took along plays (including perhaps *Tessa*?) and later recalled in a
letter to Emile:

> I remember the time when I took Bourget my plays, and
> chapters of novels and masses of verse, thinking to myself: this
> time he's going to be really bowled over! And then the following
> Sunday he'd tell me, 'You don't know French yet, nor how to
> write poetry; you haven't even reached the point of being able
> to think for yourself.' And when I read what remains of those
> old things, I can see how right he was. (E:146)

In those days Bourget was an elegant and sharp young man, vastly
different from the bland and fashionable novelist he was to become.
His smooth and worldly scepticism gave him, in the eyes of someone like Laforgue, limitless prestige. He would sit relaxed in front
of the fire and read his adaptations from Shelley and Tennyson
(not very good and later to be published in *Les Aveux*) and one
can imagine the effect on the young visitor. Perhaps Laforgue's
love of England sprang from these mornings. Bourget himself,
recalling them, referred to Laforgue as 'my little pessimist' and it
does seem that he had genuine affection for the younger man, to

whom he gave such real and generous practical help throughout his life. It was all the more remarkable when one realizes that he never really liked Laforgue's work, neglected to cut the pages of his books, and sold an inscribed copy without qualms to one of the quayside vendors. More serious still, he apparently placed a publishing ban on every letter Laforgue ever wrote to him. Could there have been an element of jealousy here? Was Bourget instinctively aware that in the eyes of posterity he was going to be eclipsed by his little pessimist?

Kahn was sent to North Africa in November, 1880, and the following month Jules wrote him a letter. Laforgue's letters to Kahn were published during the last war and, because of the German Occupation and the fact that Kahn was Jewish, they were given the title: *Lettres à un ami* (*Letters to a Friend*). Here is the first of them:[10]

Today is Sunday, and you know what Sunday is like in Paris. I'm bored, with nothing to do, and so I'm writing to you: that's not a very polite way of putting it but there you are. . . . You complain about your Algerian sun, and I complain about my lack of it and this eternally dirty, muddy autumn sky. For a change we've had a few foggy days, but for the middle of December it's muggy, muggy. Fate must know that my finances won't run to furs. (One of my dreams: furs.) And what about you? You've got the sea, ungrateful one . . . and I've got the Pont Saint-Michel on Saturday nights, with the tumult of bells from Notre-Dame's two sonorous towers. The din of the Boul' Mich' drowns the music of the bells, which is highly philosophical: it symbolizes the end of Christianity. This has killed that—this being the horns of the trams, and that the voice of the sad bells. What about it, eh?

While you're smoking and eating dates in Arab cafés I'm bent over my books at the library, occasionally tearing myself away from the study of Hartmann to contemplate the fantastic silhouette of M. Henry as it passes by. Then I go for bored strolls along the boulevards, looking in at the art dealers—Goupil, Bingham, Everard et Cadart—or the *Vie Moderne* office, rue Taitbout. Not often do I visit the Café du Palais, that lukewarm place. But I go to Bourget's at 7 rue Monsieur (third floor in case you're interested). I like him a lot. I've taken him all I've done to date of my poetry book, about nine hundred lines. He reads me sonnets, etc. and translates for me (sitting there in front of the fire in his slippers) jewels from Tennyson and Shelley. He's just off to London to write a book. Since you left

I've seen no one, or hardly anyone. A German philologist and three medical students: nobody I can talk literature or art with. I read some verses to those medical students and they said I had facility! It's not a word that would have occurred to me and I offer it to you for one of your novels if you insist. . . . Well, there you are then. A hurdy-gurdy's started up in the courtyard. Bourgeois citizens pass by in their Sunday best, dragging their wives who in turn drag the kids. I'm so bored that my legs are caving in. (Luckily you're not here to make a pun of it.) I'm still pressing on with my philosophicals: one part's finished, twenty-five sonnets. Now I'm going to tackle the big set-pieces. I'm also planning a book, in a style full of artifice, about painters who created a world of their own. . . . A series of studies where, by accumulating words carefully selected for their sound and meaning, I shall try to express the feel of each particular artist's world. In my 'Watteau', for instance, I'm quoting one of Verlaine's *Fêtes*. How about that? Then there's my novel. A painter, who is a disciple of Schopenhauer, kills himself for fear of going mad because he can't realize his dream: the macabre adventure of humanity in three great panels, corresponding to Hartmann's three stages of Illusion. I'll write a prologue describing the first days of humanity and an epilogue imagining the last, when Illusion is dead, the cities deserted and Man, his head shaved and covered with ashes, awaits Nothingness. What a lot of plans and how short Life! I leave you now in order to read my good friend H. Heine. (C:17-23)

The book of philosophical poems which he took to Bourget—nine hundred lines completed—was the *Sanglot* already referred to. For the moment he was 'pressing on' with them, but not for long. Significant is the allusion at the end to his friend Heine. The *Sanglots* and H. Heine were incompatible, and there was not much doubt about which would win. Three weeks later he wrote to Kahn again:

I'm forgetting you, aren't I! But you know what it is like when you're living with your family, especially over Christmas. I only have the Sundays free, and today's Sunday. Even so they're calling for me in half an hour. Guess what, I've just had something published in *La Vie Moderne*, a triptych in prose called 'Les Fiancés de Noël'. Yes, I'll put Manet in the book as you suggest, but first of all I must see some Manets. . . . Do you remember a grey afternoon on the outer boulevards, the day you ate too many tarts and I spoke vaguely about a *Prometheus* I was planning? Well, it's becoming clearer in my mind, and one of these days I'll do it. A modern *Prometheus* in a dress coat . . .

Will you be here for the Salon? . . . My brother will send a drawing as usual, and as usual it'll be refused—but with his receipt I'll get into the private view. . . . Soon I'm going to draw lots for the call-up but, as you know, I'm excused anyway. . . . The other day I saw Leconte de Lisle with his gloves on in a bus. . . . Do you know of the Impressionist landscape painter Pisaro [*sic*]? Is he any good? His brother's a close friend of my father. Apparently Zola thinks a lot of his work. . . . They're just calling for me, so I must fly. One of these days I'll go and look at your empty seat at the Café du Palais. (C:24-8)

It is interesting that at this point he hadn't seen any Manets and couldn't spell Pissarro's name. His first published prose, 'Les Fiancés de Noël', did not set the Seine on fire. A fortnight later he wrote again:

I'm writing you from the Bibliothèque Nationale but your friend Henry isn't here. I've just come from Bourget's. We talked about *La République des Lettres* containing Mallarmé's prose poems which he very much likes. He's keenly interested in style. Meanwhile Paris is sloshing about in the slush after a week of snow. . . . Yesterday Taine, whose lectures I follow religiously despite that Ingres fresco in the background, was amazingly good on Angelico. (You like and understand Angelico, I hope?) Do you know those adorable English gift-books illustrated by Kate Greenaway? It's time I started earning some money from journalism, so that I can buy all that tempts me in the shops. . . . Where can I get a set of back-numbers of *La République des Lettres*—or even the odd issue? I've tried all the book boxes along the quays, and there's nothing doing. . . . I'm drawing the lots tomorrow. . . . I'll send you that number of *La Vie Moderne* next time, but it's nothing, you know . . . and let me have some of your colonial literature. . . . Do they allow you a briefcase to keep your papers and notes in? . . . All these last few days I've been in love again with Baudelaire. My copy's one of those awful Calmann-Lévy jobs—when will Lemerre take him over? I bound it in the sombre lining of an old suit and take it around with me everywhere. . . . How well he understands autumn! Of the thirty or so sonnets I've done for my book four are Autumn Afternoons; they're the ones I've worked hardest on and like the least. I just haven't managed to express the melancholy—perhaps because I remember only too well one of Mallarmé's prose poems on the subject! . . . Do you remember once promising me your copies of *The Hydropath*? . . . Well, I still haven't had them! No, it's no good asking for news of people, I never see anybody. I'm always either at home or at the Beaux-Arts or the Nationale. . . . Last Sunday at the Sorbonne there was a lecture on Women by Legouvé. You should have been there, just to hear some of the metaphors. Have they let you keep your great forked beard with the unequal points? (C:29-34)

Kahn had to wait over a month for the next letter.

Forgetting you, aren't I! But what can you expect? When I feel like work I go to the Library, and when I feel low I visit the sad suburbs and listen to hurdy-gurdies. . . . Today it's Shrove Tuesday. I'm bored, alone and it's snowing. There's nothing happening on the Boul' Mich', so I'm writing to you. How well up are you with literary news? There's a new novel by Huysmans called *En Ménage* [*Living Together*] which is terrific. I did a review of it for a German paper *Magazin für die Literatur*....Haven't seen Bourget for a fortnight. . . . I drew some number or other for call-up, but I'm free anyway. . . . Carlyle is dead (in case you hadn't heard). I should like to have known him. I've now done 1,800 lines of the *Sanglot* but it's beginning to get me down, so I've gone back to the novel. Can't begin at the beginning because I haven't planned it. I can just more or less see my characters, and I've been all over the place doing descriptive pieces. (C:35-7)

These descriptive pieces were evidently planned as background atmosphere to open and close chapters, etc. Some survive in manuscript and one I have is typical. Meticulously written in tiny handwriting without a single correction, it is a highly professional description in two hundred and fifty words of a singer in the courtyard at 5 rue Berthollet. (cf. K:44-5)

If you can, do read that Huysmans novel. It really shook me, I think it's brilliant, really brilliant. But since you speak German I'll send you the article I did on it. . . . They're publishing *Nana* in serial form with illustrations by Bellenger which I'like very much. . . . Why doesn't Forain exhibit somewhere? . . . Aren't you homesick for the boulevards? But with you one can never tell. Inform me once and for all: is your military service of the voluntary kind for one year only? In which case will you be back next November (since you left last November)? Don't you want to come back? Haven't you any ambitions? . . . The truth is that I'm fed up and want to have you here. On grey days we could go to Montmartre and inspect the cafés. We'd sit on a bench and you'd read me excerpts from your novel. And I'd rejoice in your monumental fooling as we roamed the throbbing streets. Come back. . . . Soon it will be spring and the boats will be back on the Seine. On afternoons of spleen I shall go from Paris to Saint-Cloud, and from Saint-Cloud to Paris, on the water, dreaming about life. (C:37-9)

So the *Sanglot* was beginning to pall, but what about that 'terrific' novel *En Ménage*? It is about a man who leaves his wife, goes to live with a former mistress, doesn't like it and returns to his wife. Moral: a wife is a somehow-necessary thing. But, for Laforgue, the point was only partly in the plot. The book impressed him because it put forward a new artistic theory, a justification of what was then being called modernity. It sought and found a strange new urban beauty in the 'uglier' parts of towns. To a lover of Baudelaire like Laforgue, this was an idea to be welcomed enthusiastically. One can imagine his excitement when he read:

> According to the painter Cyprien, the true accent of a landscape was provided by the factory chimneys which rose above the tree-tops to spew their flakes of soot into the clouds. He admitted to moments of wild exultation when, seated on the brow of the ramparts, he looked into the distance and saw the gasometers raise up their carcasses filled with sky, like circuses built of blue walls supported by black columns.[11]

Only a few months before, Huysmans's famous piece on the sickly Bièvre river, which wended its way through the south of Paris, had been published in his book *Croquis Parisiens* (*Parisian Sketches*) with an illustration by J.-F. Raffaëlli, a painter who was to make his name with pictures of the so-called 'Zone', the ring of poor districts on the extreme edge of the city. That Raffaëlli view was of a distant Paris seen from the southern fortifications, with the

J.-F. Raffaëlli: illustration to Croquis Parisiens

domes of the Panthéon and Val de Grace framing a foreground of factory chimneys. Huysmans and Raffaëlli now became for Laforgue the chief exponents of a new type of sensibility with which he identified himself completely. His highest praise for a landscape now was to call it, in the words of Cyprien, 'consumptive and charming'. A far cry indeed (as Huysmans said) from the plump and prosperous type of landscape, with splendid view carefully arranged, that was then encouraged by the Beaux-Arts.

About this time (March 1881) Jules wrote to Emile:
You know that just lately we've had municipal elections here in Paris. Well, listen to this: it happens in Passy. Four days before polling day the sitting councillor, a radical, is haranguing a meeting when a voice asks for permission to speak. Granted! So a small gentleman mounts the tribune: it's Delcassé, Théophile, acting, it seems, on the suggestion of Gambetta himself. For an hour and a half he improvises, and then, amid shouts and acclamations, he's made an official candidate. He has only four days to play with, so he calls a meeting and papers the district with posters announcing his programme. (He gave me some.) The great day arrives and he does so well that congratulations flood in from the Ariège department inviting him to stand next year for parliament. Do you know, that fellow is quite capable one of these days of sitting in the Chamber of Deputies. (E:134-5)
Delcassé, Théophile, was on his way.

At this point Paul Bourget, always with an eye on Jules's welfare, had a quiet word with his friend Charles Ephrussi of the *Gazette des Beaux-Arts* who was just then writing a massive tome on Dürer. Ephrussi agreed that he could certainly do with a bright young assistant, so from mid-July Jules began to spend his mornings at 81 rue de Monceau.

Ephrussi was then thirty-two, slightly older than Bourget, and already well-known in the art world. George Painter has claimed him as the 'lesser original of Swann'. He certainly knew Proust well, as he did all of Paris. It was a godsend at this particular moment for the shy, somewhat poverty-stricken Jules to be taken into an atmosphere where he could blossom. Ephrussi, it might be said, was the man who educated and groomed Laforgue for all that was to follow. And his biggest influence was through paintings.

Laforgue could never afterwards forget the room where he worked in Ephrussi's house; where the colour (yellow) of an armchair sang out, and the walls were hung with paintings by Manet and Berthe Morisot. Ephrussi, as a man of the world, loved Manet and Morisot above all others. He had no use for what he would have called the miserabilism of Huysmans. His darling Morisot he would compare to Fragonard, while Huysmans merely thought her superficial, far preferring Pissarro or even Raffaëlli. Laforgue now found himself being tugged continually between Huysmans and Ephrussi, the plaintive and the worldly.

When Laforgue is recalling memories in a letter to Ephrussi later that year (D:42) it is no accident that he names three pictures by Berthe Morisot. He knows, of course, that they are Ephrussi's favourites, but he has also grown to love them himself:

(1) 'On a deep, fresh carpet of grass: a seated woman, her child, a black dog and a butterfly-net';

(2) 'A nurse and child in colours of blue, green, rose, white and sun';

(3) 'That very capricious woman with a muff, and a deep red rose in her button-hole, against a background of wittily whipped-up snow.'

These three pictures can be identified in the Bataille and Wilden-stein catalogue as:

(1) 'Sur la pelouse' ('On the lawn') (1874). Pastel. No. 427.

(2) 'Jeune femme et enfant sur un banc' ('Young woman and child on a bench') (1872). Watercolour. No. 620.

(3) 'Hiver' ('Winter') (1880). Oil painting. No. 86.

All three are delightful, but 'Sur la pelouse' is one of the best things Morisot ever did. It must have been a pleasure to work with it in the same room.

On those summer mornings of 1881 Laforgue found himself living among Impressionist pictures that had only just been painted, like that Morisot 'Hiver' of 1880, or Renoir's picture of a little girl, 'La Bohémienne', which had been done near Dieppe in 1879 and bought the same year by Ephrussi. Then there were Monet's 'Pommiers' ('Apple-trees') of 1878, Mary Cassatt's 'Lydia' (1879) and the Degas pastel (1879) of Duranty. For the young man who, six months before, had wondered where he could see some Manets, it must have been a revelation. There on the wall was the 1880 pastel of Constantin Guys, and the lithograph of Mr Punch. Any time he liked he could go down to Manet's studio in the rue d'Amsterdam and see many more; for Ephrussi was one of the painter's greatest friends and was to care for him in his last ailing days. It was indeed Ephrussi's brother Ignace who had the honour to bring the roses for Manet's last painting on 1 March 1883. But the most telling incident of all is the one connected with Manet's 1880 painting 'Une botte d'asperges' ('A bundle of asparagus'). The painter asked 800 francs for this masterpiece and when Ephrussi gave him a thousand, he was so touched that he did a small additional picture of one solitary asparagus, which he sent to Ephrussi with the note: 'This seems to have slipped from your bundle.' Now in the Jeu de Paume museum in Paris, 'L'asperge' (1880) is sometimes said to be the finest of all Manet's still-life paintings.

Ephrussi also gave great help to Auguste Renoir and in the summer of 1881 the painter responded by putting him into the famous 'Déjeuner des canotiers' ('The boating picnic'), which shows a party in a river restaurant at Chatou, near Paris. But Laforgue's favourite painting of all those to be seen on the walls of Ephrussi's house was the Monet 'La grenouillère' ('The paddling-pool') of 1869, which is today in a private collection near London. Number 135 in Daniel Wildenstein's 1974 catalogue, this, too, is of a famous boating place on the Seine near Chatou and is one of a series which includes that other better-known 'Grenouillère' in the Metropolitan Museum of Art, New York. One has the feeling that whenever Laforgue wrote of Impressionism he was thinking of Ephrussi's 'Grenouillère'. Indeed in his letters to Ephrussi he constantly returns to it: 'Best wishes to the Monet. You know the one I mean' (D:30); 'What plots are you hatching, there between your Grenouillère and the Manet Constantin Guys?' (D:88); 'I hope no one's run off with your Monet and those gloriously imagined boats. I want to see it again!' (D:116-17)

Laforgue had now moved into a world he could never have dreamed of in Tarbes. He was on the fringes of that international society of Jewish bankers who were also men of great taste. Charles Ephrussi's brother Jules was himself such a banker. He had married Fanny Merton, the widow of an even richer banker and, according to Edmond de Goncourt in his *Journal*, Jules Ephrussi had to spend a month of nights dancing till dawn to win his prize. Once together, the Jules Ephrussis built a fabulous house for themselves at Meggen near Lucerne, where Charles Ephrussi and Paul Bourget were frequent guests. Fanny herself was a particular friend of Bourget's; she was of Austrian origin and was often to be seen in Berlin. Charles Ephrussi himself, though born in Odessa, had come to Paris via Vienna. Another banker of the Ephrussi family was Charles's cousin Maurice who was to marry Béatrix, second daughter of Baron Alphonse de Rothschild—a lady who, as the Baronne d'Ephrussi-Rothschild, contributed so much to the fortunes of Diaghilev's Russian Ballet.

Towards the end of 1881 (says Emile in the notes), 'our father fell ill and returned to Tarbes with the whole family.' But, perhaps because the rue Berthollet lease had a few weeks to run, he allowed Jules to remain behind in Paris with Marie to look after him. These were precious August weeks for Jules and his confidante, almost the last chance they ever had to exchange views on books and poetry. But soon the time came for Marie to join the rest of the family in Tarbes, and for Jules to decide his future. He decided to remain in Paris and took a room in the Latin Quarter.

Much has been made of Laforgue's life in this garret. Always ready to stress the pathetic side of his life, critics have exaggerated his so-called sufferings out of all proportion. Laforgue himself is partly to blame: he was living in a cheap hotel and, if this does not seem too terrible, one must remember that it was the first time he had done such a thing. The fact is he was feeling quite absurdly sorry for himself. The letter he wrote to his sister at the beginning of September 1881 starts with a dig at Pascal Darré: 'For you alone to read before going to sleep. Tell the cousin I'll pay for the light.' It goes on as follows:

Poor dear sister, how sad the station was on the night you left— with you hidden right at the back of the compartment. I could see you were crying and I called to you, but you didn't reply and I had to leave. . . . I rushed off heart-broken: alone in Paris. I came straight back here and climbed to my sad, ordinary room, where nothing belongs to me and nothing knows me; where so many others have been. I couldn't have slept—I had a heavy heart and a tight throat—and so forgive me but I did what you told me not to do: at one in the morning I went to Rieffel's. He was alone, so I sank into an armchair by the bed and, wrapped in a blanket but shivering with sadness, I waited for morning. . . . I let the concierge have some of the books, including a primer for his son. In exchange he made me pay eight francs for two missing keys. . . . On the first of the month, when I got paid by Ephrussi, I bought three flannel vests at the Bon Marché. I asked for red ones and the assistant looked at me as if I'd arrived from outer space. I also ordered (don't be angry) a new suit in cheviot, that tweed material you like so much. . . . One day, after a lot of hesitation, I went into a one-franc restaurant. I came out with burning cheeks and a heavy head. If you only knew what cheap food is like, the cooking done anyhow and topped up with pepper. At home we always had bowls of coffee and milk and enormous plates of stew if nothing else, and it was well cooked . . .

If only you'd seen me the other evening. There I was, all by myself, watching the Sunday crowds: they were coming home, taking the trams by storm. And I noticed certain details that made me feel my loneliness even more intensely: a woman, dressed to the nines, coming out of a baker's shop and holding in both hands a steaming roast on a table napkin, the Sunday joint. You'll never guess how I dined myself. Oh quite well: all I needed was a baker, a delicatessen and a greengrocer. I have all those shops close at hand in the street, almost next door. But I didn't want to be seen by the local concierges. So first I walked miles to a baker's and bought two *sous'* worth of bread, which promptly disappeared into the cavernous depths of my pocket. For the delicatessen it was more difficult: I walked back and forth, not daring to enter: I was scared because, behind the counter, there were two young girl assistants with pink shining cheeks and immaculate sleeves laughing together. Why should I disturb them?[12] At the next shop I hadn't the same excuse, since the assistant was an old dear with a moth-eaten astrakhan tippet, but I still hesitated, wondering if the thing I wanted was really called galantine. Finally, at the next one, I went in. A one-eyed man in an apron advanced towards me, a sharpened cutlass at his side. 'Some galantine, please,' I stammered.—'How much?'—'Six *sous'* worth.'—'With or without truffles?'—Great heavens, I thought. I've never tasted either; and, in a flash, under the searching gaze of the pork-butcher, I made this small calculation: If I take it with truffles, I may not like the truffled part and I'll have to throw it away and there'll be that much less to eat. On the other hand, I think I'll like it non-truffled and, without the truffles, there'll be more non-truffled to like. So in a loud and clear voice I declared, 'Without truffles.' The butcher hurled himself at the amber-coloured jelly and a large thin slice of it joined the two *sous'* worth of bread at the bottom of my pocket. Then at a greengrocer's, for the moderate sum of ten centimes, I bought a slice of melon and came home. I double-locked the door and, while eating, I thought of life, and of you who haven't written to me. When I'd finished, not wanting to leave the melon rind in my room (which would have revealed my poverty to the man who cleans it) I picked up my hat, stick and gloves . . . and also the melon rind which I slipped in my pocket. I went down into the street and, pretending to stroll beneath the arcades of the Odéon, I waited for the right moment, dropped the rind on the ground and went round to Henry's for a coffee. . . .

Poor and good sister . . . try not to worry, relax a little. Observe those provincials carefully, despise them and wait. . . . I'd send you here and now my twenty francs from *La Vie Moderne* but you're living with thieves who are ex-bakers and Gascons as well, a formidable combination. . . . Yes, relax, arrange yourself a sort

of small resigned life. Take a lofty view of Tarbes, your friends
and everyone. Think of the characters, the women characters,
of our great Balzac. . . . Become a superior woman, worthy of
the world we shall one day live in. . . .

Very often, in the twilight when I come home, I just dream
without thinking, looking at Notre-Dame over the rooftops and
chimneys in moments of forgetfulness. . . . It's a funny thing
but, though I'm quite free, certain habits cling to me. For
instance, when I come out of Ephrussi's at midday, what's to
prevent me having a snack in that district and then going on to
the Library? But no, my legs take me quickly and automatically
to the place where we used to live: without knowing why, I
prowl around the rue Berthollet, where I've no reason whatever
to be. And, again, when I come out of a reading room at ten in
the evening, I hurry to that old district of ours, as if you were
there waiting for me. . . . How sad your letter is, my poor little
Marie! But these separations and sadnesses are necessary from
time to time to prove to ourselves that we still have a childlike
softness of heart. . . . Dear poor little one, I enclose a stamp.
Try to persuade Papa—for you're the only one who could do it
—to see a doctor, follow a proper diet and start to live again. As
a father he's all right, you know, even if he did read too much
Jean-Jacques Rousseau. What can I send you as a souvenir? I've
cut a piece of wallpaper from behind the chest of drawers in my
room. Keep it preciously . . . (D:3-13)

We know that Laforgue's hotel was in the rue Monsieur-le-Prince
but there has been a certain amount of conjecture about the number. Ruchon, in the 1946 edition of *Stéphane Vassiliew*, said it
was number 21. This was the Hôtel du Perron, so called after a
flight of steps that leads down at this point into the rue Antoine-
Dubois. From the top rooms on this side, looking across the Ecole
de Médecine, you can (as described) see Notre-Dame. But in his
livret militaire, issued in 1881, a different number is given: 43,
which was the Hôtel du Réservoir. From here also, looking across
the gardens of the Lycée Saint-Louis, you can see Notre-Dame.
When Laforgue says that he has the three shops, including the
delicatessen, 'almost next door', it is worth noting that the only
delicatessen in the street in 1881 was in fact number 41—and it
was later to become popular as a restaurant, with Valéry and Gide
as clients. In fact the little street is almost awash with celebrities,
for it was here in May and June 1872 that Rimbaud wrote the
brilliant group of poems which includes 'La Chanson de la plus

haute tour' ('Song of the Topmost Tower'). Rimbaud's room, coincidentally, gave on the same garden of the Lycée Saint-Louis, and he has described what it was like on a May morning:

Last month my room in the rue Monsieur-le-Prince looked over the garden of the Lycée Saint-Louis. There were enormous trees under my narrow window. At three in the morning, the candle-light grew pale and suddenly the birds, all at the same time, began twittering in the trees. It was all over: no more work. I just had to contemplate the trees and skies, caught up in this inexpressible hour, the first hour of morning. I could see the lycée dormitories, absolutely quiet. But already there was that jolting, sonorous, delightful noise of wagons on the boulevards. I smoked my pipe and spat on the tiles, for my room was an attic. At five I went down to buy some bread and timed it well, the workmen were bustling about everywhere. For me it's usually the time I get drunk in the wineshops. I came back to eat and went to bed at seven, when the sun was beginning to drive the woodlice from under the tiles. The first morning of summer, and evenings in December: that's what has always delighted me here.

Laforgue never saw the street in the same rosy light as Rimbaud, nine years before. But however painful the experience, it didn't last long: certainly not more than three months. The stories of his years in a garret are fanciful.

On 18 November Bourget and Ephrussi made an important announcement. They had been getting together again for the inter-national betterment of Laforgue and were now in a position to reveal their plans. Both were well aware that the situation of Laforgue was precarious. The family had gone to Tarbes and the Dürer book was nearing completion. So they decided to transport him to the Imperial court of Prussia, where he would act as French Reader to the Empress Augusta. This was a promotion indeed for a poor journalist currently living in a Latin Quarter garret (and we say journalist advisedly since it is the term used in his military pass-book, though clerk or secretary might be nearer the mark). His salary would rise overnight to the princely sum of 9,000 francs a year, which was equivalent to the pay of a French MP, and he was to join the court at Coblenz almost immediately.

By a sad coincidence, on the very day he received this scarcely credible news, his father died at Tarbes from angina pectoris: 'at nine in the morning, chez Daroux, 9 place de la Préfecture', according to the death certificate. So Laforgue, who had been walking round in a daze of bewilderment at his own good fortune, was pulled up with a jolt two days later when the news came through in a letter

from Tarbes. (No one seems to have thought of sending a telegram.)
He quickly considered his position and decided that he must at all
costs take up the German appointment. And as he had been told
to stand by for instructions, it was not even possible for him to go
to Tarbes for the funeral. As things turned out (though Laforgue
handed over all that was due to him in his father's will) the main
family worries and responsibilities were thereafter shouldered by
the indefatigable Marie. Jules wrote to her on 20 November 1881:

What can I say? . . . I received the cousin's letter today Sunday
at noon. And Papa died Friday morning. So I lived through
Friday and Saturday without knowing; going about my ordinary
business, and all the time, down there, Papa was dead. . . . At
two o'clock this afternoon I went to the aunt's, expecting to
give them the news, but they all thought I was in Tarbes. It was
a day of weeping. . . . I left at six and sent you that telegram; so
economical and curt it made me cry. . . . So now we're eleven
orphans. . . . And you, poor Marie . . . you probably haven't
eaten or slept for days . . . and your happiness now is all I want
to think about. I'll try and make the others happy but for you
it will be adoration: if you died, I would die too. (D:14-18)

He wrote again two days later:

What are you going to do? . . . I know nothing of Papa's affairs.
I've heard him talk of a M. Carbonnel but that's all . . . and if
there's one thing I'm incapable of it's making sense of our
financial position and looking after it. . . . I haven't yet had the
word to leave for Germany. It might in the end be eight or ten
days but I can't come to Tarbes in the meantime, I have to wait
here . . . (D:20-2)

A week later he got the word and on the eve of departure left this
note for Ephrussi:

Your brother will have told you that I called at 12:30 today.
. . . I found your note but it was impossible for me to be at
Manet's at three o'clock. . . . I leave at seven tomorrow morning
and arrive at ten in the evening. . . . I feel the train is going to
transport me into a great dream. Perhaps my heart will beat a
little quicker but deep down I just let myself drift, for I believe
that everything is written and decided in advance. It was written
that I should meet you in my life; it was written that I should
go to Coblenz; and what I shall make of this great chance has
also been written since eternity. But I shan't be any less grateful
to you all my life. . . . (D:23-4)

Part 2:
A POET AT THE COURT OF QUEEN AUGUSTA

CHAPTER 3
Berlin (1882)

I had a comfortable journey in first-class, all padded and mirrored and heated, with lunch at the Belgian frontier and dinner at Cologne. At Coblenz station a kind of ancient coach awaits me with a solemn coachman. A footman bows to me, opens the door and I get in. Very soon we enter the grounds of the Château. After a maze of paths and lamp-standards and guards in pointed helmets we reach a flight of steps and a door, which a great braided footman opens for me. It is my apartment and inside are my servant and his wife; while waiting for me they have lit a big fire and prepared my dinner.

Let me describe my Coblenz apartment: an ante-room leads to my study, which is a big room with a very high ceiling. On the left, a chest of drawers with a mirror and candlesticks and two big windows; at the far end, my desk all ready for writing with a fine inkwell and a complicated lamp that I haven't yet understood, a fat armchair, a spittoon and a footmuff; on the right, a divan-bed, two armchairs, eight other chairs, a wide table covered with cloth, and on a silver tray a dinner of cold meats, a gilded plate with petits fours, a tea-pot, a sugar-bowl and silver tongs. Finally comes my bedroom, where also they have lit a fire and where I find my trunk, with wash-stand, etc.

The servants bid me goodnight and leave. I warm myself and dine melancholically, with a heavy heart and just picking at things here and there. These sumptuous dinners, you know, seem pretty insipid to a stomach like mine, which has had to put up with a lot in its time. The whole place is asleep: all I hear is the ticking of the clock. I ask myself if it isn't all a dream. I open the curtain and see the long façade of the château lit by a thousand lights, and the solemn sentries marching up and down with rifles on their shoulders. I go into my bedroom where thin candles are burning in the silver candlesticks. I arrange my trunk a little and then go to bed. Ah, that wonderful bed with sheets as delicate as silk, and a blue eiderdown. I try to gather my wits and see things as they really are but, tired out, I fall asleep, with the thought that at this very moment you, too, are in your bed thinking of all that is happening to your poor Jules. Dear Marie, you haven't told me yet what you think of all this.

At eight o'clock I wake up, just as a maid brings in a tray with coffee and milk and the rest, including several kinds of tiny roll. I wash myself, put on my dress coat and white tie, patent-leather boots, gloves and top-hat. A valet with splendid calf-muscles brings me a letter on a tray which announces a visitor for ten o'clock. While waiting I watch the guards on horseback drilling in the château courtyard. At ten it is the Secretary of the Queen's Household who arrives: I am to be presented to Her Majesty at eleven. How my heart beats! Imagine your poor Jules! At eleven I go upstairs: I walk through corridors full of portraits and mirrors, past rows of armed sentries, and arrive in an ante-room which is a veritable garden of exotic plants. Here I am presented to Countess Hacke, a kind motherly lady, the principal Lady in Waiting. She's heard about Papa's death, etc. and speaks to me very affection-ately, points through the window at the Rhine, shrouded in fog, and tells me not to be afraid.

Two footmen approach and I am ushered in. Imagine the splendour! I am dazzled! The Empress is there and she rises to welcome me, asks questions about my career, sympathizes at length with me on the death of my father, asks me who is to look after my young brothers and sisters and to keep her informed about them—and it was all so sincere, I was dumb-founded! I came through it quite well, I think, making very simple replies. Then: 'Countess Hacke, show Monsieur Laforgue the Portrait Gallery.' Countess Hacke conducted me round. She's so kind—she said I could go and see her when I wished. Well, finally back to my apartment where they brought me lunch: numberless delicacies again but I'm only hungry in France. . . . Then more letters: an invitation to dine with Dr Velten, the Queen's physician, and another to go and read to the Queen at half-past eight. . . .

And so at six I change my shirt (not that the one I put on this morning isn't still immaculate) and a servant takes me to Dr Velten's, where a charming old gentleman grips my hand, helps me off with my coat, sits me down and starts talking French. I

mention some of the vast number of famous medical works that
I read during my years of humble toil in Paris libraries. This
touches him and he serves me himself, suggests that I don't eat
enough. (By this time I have given up counting the courses.)
Tomorrow the Court leaves for Berlin at nine in the morning,
and we shall be in the same coach. In Berlin we'll see each other
every day, we'll go to the Opera together and he promises he'll
teach me perfect German. Ah, what a nice doctor! Last winter
when I had my palpitations I never guessed there were people
around like him. At eight I was back in my apartment. In half
an hour I would be reading to the Queen. . . .

The rain's coming down in torrents and every so often they
come and top up my stove, a big contraption that reaches to the
ceiling. In my dress coat I walk up and down restlessly. At last
the moment arrives: imagine me, for heaven's sake, as I stride
up the great white staircases, accompanied by a valet. Down
innumerable corridors, between rows of sentries I pass, and as I
enter the room I manage not to fall head over heels. Seated
round a table are two young princes, four princesses, Countess
Hacke, and the Empress in evening dress. The princes are looking
at albums, the young ladies embroidering. The Empress herself
is doing a watercolour. There is one empty place, which the
Empress invites me to occupy. I'm between Countess Hacke and
one of the princesses. I read as if in a dream, trying to control
my voice. Little by little I gather my wits and begin to think
that I'm reading quite well when oops! I see a risky bit just
ahead. Countess Hacke looks at me nervously, or so I imagine.
In masterly fashion, so that it isn't the least bit obvious, I skip
the risky bit. Saved! Oh my God! The countess must have been
the only one to notice, and I seem to catch her look of relief.
My life has certainly had its odd moments.

Later the Empress asked me for details of Paris art exhibitions,
and I replied with composure. Then we all rose, and I returned
with a light heart to my study, where a good fire awaited me
and, on the table, a supper which I haven't yet touched (pâté, a
leg of chicken, petits fours). And here I am writing to you: it's
midnight, it's raining and the Queen's windows are still lit up.
Ah, my dear Marie, the worst is over, I'm saved. I'll let myself
live amid all this opulence, I'll get used to it, relax a bit, spoil
my stomach, care for my appearance and work on my books,
my beloved books which despite everything are my only real
ambition.

Well, what do you think of it all? . . . If little Adrien were six
years older he could succeed me in four years' time. Can't you

just see him in ceremonial dress, reading to Her Majesty and skipping the risky bits. Tell him from me to be good and to adore you.

Sorry but I dare not tear off a piece of the gilded wallpaper to match the one I sent you from my other room two months ago.

I imagine myself for ever surrounded by footmen. Write to me: M. Jules Laforgue, care of Her Majesty the Queen-Empress, Palace of the Princesses, Berlin, Germany. (D:31-9)

He then wrote a note to Charles Henry:

I am behaving with great correctness, my evolutions are supple and perfect; I think it's because I don't know a word of German. I am superbly lodged, exquisitely nourished with multiple insipidities. . . . It's footmen, lights, great white staircases and mirrors, followed by mirrors, great white staircases, lights and footmen. I haven't had a moment's time for thought which is just as well, otherwise I might pass out in ecstasy. (D:25-6)

A note was also despatched to Ephrussi:

I got through everything all right. In fact I was less timid than I am with you. Why is that? I'm still too shaken to analyse the psychology. . . . My voice didn't tremble. What's the explanation? Remember how I nearly fainted when Mme C. spoke to me in your study? I would like to tell you everything in detail, dear Monsieur Ephrussi . . . you to whom I owe so much, you through whom I am here, you so good, you so tactfully good....(D:27-30)

The German Empress Augusta was a seventy-year-old Franco-phile for whom the war of 1870 had been an unmitigated disaster. To show her displeasure she now insisted on speaking the French language whenever possible. And she despised most things German, including beer, Wagner and even perhaps her eightyfour-year-old husband the Emperor. Almost her only consolation for being the first lady in Berlin was that it gave her the privilege of having French chefs and a French Reader all to herself, with whom she could converse wittily in his own language. He must also read to her, every morning at eleven, carefully chosen snippets from the *Figaro*, the *Journal des Débats* and the *Indépendance Belge*. She swore that it was only through the French papers that she could understand German politics. In the evening at 7.30 books and the *Revue des Deux-Mondes* were more appropriate, but first the pages had to be formally cut by her French coachman M. Corbeil.

She had spent her youth in Goethe's Weimar but, as the daughter of a Russian Grand-Duchess, her education had been French. She .saw herself, in fact, as a French grand lady of the Ancien Régime. Thanks to a platonic, almost mystical affair with the Frenchman Adolphe de Bacourt, she had developed strong Catholic sympathies, rumours of which did nothing to endear her to Berliners. As Laforgue himself wrote, after he had lived with the lady for five years:

The Empress is unpopular in Berlin. It isn't so much for her French sympathies, of which the masses are largely ignorant and about which the Germans are in any case less susceptible than we might be in similar circumstances. No, what the Germans object to is that she does not show herself enough in public, which seems to them to make a mockery of her role at the side of the Emperor. And then she's rumoured to be a pious Catholic, an enemy of Bismarck, a stickler for etiquette and one who despises not only beer but all those simple familiarities dear to the German heart. She's incapable of *Gemüth*, in a word she's 'not one of us'. (G:45)

Laforgue defined *Gemüth* as 'the misunderstood German soul, made up of poetry, nature and family life all rolled into one'. (G:124)

Even her French Reader thought that the Empress sometimes went too far in her love of France and the French language. She would talk French ostentatiously with her daughter at German public gatherings. Sometimes she would arrange witty asides for the benefit of Laforgue himself, as when she said of something or other, 'It makes my hair stand on end . . .' and added *sotto voce*, 'which in my case would be a miracle!' (G:47) Spoken in a plaintive voice, with perfect French accent, these asides could have their charm. Where she perhaps overdid things was to attend the French opera *Carmen* once a week, every week, throughout the season, as well as having it played by the bands as they marched past the palace. This is the sort of thing that, towards the end of his stay, Laforgue was beginning to find exaggerated.

There was no pretence that her marriage to William had been anything other than a matter of State convenience. After she had provided him with an heir, she went her own way—and one of her ways was never to be without a French Reader: it was the minimum requirement to keep her amused and reasonably sane. One would like to record that the French Readers in their turn rose to the occasion, but it cannot be said they were always satisfactory. The first one disgraced himself by going to fight on the barricades in 1848. He had to be dismissed by General von Unruh. Augusta's chagrin and surprise were immense; she resolved to be more careful next time. Reader number two was more rewarding: M. Fromont of Burgundy lasted twenty years and died of despair following the outbreak of hostilities in 1870. The Empress set up a monument on his grave, which she personally tended for the rest of her life. Reader number three was a M. Guiard of whom nothing good or bad is known. He bowed out in 1875 with a clean slate. François Ayme was a fleeting apparition who was engaged with the memorable words: 'Monsieur, I will not allow any language but French to be used in my apartments. Is that understood?' After which she went on pleasantly, 'I am delighted to hear that you teach my dear little grandchildren. What charming boys they are, aren't they! And what a pity, isn't it, Monsieur, that they have such a mother!' This was a reference to Queen Victoria's daughter 'Vicky', the German Crown Princess and mother of the boys in question, William and Henry. It indicates that, in Augusta's eyes, the English were hardly better than the Germans, since neither of them were French.

The next reader, Auguste Gérard, was observed closely by a bright little French girl, the great-niece of Augusta's favourite, Adolphe de Bacourt. She had first had the privilege of staying at

Coblenz in the 1860s during the readership of M. Fromont, but after the Franco-Prussian war she returned there on a visit and later, when she had become the popular French author 'Gyp', described her impressions:

I saw the same Second Empire furniture and the same green plants—huge great palm-trees and gloomy ferns—that I had so detested before the war. The place was like a boarding house for rich families. The whole atmosphere was more like a family than a court: the ladies in waiting sat about in the window seats reading or sewing, while the Empress, who was writing, occupied the very same seat, I swear it, in which I had last seen her. Nearby on a big table covered with the same frightful table-cloth—white with blue stripes and roses; the very one that had made me wince so much in the old days—a gentleman was arranging news-papers and magazines.[13]

This was M. Gérard, who lasted three and a half years till 1880 and was a very distinguished reader, except that he suffered from that fatal flaw of all the later readers (not excluding Laforgue himself): he was a writer and he wrote (so they said) too frankly about Augusta and the Court. It was never quite proved but people in the know felt that he had supplied much of the information to Catherine Radziwill for 'Count Paul Vasili's' scandalous *Berlin Society* (1883). It must be said that M. Gérard denied the whole affair and went on to become French Ambassador to Japan. Other people agreed that he was too starchy to be a good gossip, and was therefore probably innocent.

Amédée Pigeon, who held the post for the year 1880-81, was a close friend of Paul Bourget, and since Gérard had also been a school-friend of Bourget there is the obvious inference that Bourget was the guiding hand behind all the later appointments. When Pigeon unexpectedly came into a small inheritance, he quickly resigned and sped back to Paris, where he occupied the room at 9 rue Guy de la Brosse that Bourget had just vacated. By February 1882 he had already begun writing his German memoirs for the *Figaro*.

Laforgue, as we know, was the next in line and, during his tenure, he did not fail to criticize Pigeon for his gross lack of tact in writing about the German Court. When the articles began to appear they provided a new supply of 'risky bits' which Laforgue had to skip when vetting the *Figaro*. But needless to say, the moment he was released, he hurried to do exactly the same. It is also true that he had a better excuse than the others: he was starving.

Laforgue wrote to Henry:

From Coblenz to Berlin was a whole day's journey . . : through flag-bedecked stations and cheering crowds. I travelled with Dr Velten and Count von Nesselrode, Grand-Master of the Queen's Household—quite a character, that one, and there's nothing like a day in a railway carriage, face-to-face, for observing a gentleman (I saw him asleep, for instance). At Cassel I dined with the maids of honour and the Countess Brandenburg, whose smile is divine in the illuminating sense of that word (rather like Mme Mültzer's between you and me). . . .

Here I live in the Palace of the Princesses, Unter den Linden, under the limes, a smaller version of our boulevard des Italiens. I am actually on the square itself in a ground-floor apartment raised about a metre above street-level. Opposite me is the Royal Guard House, all military bands and pointing cannons. On my left the Opera and Palace. On my right a mass of columns and statues. I've got five windows looking out in all those directions. I can see nothing but monuments. And officers with pale monocles.

Try to imagine my apartment: my study is four times the size of yours in the rue Séguier [where Henry lodged in rather a grand mansion at number 16]. It contains six tables, two of them big ones, and it still isn't crowded. Plus two huge sofas, two mirrors, two armchairs, ten ordinary chairs, a bookcase and a big stove that goes right up to the ceiling. Then there's my bedroom and ante-room. There are fires all day in all the rooms. My servant is a good fellow who, knowing my ignorance of the language, manages to be everywhere at once, anticipating all my wants without a word. Come to think of it, that's not a bad idea: the servant of the future: a dumb man.

What else? Well, at 7.30 every morning I go round to the Palace, which is two steps away. I talk for half an hour with the oldest of the ladies in waiting, Countess Hacke (who tells me she spells French 'like a pig'); then the Empress arrives and I do my reading. . . . Yesterday, when I'd finished, she smiled and said: 'Goodnight, Monsieur Laforgue. We are much obliged.' I managed not to collapse; indeed I've changed so much you wouldn't recognize me. Tell Mme Mültzer I'll never be my awkward self again. . . . Reading the *Revue des Deux-Mondes* last night we came across a book called *Mathematical Recreations*. The Empress gave me a smile from behind her green make-up and said, 'How, I wonder, do mathematics re-create one?' . . . For goodness sake tell me what you're doing. Don't just let me rot or I shall throw myself into the Spree, an ignoble stream (but I've seen the Rhine and the Kehl bridge, and also M. Bismarck who looks bad-tempered). Well, goodbye. I kiss the hand of Mademoiselle [Duhaut]. . . . Have they found Mme Mültzer's dog yet? (D:45-9)

On the same day he wrote to Ephrussi:

I'm not the least bit intimidated. I read very clearly, very slowly in a very confident voice. I don't know why this should be, perhaps because I'm in Germany. . . . Is your book on Dürer out yet and will you give me a copy? You notice how shameless I am; my new-found grandeur must have turned my head. . . . I haven't been to the museum yet. I daren't go out really, I know so little German. I start by arranging my phrases with absurd slowness, but then it all goes to hell. . . . What fine soldiers are the soldiers of King William! Countess Hacke doesn't think they're anything special. During the war she knew a lot of Frenchmen and she thinks they're much more handsome (!). . . . I roam farther afield each day, but not too far: I'm afraid of getting lost and not turning up for my 7.30 rendezvous with Countess Hacke.

I'm happy on the whole, and lucky. But I still think of life as something noisy and pointless. The earth was born and will disappear, a flash in the pan. Wouldn't black eternity have been better without any Empress or Albert Dürer? But in that case I should never have met you. (D:40-4)

Two days later he wrote again to Ephrussi:

Every morning I receive the three papers (two French and one Belgian). I mark the interesting articles, and make summaries of others.[14] Then at eleven I go to the reading. She's amazingly good to me. Sometimes I'm almost embarrassed, she's so natural and intimate. She wants me to give her exercises on the past participle, so I do this . . . and then ask her questions on points of grammar and pronunciation, after which I comment on her replies. . . . For the morning readings there's the Empress and a lady in waiting [Countess Brandenburg] in a little room [La Bonbonnière] hung with engravings. But the evening ones are held in Countess Hacke's room. Oh that good and charming lady, who protects me and makes me visit her every day and wants so desperately to mother me! . . . I correct her faults in pronunciation. Can you imagine me of all people correcting someone else's accent! . . . Then the Empress comes in and asks me if I've been to the museum yet. I confess that I haven't and we start reading. I see no one else except Dr Velten and the secretary M. von dem Knesebeck, who are both near neighbours of mine. . . . Well, goodbye, I'm going to the museum today, partly for pleasure and partly so that the Empress will stop teasing me. (D:51-5)

The change in Laforgue's fortunes had been immense. He had been plucked from a garret in the rue Monsieur-le-Prince (which may or may not have been as bad as he painted it) and whisked away into one of the most desirable apartments of Berlin. At a mere 'two paces' from the Imperial palace, it was in every way comparable to the sovereigns' own residence. Laforgue's wing of the Palace of the Princesses had a forty-five-foot wide façade on the south side of the Unter den Linden, the whole width being occupied by his own apartment. Built in 1811 by Heinrich Gentz, it was distinctly less ugly than its neighbours. Even today, when the East Germans have turned it into the 'Opera Café and Restaurant', it still has elegance. The young Frenchman could look through all five windows at the very heart of Prussia's capital city, the spot where all the big parades took place, where history was made, where some fifty years later on a notorious tenth of May the Burning of the Books was to take place. His large multi-windowed study, with its olive-green walls, ebony woodwork and dark hangings, was in special demand on parade days when everyone from Dr Velten to the maids of honour would crowd in for a ringside seat. On top of all this he was well paid, had free board, a personal servant and two months' holiday. By the time he had settled himself in his new room, with his own engravings on the wall and his own books in the book-case, he was probably set up as comfortably as the Emperor and Empress just along the street. And this is important because, however much he complained about subsequent frustration, it was this dramatic change in his physical way of life that turned the 'tragic' Buddha of the *Sanglot* into the 'dilettante' Buddha of the *Complaintes*.

We ought not, however, to exaggerate the splendours of the German court which, despite Laforgue's initial dazzlement, was never more than third-rate. The soldiers might cut a fine figure, but they were the only element of style on view. The Unter den Linden itself, according to Amédée Pigeon, could well have been the pride of a small provincial town but it was not much by Paris standards.

The Imperial palace had no bath. It was a small, two-storey building, with the Emperor on the ground floor, and the Empress above with four attendants. Like most of Berlin it was painted a dingy café-au-lait colour with the usual flat roof. According to Laforgue it was furnished mostly with Christmas presents, and the administration was so casual that it was quite possible for a stranger to wander in off the street and bump into the Emperor. The etiquette was so primitive that most people greeted the rulers, when introduced, with a slight nod of the head. The Empress was

grateful indeed if anyone called her Madam. It was as if all the
order and discipline in Berlin were reserved for the military.

This was the sad reality, which the Empress did her best to com-
bat, aided and abetted by the local passion for titles, which were used
in reckless profusion to paper over the cracks. Let us consider merely
the Household of Her Majesty the Empress-Queen. It was supervised
by a Grand-Master (Ober-Hofmeister Count von Nesselrode) and a
Grand-Mistress (Ober-Hofmeisterin Countess Perponcher) who
were both too grand to be normally on view. Laforgue could hardly
have known how privileged he was to observe the Count at such
close range on the journey from Coblenz. On a lower plane of
grandness came the following:

PALACE LADIES (PALAST-DAMEN)
Adelaide Countess von Hacke
Luise Countess von Oriola

LADIES IN WAITING (HOFDAMEN)
Alexandra Countess von Brandenburg
Olga Countess von Münster
Adelaide Countess von Schimmelmann

Now comes an indefinable transition from *Damen* to *Frauen*,
where the ladies become women and finally women without even
a particle to their names:

WOMEN OF THE BEDCHAMBER (KAMMERFRAUEN)
Fraülein Marianne von Neindorf
Fraülein von Schöler

WOMEN OF THE WARDROBE (GARDEROBENFRAUEN)
Fraülein Rosa Bachem
Fraülein Dominicus

Countess Hacke, at sixty-nine, was only a year younger than the
Empress herself. The Hofdamen were younger ladies: Brandenburg
forty-seven, Münster and Schimmelmann thirty-two and twenty-
seven respectively. These were the permanent Ladies in Waiting, as
opposed to the temporary maids of honour who were called upon
to serve for short periods only, mostly during the summer months
when the court was, so to speak, on the road.

As Laforgue himself informs us (G:8, 49, 80)—and who ever
knew them better?—the maids of honour were young girls of good
family, always countesses and invariably from the provinces, who

were brought from their 'homely castles' ('naifs châteaux') for a month's tour of duty. They could just about say 'Yes, Majesty' and 'No, Majesty' but it would pass: for them it was not so much an apprenticeship as a finishing school, a seal of approval after which they would be despatched back to their naifs châteaux, with a present from the Queen, to wait for a husband. Unfortunately for the historian, they do not figure on any official list: we know that Laforgue carried on mild flirtations with these innocent butterflies as they came and went—and their Christian names flutter through the pages of his 1883 diary—but it is difficult to identify them or pin them down.

The four personal attendants, however—the women of the Bed-chamber and Wardrobe—were once more permanent officials of the household and as such well authenticated. This is just as well since Laforgue was to be involved with one of them, and on that affair at least we have some intelligence. It is worth noting, though, that all four lived close to the Empress in the Imperial palace and were therefore restricted in their movements. Added to which the Empress had what can only be called an obsession about sex on the premises: to the extent that even married couples were forbidden to live together in the Royal palaces. Servants like Corbeil the coachman could be married only because they lived elsewhere. The Empress's intimate staff was completed by Sister Placida, who belonged to a nursing order, the Soeurs Grises (Grey Sisters, or Soeurs de la Charité de Saint-Vincent de Paul). On a somewhat different and separate footing came the secretary M. von dem Knesebeck, the physician Dr Velten, and the French Reader M. Laforgue.

It is interesting to see Laforgue getting on so well with Countess Hacke, whom others found a very formidable lady. 'Count Paul Vasili' describes her thus:

She's a hunchback and, though she hasn't the lively wit that normally distinguishes that variety of the human species, she has all the vindictiveness. She has great influence on the Empress, whom she sometimes even bullies. She is, in fact, the sovereign's alter-ego, the one person who is permitted to replace her in certain circumstances. What she loves is intrigue, bustle and noise. Her soft voice, in accents both false and affected, mouths 'My Dear' to men and women alike in madonna-like tones that go ill with her features. Secretly, in an underhand way, she's always ready to attack this one's reputation, put in a bad word for that one, make a discreet allusion to Madame X's faults or underline the weaknesses of Monsieur A. On one side she dis-tributes the poison of her perfidious insinuations, on the other the venom of her outrageous suppositions. She does evil without knowing it and does wrong to others, not through malice but by a natural impulse which, because it is ugly itself, can admit no good in anyone else. (G: 152)

According to Marie von Bunsen in her book on the Empress Augusta (Berlin, 1940) Countess Hacke used her rank to accumulate a vast fortune. The same author says that one day the Empress came upon a maid of honour who was crying at the prospect of being placed beside Countess Hacke at a reception. 'Surely you can bear it for two hours,' said the Empress. 'I have had to for thirty years.'

Of the permanent Ladies in Waiting no one had anything but good to say of Countess Brandenburg—and Laforgue, as we have seen, admired her smile. Of Olga von Münster he confided in his diary, 'What eyes!' and they may have had some joke together about a secret rendezvous in Ostend. (F:246) She was the daughter of the then German Ambassador in London and died at Cannes in February 1888 at the age of thirty-eight. As for Countess Schimmelmann she was of Danish origin and had been a Hofdame for ten years (since she was seventeen). She seems, moreover, to have been in a particularly privileged position. 'I was allowed to come and go as I wished,' she has written in her *Memoirs* (London, 1896). After the death of Augusta in 1890 she went to work for the poor, but her family maintained they were anarchists and tried to have her certified insane because of a miniature revolver she carried in her handbag. 'I carried it for eighteen years at the Berlin Court,' wrote the countess, 'and nobody dared to suggest I was mad then.'

The first Woman of the Bedchamber, Marianne von Neindorf, has been given the full treatment by 'Count Paul Vasili'—and rightly so for, on a lower plane than Countess Hacke's, she wielded almost comparable power:

She is in her way a personality: she knows all the secrets of her royal mistress, for whom she writes letters and transmits messages. Though imagining herself to be a devoted servant she is actually a mortal danger, because of her indiscretion and intrigues. She is flattered and adulated by all those ladies who want to keep in with the Empress. Sometimes she makes them wait for hours which—especially in the case of a countess or even perhaps a princess—is most satisfying to her amour-propre. More of a friend than an attendant, she combines the servility of a servant with the veiled and affectionate insolence of a confidante (who knows that her employer will always be afraid to dismiss her). The Empress sees through this woman's eyes and lets herself be influenced by her to an extent that altogether

undermines the royal dignity—especially as Fraülein von Neindorf, like many in her circumstances, has not the sense or tact
to conceal in public her intimately privileged position. (G:153-4)
Laforgue himself said of her: 'Of the whole Court she is the one
who could write the most curious and most complete memoirs—
but she will never do so.' (G:50)

The comparative status of Neindorf, Schöler, Bachem and
Dominicus can be neatly gauged from the Empress's will[15] in
which they were left: Neindorf 50,000 marks; Schöler 30,000;
Bachem and Dominicus 10,000 each. How much would Laforgue
have received? Corbeil the coachman got 6,000. They all received
pensions as well. Corbeil, in addition, was left a couple of houses
in Berlin and Baden-Baden, but William II decided his pension was
quite sufficient. The Empress had lent Corbeil to Napoleon III
when the latter was a prisoner in 1870, and ever since then he had
become rather self-important. This shows in his *Memoirs*,[16] the
most interesting fact that he has to relate being that the Empress
was superstitious: she would never travel on Mondays or Fridays.

The presence at Court of Sister Placida, a Catholic, was the unwit-
ting cause of many rumours, according to which the Empress was
about to be converted. All of them (according to Corbeil) were
without foundation. The Emperor thought, however, that Placida
was an unnecessary luxury: he sometimes felt that his wife had too
many attendants and that they were driving him out of the palace.

THE GRAPHIC

MARCH 10, 1877

THE EMPEROR WATCHING THE REHEARSAL OF THE COSTUME PROCESSION   THE REHEARSAL—ENTRANCE OF THE EMPEROR
Fac-simile of a Sketch by our Special Artist, Mr. C. E. Fripp.   Fac-simile of a Sketch by our Special Artist, Mr. C. E. Fripp.

Laforgue wrote to Ephrussi on 11 December 1881:

Terrible weather. You know Berlin, don't you? Well, my windows give on the Platz am Zeughaus, full of puddles and swept by gusty showers. At least there'll be some water in the Spree! . . . My days are all much alike. I give a reading in the morning or evening, sometimes both. . . . I no longer swallow my words; my voice is loud and clear. . . . Countess Hacke likes to play at being my mother. I give her dictation; each day I bring a collection of extraordinary words and phrases to test her spelling. (D:60-4)

The next day he wrote to Henry:

Cold this morning: it's nine o'clock. The Berlin shopgirls hurry by, with red noses and holding their muffs in a way which makes me regret the Paris ones. I haven't yet seen a single pretty foot here, not a solitary pair of those memorable little bird-feet like the ones I saw one blazing hot afternoon last summer in the rue du Quatre-Septembre, as I was airing my famous disgust with the universe. It's cold and it's been snowing. I've had my coffee, read the *Débats*, the *Indépendance Belge* and the *Figaro*. At eleven I go for my reading . . . and I'm writing to you by the fire, my big German stove, where sad enormous blocks of coal are beginning to redden. . . . I smoke three cigars a day. . . . I'm pressing on with my novel and write a page every morning. For that I get up at five; my servant is amazed when he comes in at seven and finds no one in bed, and me in my study with lighted lamp and papers everywhere. The result is that Countess Hacke, who likes playing mother, has ordered me to go to bed at ten, rise at eight and go for a walk in the park, which is five minutes from the palace. I haven't been there yet but I'm going quite often to the museums: there are two of them corresponding to our Louvre and Luxembourg. . . . A splendid collection of primitives, especially the Van Eycks. . . . But in the new museum . . . nothing to convince me yet that the Germans are artists in the way that we are. . . . What a city it is that can produce Degas, Forain, Monet, Manet. Ah Paris! . . . I'm absolutely full of love, absolutely but vaguely. My heart glows with the sun of Sunday and the sound of bells in the country, when one is watching the white dresses and ivory prayer-books file out of the door marked: Deo optimo maximo. Adieu. (D:56-9)

He wrote to Henry again on 30 December:

Today Countess Hacke took me with her in her carriage. The coachmen wore silver aiguillettes and uttered strange shouts as they passed the barracks, upon which the soldiers scrambled to fall in and present arms to the rolling of a drum, while the officer flashed a salute with his bared sword. And even the

bystanders doffed their caps! All highly amusing to this ex-
tenant of a rue Monsieur-le-Prince lodging house. We drove on
like that for hours and hours. We were visiting the Queen's
boarding-school, an adorably chaste birdcage. (D:73)

These two remarkable caricatures by Laforgue from the collection of Mme
Elisabeth van Rysselberghe (and first reproduced here) may well represent the
Ysaÿe brothers, Eugène (left) and Théo (right).

In the course of the above letter Laforgue asks, 'Ever heard of Lindenlaub?' (D:74) and in his next letter (4 January 1882) he returns to the subject: 'I have a friend here, a young M. Lindenlaub, who knows you and whom you astonish. . . . In fact he's enlightened

me quite a bit on your account.' (D:83) Théodore Lindenlaub was
the Berlin correspondent of a French newspaper who had known
the two previous French Readers and in fact had called at the
palace expecting to see Pigeon. At first he couldn't make out
Laforgue at all: his immediate assumption was that the old Empress,
with her well-known weakness for Catholics, had fallen for a little
Rhineland priest and engaged him as her new Reader. Then he
looked at Laforgue's blue-grey 'Breton' eyes and decided that that
could not be. To everything that the journalist said Laforgue
apparently replied with a 'That's odd, how strange!' as if there
were something predestined about Lindenlaub arriving in his life
in this way at this time.

Lindenlaub lived in the south-east corner of Berlin (beyond
Spittelmarkt) in a street called Prinzenstrasse. He shared a flat
with two Belgian musicians, the Ysaÿe brothers: Eugène (twenty-
three) a violinist, and Théo (seventeen) a pianist. Their landlady,
who played a considerable part in their lives, was Frau Hesse.
Eugène the violinist was star soloist and conductor of the Bilse
orchestra which played every night: in winter at the Konzerthaus,
48 Leipzigerstrasse, and in summer at the Flora Garten, Charlottenburg. The great attraction of the Bilse concerts was that you could
eat and drink while listening to the music. But Eugène, a brilliant
performer, was to be discovered by the celebrated pianist Anton
Rubinstein and whisked away to greater things. Before he left,
however, the four of them used to spend a great deal of time
together, and one of their amusements was to read aloud from
Murger's *Scènes de la Vie de Bohème*, in which Laforgue was invariably given the part of Colline, the philosopher who carried
books everywhere and used long words. It would appear to have
been excellent type-casting, especially when one reads Murger's
description of that 'steady look in his big blue eyes, which seemed
always to be searching for something and gave his features the
innocent placidity of a seminarist'. When the others left Berlin later
that year. Théo stayed on for three years longer and moved to the
Kanonierstrasse to be near Laforgue. Jules used to go regularly to
Théo's room while he was practising: while Théo played the piano,
Jules would read or write. In this way he developed a love for and
knowledge of music, just as he had learnt about painting from
Ephrussi. In the evenings they would go to the Renz Circus or
the Café Bauer together, as well as to other less innocent establishments—sometimes to ordinary brothels but more often to the kind
of low-class nightclub which in the Berlin of those days was called
a *tingeltangel*. Here you could see a fairly crude type of all-women
music-hall, the then-equivalent of a striptease joint today, but with

the difference that the performers mixed freely with the audience
between acts and/or went home with them afterwards. The taw-
drier these places were, the grander their names: one of Laforgue's
favourites was 'The Academy of Music' and another 'The German
Imperial Saloon'. Both were in the Friedrichstrasse. When Théo
finally left for Paris in 1885 it caused a major crisis in Laforgue's
life. Théo's appearance has been described by Madeline Octave
Maus as 'a thin face scraped back by a huge mass of exotic hair'.
Laforgue used affectionately to call him 'the Nubian'.

On the last day of 1881 Laforgue wrote to Ephrussi:
Just back from my eleven o'clock reading. Nothing in the papers
but the Empress very much approves of the Etincelle articles
and the Kingdom of Clothes particularly delighted her. I've been
given the extra job of hunting through the papers to find snippets about fashion for the first Woman of the Bedchamber,
Mlle de Neindorf. . . . Today is a day of spring with sun and a
clear blue sky and tall shining soldiers everywhere. . . . There are
several sorts of articles to be written about your book: the first
would be on yourself, your silhouette and your youthful fame
(as a scholar-dandy), your work, your collections, all very
Parisian. Another might compare three kinds of art critic: Taine,
Goncourt (on Watteau) and you. A third might question how
far a Parisian of 1882 who collects Impressionists and goes to
Brussels for a first night and has his seat at the Opera and eats at
Brébant's and smokes on the boulevard and wears a top-hat can
actually understand Albert Dürer's soul. . . . And on that I leave
you and—since it's the custom despite my convictions—allow
me to wish you a happy new year. (D:79-82)
In this letter to Charles Henry of about 6 January 1882 he was
once more on about Lindenlaub:
A charming fellow, with a mind that's curious and informed
about everything. He admires you profoundly: he thinks the
epithet that best fits you is 'singular'. Whenever we're talking
about you he pauses and shakes his head: 'What a singular chap!
What a singular existence!' . . . Let me tell you that Berlin
placidity exasperates me and I'm getting to be so afraid of it that I
don't write a single phrase or line of poetry without making it
overshrill to convince myself that I'm still alive. But no doubt
what seems like alcohol in Berlin will pass for herb-tea in Paris!
. . . My days are all much alike, except for the hiccup of the New
Year when we had a spate of receptions and processions featuring
state coaches of a kind I thought had long been relegated to the

bric-à-brac of other more pompous centuries. . . . Tell me, yes or no, is it cold in Paris? Because here everyone's in a daze: we have blue sky and warm air and April showers, delightful weather which fills the smarter streets with pretty women who think the spring has arrived. My windows give on the best frequented promenade and I observe them. Some are adorable: I spend hours watching and dreaming. Then I think that these angels have knickers and genital organs—pouah! pouah!—it's the bane of my life, Monsieur, indeed it is! (D:91-2)

Laforgue often played the world-weary young man, making Melancholy Jaques remarks of this kind. It was a pose not to be taken too seriously. Usually when he 'dreamt' it was of the Alcazar, the establishment in rue du Faubourg Poissonnière, Paris, where he'd been accustomed to haunt the Promenade.

Two times out of six my dreams are of the Alcazar. I've spent so many contemplative evenings in that sort of place that even in dreams it has become the natural ambiance in which my brain strangely blossoms. An Alcazar where on the stage unusual acts are unfolding, and at the same time in the corridors one is involved in absurd or swooning meetings with various gentlemen and ladies. (J:40)

Laforgue made no secret of the fact that he was something of a voyeur and he also admitted his 'ardent fantasies of underclothes' ('mon imagination ardente des dessous') (J:46). One would like to think his fantasy dreams were peopled with the girls of Forain and Willette romping around in the knickers of the time, which were voluminously white and billowing down to the knee over contrasting black stockings. Recently the closed knicker had made its appearance and become a talking point. Some thought them indecent. Up till then knickers had been either not worn at all or open at the crotch. There is no evidence as to which style—the old or the new—Laforgue preferred, the subject having been unaccountably neglected by thesis-writers, but there is no doubt that underclothing in general delighted him.

It would be interesting to have attended one of those erotic fantasies in Laforgue's 'strangely blossoming' brain. He even invented the word 'anomoflore' ('weird bloom') to describe their special nature. One can be sure that a Laforguian fantasy would be nothing less than stylish and probably owe a good deal to the (so-called decadent) painter Gustave Moreau, whose ravishing creations (he was indeed an inspired dress-designer) had delighted Laforgue ever since he saw the 'Galatée' at the 1880 Salon. One imagines such dreaming would be full of those 'enchantments of precious stones like those in the cavern of Moreau's Galatée as she sleeps under the watchful gaze of Polyphemus, with happy corals living in a dreamless state and strings of rubies waving like weeds.' (J:41) And when later he dresses his Salome in 'diaphanous mousseline of jonquil and black' it is pretty clear he has borrowed the dress from Moreau's own 'Salome'.

Laforgue was extremely frank in the expression of all kinds of sexuality—he was one of the first poets to introduce the clitoris into French verse (A:323); and he also wrote an explicit, and not very good, poem about childbirth ('En avant! Ah, Maman . . .') (A:55-6). But, though he could deal with sex in poetry, the sex in his life was more recalcitrant. What he called his 'skill as an observer' (J:118), thanks to which he kept his fantasies fresh, alternated with crudely experimental sex ('la débauche expérimentale') (J:118), neither of which was especially satisfactory. This was due partly to his own personality and partly to the age in which he lived. His friend Gustave Kahn could cope well enough in his rumbustious way (Laforgue likened him to an oriental pasha) and so could Charles Henry in a colder, more calculating manner. But Laforgue was at a temperamental disadvantage: his direct simplicity was not what was needed in the nineteenth century. It was a difficult age to live in, with tremendous pitfalls on all sides. Many good men and women were brought down by the sheer size of their families. His own mother had died while still in her thirties from the effects of a twelfth pregnancy. On the other hand it was almost a rule for writers to have syphilis. To steer a way between Scylla and Charybdis you had to be tough and sure of yourself: Laforgue was neither.

Laforgue had been awarded the job at the German court partly for his tact, and he was soon called upon to show it. This was in respect of his neighbours the Crown Prince and Princess who lived in the palace next door, on the right as he looked out from his study windows.

There was no love lost between the old Emperor William I and his son Frederick who was still waiting patiently to succeed to the throne. It was obvious now that William was going to hang on till the bitter end, while refusing to delegate any authority whatsoever. Frederick's predicament was made worse by the character of his English wife 'Vicky', who got on the nerves of the Prussians with her high-minded attitudes. In what seemed like a perverse effort further to annoy their son and daughter-in-law, William and Augusta went out of their way to spoil their grandson (Frederick's son William), thus fostering the idea that the succession, when it came, might well skip a generation. In the event this is exactly what happened; when Frederick finally succeeded he was a dying man who reigned a few weeks only, to be followed almost immediately by William II. The role of Laforgue in all this was to step very carefully and to accept the fact that the Empress could not stand her English daughter-in-law. But it was difficult, for secretly he had an intense admiration for the English princess. He venerated her for being both an art-lover and an Englishwoman—two qualities he always found irresistible. Even her age—Vicky was forty-one—was attractive to Laforgue, who was highly susceptible at that time to the 'femme de 40 ans' whom he compared favourably with the type of bird-brained maid of honour. Vicky for her part had a weakness for the French, having never forgotten a week she spent in Paris at the age of fifteen. In short they got on famously—but he was careful not to boast of it to the Empress. To Ephrussi, however, on 9 January 1882, he could reveal all (he refers to her as Princess-Royal, as she styled herself—though Germans preferred to play down her English connections and call her Crown Princess):

I have just been introduced to the Princess-Royal. She has the most charming simplicity and friendliness. I came through it all right, I think, except that I may have been a little too talkative. But can you blame me? For our subject of conversation, chosen by the Princess, was you! So do tell me, won't you, what M. Seckendorff relays to you about it (that is, if the meeting has, to the outside world, the importance it has for me). The Princess mentioned you at once. (I'm no longer timid, I observe things.) I can still see her gesture as she vaguely and smilingly indicated a work-table, saying, 'I've almost finished it.' And 'it' was your book. . . . Apart from that I'm working, working: a fair amount of German, a lot of poetry and a discourse on love, that driving force in our lives which is so eternally charming, dirty and absurd. After which I feast my eyes on a pile of Japanese prints left here by Pigeon. . . . I miss so much the arcades of the Odéon the sick skies that one sees from the Pont de la Concorde, and the beautiful puddles in the *place* of that name. (I was once in love with the statue of Nantes, which symbolizes robust and healthy chastity.) I miss, too, the funerals at the Madeleine and the resigned and sleepy cab-horses. . . . I hear your book has been seen at Tarbes (Hautes-Pyrénées). (D:85-9)

Four days later he had more to tell Ephrussi about the Princess-Royal, who invited him to an evening tea-party (at nine o'clock, after the reading):

I've just come from there, it's half past eleven. I chatted for hours, about you and everything. . . . I was a bit nervous at first but after five minutes I'd recovered and was busy observing the various characters, including, I may say, some very curious ones: like Werner, who did the paintings at the Café Bauer. . . . I met old friends like the amiable M. de Seckendorff, and made new ones. From nine to eleven I was all ears and eyes, despite my air of melancholy wanderer. At one point the Princess-Royal came and spoke to me. It seemed that all eyes were upon me, but I wasn't worried: I was as smooth as they are in Stendhal novels. And I gathered pages of notes: an English diplomat's curious profile, for instance, and several decrepit old men bedecked with gilded decorations. Not forgetting the women, of course. I indulged in mephistophelian reflections.

There was one incident. It happened about ten o'clock. I was with a group of people, and I was watching a splendid military gentleman moving around, talking to this person and that. I didn't know him. Suddenly he came up to me, shook me warmly by the hand and began chatting and laughing in a very friendly way. I responded, of course, and was soon beaming at this large, affable stranger. So we chatted on about various things and when he'd gone I asked Dr Velten who he was. Only the Crown Prince!

Laforgue completed the letter the following day:

This morning the Empress gave me a very wry smile and said, 'I hear you met my son at yesterday's tea.' (Dr Velten had told her.) . . . And you, what are you doing? What does one do? Does M. Jacques-Emile Blanche follow your advice not to put water in his wine? Is the beadle of Saint-François-de-Sales still the serious art connoisseur that we know so well? (D:94-7)

But the Princess-Royal was not the only 'older woman' in Laforgue's thoughts at this time. Just before leaving Paris he had spent two November Sundays at the Salon of a lady poet called Sanda Mahali. Her real name was more prosaically Mültzer; she was thirty-three years old with a son of fourteen and separated from her husband, an architect. She would have been an ideal lady for Laforgue to gain experience with, had he so wished; but it turned out to be a purely literary exercise. One cannot help thinking that T. S. Eliot's 'Portrait of a Lady' must owe as much to Sanda Mahali as to the

Harvard hostess who is usually credited with being the source of inspiration. The letters to Sanda are spread over the whole of the year 1882. They contain a number of true confessions which do not appear anywhere else in his work, perhaps because these are the only surviving letters to a woman other than his sister. On 23 January he wrote:

I long to see Paris again in April, when the trees in the Luxembourg have tender young leaves transparent in the sun, and even the manuscripts in the Bibliothèque Nationale smell of spring. Every Sunday, dear poet, as evening falls, I suffer agonies of despair, just imagining Paris and our special part of it at that hour: the rues Denfert, Gay-Lussac, Berthollet, Monsieur-le-Prince. Do these streets still exist? Even now I can see Henry, like an elegant grasshopper, dashing down the rue Denfert to chat with you in your little salon—and I'm very jealous. Shut the door in his face, won't you, just once in a while. Here I live in a street full of palaces and monuments, which means that I never hear the hurdy-gurdies, those street organs which were my good Paris friends. (In Berlin, oddly enough, one only hears them in the park.) I long to hear the one that's always outside the Luxembourg gate at five o'clock. The rue Denfert's not so far from there: shall I come and see you in your intimate dark salon with the severe furniture? In my heart I can still hear that evening shower, the last evening we met. Though sad, thinking of my departure, I talked and smiled—while you, your eyes were still full of tears for that curious sort of dog, snatched away in such mysterious circumstances that same 27 November 1881. . . . My servant collects stamps. . . . If you've got any, do let me have them. (D:101-5)

On 5 February he wrote again:

Dear poet, what's this odd bit of letter I've just received? First of all it begins with nothing: no Dear Sir or Dear Friend, nothing: Is there no form of address appropriate to our relationship? Doesn't one exist, or are you just afraid to name it? It ends with nothing too: no signature. Luckily it mentions an all-too-famous dog, so I was able to guess the sender's identity. And now, if you will allow me, I will quote . . . your final phrase: 'I'm very, very sad about very many things that one can't lose like one loses one's dog because nobody wants them.' Tell me, dear poet, what do you want to have stolen? Your Italian painting perhaps? Or your illusions? Or your verses? Or the eastern magic of your pseudonym? . . . As for me I still lead my dilettante life. . . . I'm dilettante in everything now, with only occasional little outbreaks of my universal nausea. I watch the carnival of life pass by:

policemen, artists, rulers, ministers, lovers. I smoke pale cigarettes, write poetry and prose, do the odd engraving and wait for death. Do you adore the circus? I've just spent five nights there. Clowns seem to me to have attained the only true wisdom. I ought to have been a clown, I've missed my vocation. And it's too late to start now, don't you think? As a matter of fact I've had to stop going to the circus: people leap to the conclusion that one has designs on the bareback rider, with the result that they try and sell you enormous bouquets to throw at her. . . . P.S.—Thank you for the stamps . . . but who have you got in Egypt? (D:121-4)

Then, on 25 March, he wrote:

Madame, Dear Colleague, Dear Friend, Dear Madame and Friend (?), My metal throat speaks every tongue[17] . . . . A thousand thanks for the stamps and for your assurance that there's nobody in Cairo. . . . Tell Henry to take himself off to the countryside. He needs a whole green summer listening to the rustle of leaves, with nothing to dazzle his eyes except the parrot-green fields. Let him breathe dung and give his eyes a rest from gas with humble spluttering resins. Then he can come back to Paris and write a book to the greater glory of art. . . . I told you of my sorrows and you take them with a smile. You say what everyone says: 'You're so young!' . . . I could say a lot about that. . . . Once upon a time I wanted to weep on the Holy Sepulchre. Now I'm a dilettante who's got no illusions left. I'd go and smoke a cigarette on Golgotha while observing the extra special sunset. . . . It's true I sometimes suffer even now. But I no longer need to deafen with sublime cries my fellow citizens on the boulevard and around the Stock Exchange: I'm content to squeeze my heart delicately so that it shall drip curiously shaped pearls. . . . And there you are: if I had any money I'd collect ceramics, Japanese prints and certain canvases of the Impressionists. I'd travel. I hate crowds and universal suffrage; all I like is art and myself. . . . And you, what are you? I'm presumptuous, aren't I! My God, do you exist? Do I exist? . . . Do I displease you? If so, please tell me and I'll . . . take myself off to the most distant recesses of my room. . . . However, I think I may come and ring your doorbell in September . . . and I would like you to send me, just because I want it, your photograph. (D:125-31)

Another letter followed on 9 April:

No one writes to me. Neither you, nor Henry, nobody. . . . Really! What is he doing that he can't write me? Is he caught up in the mesh of some passion? He needs watching. Just now I'd like to roll among flowers, or go on a riverboat to Saint-Cloud at eight in the morning . . . And your photograph? If I don't have it in

a week, I'll never see you again in my whole life, which won't
be long anyway. . . . (D:135-7)
As these letters show, Laforgue was approaching the end of his
'Sobbing Earth' phase and regarded himself already as a full-blown
dilettante. Certain poems like 'La Cigarette', which seem to belong
to this period, illustrate the transition from 'sublime cries' to the
Complaintes. 'La Cigarette' shows no originality in form (it is a
conventional sonnet) but it has an easy-going rakishness which is
a clear consequence of his new life-style:

> Oui, ce monde est bien plat; quant à l'autre, sornettes.
> Moi, je vais résigné, sans espoir à mon sort,
> Et pour tuer le temps, en attendant la mort,
> Je fume au nez des dieux de fines cigarettes.

[Yes, it's a flat world and the next one's only humbug, but I
will carry on regardless, even though hope is dead, and to kill
the time while waiting for death I smoke pale cigarettes in the
face of the gods.]
He was very concerned with pale cigarettes at this time. It is as
if the German blond tobacco had become a symbol of his new-
found dilettantism. Certainly the world he evoked here:

> Où l'on voit se mêler en valses fantastiques
> Des éléphants en rut à des choeurs de moustiques
> [Where one sees, lurching into a fantastic waltz, randy elephants
> and buzzing mosquitoes] (A:333)

is nearer to Rimbaud than to the *Sanglot*. Similarly, the strange
'Complainte de l'organiste de Notre-Dame de Nice' ('Lament
of the organist of Notre-Dame de Nice')—about an unknown lady
in a church he had never visited, which didn't have an organ anyway—provides a foretaste of much later poems:

> Voici que les corbeaux hivernaux
> Ont psalmodié parmi nos cloches,
> Les averses d'automne sont proches,
> Adieu les bosquets des casinos.

[And now the wintry crows are droning round the bell-towers;
with autumn almost on us, it's goodbye to casinos.]

> Le jour qu'elle quittera ce monde,
> Je vais jouer un *Miserere*
> Si cosmiquement désespéré
> Qu'il faudra bien que Dieu me réponde.

[The day she leaves this world, I'll play her a *Miserere* so cos-
mically despairing that God'll just have to answer.]
And he adds that, when she's gone, he will remain seated at the organ,

> Berçant mon coeur hypertrophique
> Aux éternelles fugues de Bach.

    [Nursing my hypertrophic heart to the eternal fugues of
    Bach.] (A:365)
which is already half way to the Laforguian Laforgue.

In 'Les Amoureux' ('The Lovers')—which is also a sonnet in
form—there are even lines which point ahead to the *Derniers Vers*,
the last poems he ever wrote:

        Seuls, dans leur nid, palais délicat de bambous,
        Loin des plages, du spleen, du tapage des gares
        Et des clubs d'électeurs aux stupides bagarres,
        Ils s'adorent, depuis avril, et font les fous!

        Et comme ils ont tiré rideaux lourds et verroux
        Et n'ont d'autre souci, parmi les fleurs bizarres,
        Que faire chère exquise, et fumer tabacs rares
        Ils sont encore au mois des lilas fleurant doux,

        Cependant qu'au dehors déjà le vent d'automne
        Dans un *de profundis* sceptique et monotone
        Emporte dans le ciel par les brumes sali,

        Les feuilles d'or des bois et les placards moroses
        Jaunes, bleus, verts fielleux, écarlates ou roses,
        Des candidats noyés par l'averse et l'oubli.

[Alone in their nest, a delicate palace of bamboo, far from
beaches, boredom and the bustle of stations and political clubs
with their stupid quarrels, they've been loving and acting crazy
since April! And having drawn the heavy curtains and the bolts,
with all the time in the world, amid strange flowers, to eat
exquisite food and smoke rare tobaccos, they're still in the
month of sweet-flowering lilac—but outside already the autumn
wind in a sceptical, monotonous *De profundis* whirls up into
the fog-dirty sky golden leaves of the woods together with
bilious posters, yellow, blue, acid green, scarlet and pink, of
election candidates drowned in rain and forgetfulness.] (A:437)

Ever since the beginning of the year Laforgue had been bracing
himself to go and call on Ephrussi's cousin, a rather formidable
professor of Roman Law at Berlin University called Charles Bernstein. Here was another extremely rich and cultured gentleman of
the international Jewish set, but for some reason Laforgue was
holding back. He need not have worried: soon he would be calling
Bernstein 'the most artistic man in Berlin', and the house at 23
in den Zelten, just north of the Tiergarten, very quickly became
one of his regular ports of call. Presided over by Bernstein's wife
Félicie and his unmarried, rather starchy, sister Thérèse, the

Bernstein flat was on an upper floor and used to shed portions of its plaster walls regularly on the heads of passers-by, much to Thérèse's mortification and Félicie's amusement. Despite the efforts of Thérèse, an expert in etiquette, to raise the tone, the atmosphere at number 23 was relaxed and almost Parisian. Of Russian origin, like Bernstein himself and Ephrussi, Félicie had a winning way with her husband's staid colleagues from the university. When, for instance, the historian Mommsen upset his glass of wine, not for the first time, she would laugh it off with a 'What else are German professors for?' Laforgue did his best to convert Félicie's husband to the virtues of so-called decadence by lending him his Baudelaire and other subversive works. But, as it turned out, Laforgue's influence on the Professor of Roman Law was not to be in literary matters at all, but in a very different field. Laforgue wrote to Ephrussi on 29 January 1882:

M. Bernstein is very kind. I spent two excellent hours with him last Tuesday. Like you he has a Goyen, a splendid one, very autumn, very sad. . . . Then we went out, did some window shopping, and on to my place. . . . M. Bernstein and I are the only people in Berlin who adore decadence in all things. . . . And you, scholar dandy, what are you doing, you the healthy-minded and well-balanced one, are you resting on your laurels? . . . The readings are going fine, twice a day now. . . . In the mornings we do stylistic exercises and, the Empress's hand being too weak to write with, she asked me to devise a special form of exercise. After much thought I found one, which allows her to be witty and to embroider elegant phrases around a given word. Am I not Machiavellian? . . . Guess what I'm thinking of now—of the way you used to cry 'Oh how horrible!' whenever Bourget emitted one of his stranger ideas or expressions. Goodbye and don't be angry. (D:106-9)

On 2 February he continued:

When I called you healthy-minded and well-balanced that's only half of it: you're a veritable sage when you deplore the disease that produces such flowers as *La Faustin* [the novel by Edmond de Goncourt which had appeared on 17 January]. Never will you feel the charm of decadence, and I promise you that when I tell M. Bernstein, he who loves decadence, he will pity you with a smile from behind his golden spectacles. Oh yes, I know that everything you say is true but, heaven help us, one has to be of one's time and even before one's time if one doesn't want to be taken for an antediluvian relic and a specimen for literary palaeontologists. (You will forgive me, won't you?) . . . I saw M. Bernstein yesterday, but only for a few minutes because he had a sore throat. . . . Incidentally, I've decided my book of poems is a collection of obscene little banalities. (D:110-12)

There was a further letter on 11 February:

Though without any personal pretensions I adore good breeding when I see it; it gives me unique enjoyment. Sincerely, though, there's not much of it here. Most pillars of the Court are pretty vulgar. I've seen young men and women in Paris who could teach them a thing or two. This century of ours stinks of upstarts, don't you think? Now the Princess-Royal, there's someone who has a complex brand of distinction which it would be a delight to analyse, pen in hand. As for the Empress, she's the perfect grand lady, dear to all of us who have inhabited, at least in imagination, the Salons of the seventeenth and eighteenth centuries. But I mustn't confide in you like this. I expect you've read Pigeon's first article: it made a fairly bad impression here. The news of it spread during a Court ball and caused quite a stir. Some of the blame for this minor act of treachery devolved on me. But I took my precautions and had a few quick words with the Empress's secretary, which will stop in their tracks any possible suspicions. Pigeon's case is, shall we say, odd—but I won't say more than that for the moment. I heard a vague rumour that he was to be rapped over the knuckles in the official Court journal, though just when that will be I don't know. . . . At last I've met Mme Bernstein. . . . She struck me as certainly kind and probably witty. . . . I'm going there after dinner tomorrow. Trying to convert M. Bernstein to Baudelaire is uphill work. . . . Well goodbye, I hope you're the same as ever: in excellent form, keeping your beard in trim, smoking your special cigarettes and laughing at de Goncourt's style. (D:113-7)

And, on or about 15 March, a rare letter to Eugène Ysaÿe reads:

Professor Doctor Bernstein

Lindenlaub and your brother just back from Hamburg. . . . Wonderful three days. (He's dictating this note to me.) Many kindnesses from Saint-Saens, as well as oysters, champagne, kisses. (Kisses from Saint-Saens, imagine that!) . . . We got your letter which is rude but not at all clear. . . . At the moment we're waiting for Frau Hesse's coffee. She's not a widow yet, despite your brother Théophile's piano. . . . He and I are off to the circus tonight. I've got a summer overcoat. (M:277)

A Max Klinger engraving from his 1880 series 'The Glove'

And at about this time he also wrote to Henry:

> Not since crossing the Atlantic (six years old, sunsets on the
> sea) have I suffered such black depressions as now. If I had
> money and no family I'd abandon Europe and go and live in
> some mad colourful country where I wouldn't need to think.
> Which is a way of telling you I've been writing poetry, but my
> ideas on the subject are changing. . . . I'm thinking of a kind of
> poetry which would be psychology in the form of dream . . .
> with flowers and scents and wind . . . complex symphonies with
> certain phrases (motifs) returning from time to time. I'm feeling
> my way carefully. In the meantime here's a final offering in my
> old manner. I'm revelling in English albums by Kate Greenaway,
> etc. I smoke lots of cigars and never a day goes by without my
> hearing music. . . . Just at this moment (Sunday evening) I'd
> like to be in Paris with you, strolling down the rue de l'Abbé
> de l'Epée or rue Séguier or along the quays. (D:65-8)

In this same letter Laforgue mentions having discovered a brilliant
young engraver, and he returns to the subject when writing to
Ephrussi on 13 March:

> His name is Max Klinger and I'm trying to write a piece about
> him. . . . When I read Ollendorff for my German I drag myself
> through it very slowly like a snail. Then I sit and think, and
> having thought, I begin to doubt. I begin to doubt whether our
> thoughts ever correspond to anything real in the universe.
> (D:118-20)

And on 31 March:

> Max Klinger is a sort of genius of the bizarre. . . . The work is
> carefully, painfully done, but resolute and profound. If you see
> M. Bernstein he'll tell you all about it, and you'll see what M.
> Bernstein looks like when he waxes lyrical. . . . I've found some
> beautifully sad places here, where I can take my melancholy
> moods for a walk: the Kronprinzen Ufer (behind the Zelten)
> and the Luisen Ufer (on the other side of Berlin). Marvellous
> effects in the evening. (D:132-4)

On 9 April:

> Did I tell you about Max Klinger's engravings. I can also see
> real-life engravings here: at one o'clock last night I was contem-
> plating a sort of narrow passage, like a black stinking stream,
> between peeling walls in the moonlight. It was an engraving and
> an intoxicating one. But perhaps you remember it: the passage
> linking Taubenstrasse and Hausvogteiplatz. . . . I'm very glad to
> hear what you say about Bourget's fame. . . . I've often thought
> about Bourget and fame. Bourget adores fame—furiously like a
> Balzac, but a Balzac with fragile shoulders and without the gift

of patience. . . . Now you, you're different, you're a sage, you construct, stone by stone, slowly and solidly, the pyramid that will eventually be topped by your neatly-bearded bust. Cheerful, aren't I! . . . My life proceeds normally. I read and write but mainly think. (D:138-41)

And he adds these words to sum it all up: 'This change to a more civilized life has turned me over like you turn an omelette. And I'm taking notes all the time.'

CHAPTER 4
On the Road (1882)

BUT the Court did not always stay in Berlin. The Empress was a lady of habit: as regularly as clockwork she set off each May on a provincial tour which, starting at Baden-Baden, proceeded to Coblenz, and then returned to Berlin in late August via Homburg and Babelsberg. The following month she would be off again, this time on an autumn tour to the same places: Baden-Baden and Coblenz, and back to Berlin on the first of December. Nearly three months of every year were spent by Laforgue in Baden-Baden and Coblenz, and since much of his work was done in those places, it is interesting to examine the conditions in which he lived.

In each town he had his eyrie, a lofty perch to which he would escape, but there is no question about which of the towns he preferred. He adored Coblenz and loathed Baden-Baden, though this did not prevent him from writing perceptively about it; even his ennui could be creative. It depended a great deal on his manner of life: in Coblenz he lived in the vast Château and had his meals brought to his room by one of the royal servants. At Baden-Baden the whole royal party, including Laforgue, lived in an hotel, where he took his meals in the public dining-room with the ladies-in-waiting. He complained of always wasting his time at Baden-Baden, of being caught up in pointless promenades and conversations, in an ambiance of semi-invalids which he detested. He even disliked the scenery, which he found too pretty-pretty; while at Coblenz the meeting of Rhine and Moselle at least had a certain grandeur.

At Coblenz he was left largely to himself, disturbed only by a servant bringing a tray of tea and petits fours. He could thus spend long productive hours in his 'gemütlich' apartment, high under the palace roof, with a fine plunging view of the Rhine. He once spent a whole night reconsidering his thoughts on life, and in the morning told Ephrussi that it had been 'rather like Jesus in the Garden of Olives, St John on Patmos, Plato at Cape Sunium, and Buddha under the fig-tree at Gaza', all rolled into one. (E:60) In short he found his *recoin* (little nook) at Coblenz extremely congenial. As long as he prepared his reading sessions for the Empress, and appeared punctually and presentably when she desired him, he could get on with his own work.

Circumstances were very different at Baden-Baden, where he now arrived on 29 April 1882. The Empress and her suite of ladies lived in the Hotel Messmer, which was more or less commandeered

Hotel Messmer, Baden-Baden

for the occasion. Her salon was a large first-floor room with balcony above the hotel entrance. *Der Balkon* (*The Balcony*) at Baden-Baden, overlooking the Kurgarten and at which the Empress made carefully judged appearances, was as famous as *Das Fenster* (*The Window*) in Berlin, through which the Emperor could be observed by adoring subjects as he worked at his desk. But *Der Balkon* exists no more, for the hotel was pulled down in 1957 and there is an account of its demolition[18] which is reminiscent of Laforgue's own poem, the 'Complainte des grands pins dans une villa abandonnée' ('Lament of the great pines at an abandoned villa') (A:99) It was to the balcony room that Laforgue went for his daily readings, just as in Berlin he repaired to the palace. But his own residence at Baden-Baden was a disappointment: instead of the elegant Palace of the Princesses, he was reduced to one small room, high up in the annexe, on rising ground behind the Hotel Messmer. This annexe was separated from the hotel proper by a courtyard with a fountain in the middle. From his room he had a plunging view, not only into the courtyard but also into the Kurgarten next door (with its eternal orchestra) and sometimes even into the royal apartments. And beyond all these he also had in his sights a vast panorama of countryside looking north-east to the Merkur mountain and its twin the Kleine Staufenberg.

The charming first section of 'Le Miracle des Roses' (B:67-72) introduces a note of nostalgia for Baden-Baden which he did not always feel. Untypical also are those touching references in the 1883 Agenda to 'blue eyes chez Marx' (F:225, 233). No doubt the girl who ran the bookshop of D. R. Marx in the Kurhaus was a happy distraction from time to time, but she could not all by herself console him for the rest of Baden-Baden. His hotel bedroom, too, was poor consolation. Room 19—with its band next door and everlasting fountain below—was at best a hide-out.

A talented artist, Laforgue describes the view from his room exactly as if it were a bad picture. 'The landscape out there,' he writes,

> offers a splendid twilight scene but is too much the picture. A pretty sky tenderly flecked with cinnabar. The two smooth hills bristling with black fir trees. . . . It's Calame, Chanoine Schmidt and all the rest of them. The weather is fine and the view is fine and there's no more to be said. These are Fénelon-like landscapes 'arranged to delight the eye'. Nature here is posing too much. Oh how I long for the sickly Bièvre river, the thin vine-shoots and the vacant lots! (J:12-13)

He refers elsewhere to the 'podgy' look of the local scenery, thus echoing Huysmans who, in L'Art Moderne, referred to a certain well-fed quality that the Beaux-Arts considered essential to distinguished landscapes: 'We are being stuffed with superabundant sites and pot-bellied Nature,' complained Huysmans.. The sort of landscape that Laforgue liked was lean and hungry: in fact it was the kind that Huysmans himself had extolled in En Ménage: the melancholy Paris suburbs with their factory chimneys, precisely the thing that Seurat was at that moment painting into the riverside background of 'Une Baignade'.

However, one day Laforgue woke on a May morning, and his description of the same landscape is almost lyrical, though he still sets it up in a painterly way:

On a certain May morning, at eight o'clock, with the windows
thrown wide open after the clammy fatigues of night and day-
break, a truly godlike spectacle: a wonderfully happy garden.
Under a cool blue sky the green of the twin mountains can
hardly be distinguished in the sun's luxurious haze. . . . In the
garden itself, flowers, lilacs, the freshness of the falling fountain.
Immediately below: a groom in buckskin breeches and red jacket
washes down the coach with its gold-painted coat of arms.
The whole scene is criss-crossed with the deafening flight of
swifts. High in the air and very slowly, as if weary from a long
journey, a great skinny bird flies by. It is a stork on the way to
Strasbourg.[19]

Elsewhere a variation on the same theme:

I get up to the sound of the fountain in the courtyard, to the
sound of the gravel being raked methodically by a groom in red,
to the trills of the birds which have made of the shrubberies an
aviary. And sharp on seven the band strikes up alongside. (J:18)

Ah yes, the band. 'The eternal band and the paroxysms of brazen
melancholy on the cornet, that odd instrument which combines
the aloof romanticism of the hunting horn with the vulgar whines
of a sleazy dance hall' (J:17-18). With such images to call upon it
is not surprising that Room 19 inspired his 'Complainte du soir
des comices agricoles' ('Lament for a country fair') (A:95). He
had been building up to it for some time, for the band had been
having a particularly gruesome season and his journal for the previous days is sprinkled with such entries as: 'The band next door
is giving its all. What an occupation! . . . Orgies from the band next
door: a salad of waltzes, overtures, rhapsodies and marches.'
(F:230) Typical of his feelings is the following unpublished piece:

These stifling evenings at Baden-Baden with the room full of
moving flowers, the windows open to all the noises of the valley:
a distant dog, distant fireworks, that stupid band in the Kurgarten, the perpetually renewed fountain in the courtyard, a
villa gate being shut. Lights dotted here and there on the twin
mountains disappear one by one. A breeze from the windows
makes all the candles run on the same side. Flashes of summer
lightning—silent, bluish, darting.

The white corridors of the hotel. Electric bells. A spick and
span maid crosses the courtyard and climbs towards the villa
with a convalescent's light meal on a tray. And always that
stupid band which, in the infinite melancholy of this place, still
wants to make believe that humanity is having fun, is glad to be
alive, and that the planet is a playground. And so it grinds out
waltzes indefatigably and deafeningly with a come-blow-trumpet

and tinkle-triangle. Timidly the cor anglais suggests a broken-hearted lament but is immediately drowned out by the drums, trumpets and strident violins, all shouting in unison. And that settles that: the cor anglais is dead; they have stuffed its lament down its throat.

But now ten o'clock sounds—successively all down the valley. The band stops playing, the poor devils stick top-hats on their heads, the latter somewhat dampened by the evening dew, and off they go—back to their tawdry everyday life. The garden dies, people slip away with macabre shivers. God, how bored is Baden-Baden with itself! The imperturbable fountain trickles on regardless.[20]

That bright little fountain became one of Laforgue's obsessions.

It is pouring with rain from a clear sky. The birds are warbling like mad and the fountain is gayer than ever. Oh well, the roofs will be washed nice and clean for the view. Heavy drops slide down the sagging telegraph wires, and I watch them from the window. It's the hour when everyone's at table restoring their strength. They are at the cigar stage, a time for dreams. The maids have seized this moment to make the beds: they stagger about beneath spare eiderdowns. And here's the flower-seller: there you are, my good soul, that's for you, when love goes right, everything's right. (J:19-20)

One of those maids, incidentally, was called Anna. It was Anna who, as he was leaving at the end of his stay, cried out to him, 'Adieu, Collègue!' and he was touched enough to record it in an unpublished note.[21] On another occasion he writes:

All the incomprehensible, intangible desolation of the autumns of my life has gathered in my heart and burst . . . because of the wind that howls today. Nothing that I can think of will ever repair the devastation it has wrought inside me. . . . And yet people are still working, the louts. Somewhere the floor-polisher is waxing the parquet. I can hear the sound of dishes. And that pathetic bell of a thousand little German railway stations. The poplar shadows grow long and faint in the twilight of half-past-six. And all those ends of cigars that I've smoked! . . . I desire nothing and nobody—except perhaps not to be alone. God, how they slam doors in the corridors of this hotel! If only I could do something useful, like going to sleep. I light another cigar. But that's not original. (J:43-4)

Laforgue paid only one autumn visit to Baden-Baden—he used normally to be on holiday in France at that time of year—but his one November there gave him the line about the slow drizzle in 'L'hiver qui vient' ('Winter coming on'):

> . . . the rain as patient as angels ['Voici venir les pluies d'une patience d'ange'] and that same bell from May afternoons, but now the Kurgarten is whipped by squalls. The two hills wear their deepest eternal green. . . . What an interruption and what melancholy! My table and lamp in Room 19, Villa Messmer. My wax sculpture by Henry Cros back in position and smiling at me. I have just dined in the white restaurant, the fountain is still there below and a piano plays fugues. Everything calls on me to surrender and yet I dare not. What a poor anxious idiot I am! (F:257)

Here he is looking back on the previous summer with nostalgia, having forgotten that in the same journal and the same room he wrote: 'Sheer terror at the collapse of my brain!'—an entry which has never been explained. Far from going mad, he is soon his old bored self again when he writes to Ephrussi, 'It's two o'clock in the morning. My lamp is the last burning in Baden-Baden. Everything is dark, the dogs are howling at the moon and the fountain in the courtyard flows on for ever.' (E:81-2)

Years later, but still in Room 19, he had these thoughts on death:

> I shall cease to live, as surely as the mosquito that's just burned itself on my lamp—as surely in my turn as my mother, as surely in my turn as my father. I shall cease to live as surely as my niece Juliette began to live last night. And it's amazing how unperturbed I am by the idea . . . which only goes to show that a human being, whatever he cares to think of it, is designed with a view to happiness—though some might call it illusion. (K:15)

On this first visit to the place he wrote to Ephrussi on 12 May 1882:

> Do you know Baden-Baden? As a setting of landscapes and as a tourist resort its banality is indescribable, it's absolutely deadly. I go every day to the Kurhaus, decorated by a lot of twopenny-halfpenny daubers. I go to the Reading Room, where I hunt out those good bits that are always to be found in back-numbers of The Graphic. Meanwhile the so-called 'smart set' walk up and down the Kurgarten listening to the band. Not a decent costume to be seen anywhere. The dowdiness of this place is such that you can't even wear a top-hat in the streets or in the Kurgarten without drawing attention to yourself—it's considered normal only for very old old-men. (D:159-60)

And to Henry he wrote: 'I lead a stupid life here. I pass my time castrating dull books and contemplating pine-trees, while awaiting the fifth incarnation of Vishnu.' (D:165) 'Luckily I like poetry and certain books and real pictures and good engravings; certain aspects of nature, women's clothes, unusual characters . . . in short the whole kaleidoscope of life. But it's not much of a prospect when life is reduced to a kaleidoscope.' (D:157) 'You'll find enclosed one of my 1880 sonnets . . . at that time I wanted to be eloquent, but today that sort of thing gets on my nerves. Being eloquent seems to me such bad taste, so naive.' (D:163-4)

But his letters to Henry at this time, while protesting all the while that he is not really interested, are very often about women. Things were not going well between Henry and Léonie Duhaut and he seems to have confided his problems to Laforgue; while at the same time urging him to find a girl-friend of his own if only as an antidote to boredom. Laforgue explains carefully that in Berlin he used to accompany Théo on his 'two-mark-fifty idylls' but that he does not feel this to be the answer. The effect of such visits to the Friedrichstrasse was to make him long for pure young girls, preferably English because they were the purest and most unsullied. But the pure young girls were just not available—at least not to Laforgue. Time after time he would beg them (in his notes) to come off their pedestals and mend their mincing ways, but they always failed to get the message. Finally he decided it was neither his fault nor theirs—their regrettable behaviour had simply been imprinted in them at birth. And at this point he comes so near to the ideas of today's Women's Movement that he has been hailed as an ally by no less a person than Simone de Beauvoir. 'In all his work,' she says in *Le Deuxième Sexe* (1949),

> Laforgue expressed his rancour against the mystification for which he held men as responsible as women. His Ophelia is a pathetic creature, of whom Hamlet says: 'That's how Ophelia would have loved me—as a possession which she judged to be socially and morally superior to the possessions of her friends.' (B:27)

Woman makes man dream dreams, while all the time she herself thinks only of her own well-being and comfort. People speak of her soul when she is nothing but a body. Man, in his belief that he is pursuing an ideal, is the plaything of nature which uses all his mystical illusions for its own reproductive ends. Woman truly represents the ordinariness of life: insipidity, prudence, meanness and boredom. All this is expressed in Laforgue's 'Notre petite compagne' ('Our little companion') (A:259) and other poems.

There are a great many quotations from Laforgue in *Le Deuxième Sexe*:

> Women are a mirage. Either they must be dismissed from our

minds, because impossible to grasp—or else we must treasure and educate them . . . make them our truly equal companions, our most intimate friends, our accomplices in the world; we must dress them differently, cut their hair and talk to them absolutely freely. (K:48)

Because we have let Woman linger in slavery and idleness, without any occupation . . . other than her sex, she's blown it up out of all proportion . . . till the whole thing's become a lie. . . . Up till now we've played dolls with women . . . and it's gone on too long. (K:52)

When will the girls become our true brothers, so that no one exploits anyone else and we can at last exchange an honest handshake? (K:48)

They all have it: that delicate air of please-don't-touch-me, which is the product of a whole past of slavery—with no other salvation or livelihood for them than that same little air of being seductive without meaning to be, and biding one's time. (K:49)

No! Woman is not our brother. By teaching her idleness and corruption we have made of her a thing apart, a quantity unknown, having no other weapon but her sex—which not only leads to endless war but involves something that should not be used for war at all. Either adoring or hating but never our frank companion, she and her like close their ranks in a freemasonry which is based on the suspicions of the eternal little slave. (K:47)

It is strange to find Charles Henry (in the interview he gave to Jules Huret in 1891) speaking with almost the precise accent of Laforgue and Simone de Beauvoir. He replies here to a question about the future of love:

The kind of love affairs that are so much on our minds today result from our particular social condition . . . which requires that the act of love shall be protected and guaranteed. It is obvious that this will become incomprehensible as soon as society is organized differently: when children, for instance, become the responsibility of the state, and when women, assuming complete control of themselves, are free to choose and to love the sort and number of men they want to.

Laforgue's predicament was put in another way by Alain-Fournier in his long-running correspondence with Jacques Rivière. Fournier had an immense admiration for Laforgue, which he tried vainly to make Rivière share. But it was only after his friend's death in the 1914 war that Rivière admitted:

I can see now all that he discovered of himself in Laforgue. Like Laforgue he had a huge longing for women . . . but the union of souls had to come before the union of bodies, and he needed love to be absolute. All the exigencies of Laforgue, Fournier recognized as his own, and he knew at the same time that such a dream was scarcely realizable.[22]

In his *Lettres au Petit B* Fournier says: 'Jacques criticized me the other day for my so-called purity, for overstressing purity in my worship of women. That isn't really the point at all. Like Dostoevsky's Idiot I have for women a look that goes first to the soul.' Laforgue, also, in this sense was an Idiot.

None of Laforgue's letters to young girls survives but one imagines that, if they did, they might resemble this note by Fournier breaking off with a student called Henriette:

What are we doing together? With your little body, straight as a whistle from top to toe, you're made for dancing and giggling and having fun. What's the point of our liaison? If I'd been honest I'd have broken off long ago. We were going in opposite directions and held out hands . . . but now it's time to move on again. I would like our love to have been the tale of two children who cut school and stole nuts together—a game we played, soon over and no regrets. I like you very much but the trouble is: your happiness isn't mine.

Laforgue girls tended not to giggle. They had more in common with the Jean Anouilh type: the 'petit soldat' who is brave, honest and uncompromising, and inevitably comes to a sad end.

For want of anything better to circle around, Laforgue's thoughts returned to his old pen-pal and fellow poet Sanda Mahali. 'Describe her to me,' he asks Henry. 'I mean, the way she speaks and moves, as if I were a very bald old lecher. I mean it. And send me a newish photograph and tell her to write me.' (D:162) Then later he complains:

The photograph you sent me seems a bit old. Surely she's younger than that. But what a curious mouth! I remember the smile well, and those mad eyes and sensual nostrils. And, with all that, childish breasts! Do you like flat breasts? Really flat? I don't mean for Louis Bouilhet's reason—because 'flat bosoms are nearer the heart'—no, I'm talking of a really depraved taste for thinness. For instance, have Memling's virgins sometimes set you wondering in the Louvre? (D:155-6)

The court had now moved on to Coblenz and Laforgue was back in the great Château which was his first taste of Germany when he arrived there six months before. On that occasion he had been given temporary rooms on the ground floor, but for his nine subsequent visits he seems to have been placed high under the rooftops, just as he was at Baden-Baden, and he was delighted with the arrangement. From the evidence of various letters and fragments he seems to have arranged things in a very cosy (gemütlich) manner in the Château's north wing, near the so-called English chapel, which the Empress had set aside for English residents and tourists. To Laforgue, who regarded English girls as delightful beyond all others, the Empress could not have paid a more charming (though involuntary) compliment. He now had a plunging view, not only of the Rhine but also of crocodiles of schoolgirls wending their way into church. He was in seventh heaven, though he played it down in his first Coblenz letter (26 June 1882) to Sanda:

I am lodged near the Château's English chapel and spend my Sundays, like yesterday, working behind closed curtains while listening to continuous and truly lamentable litanies accompanied on the organ. This lasts for two hours, during which I am overcome with sadness, abjure my wretched life and consider entering a monastery. Then the voices stop, I go to the window and watch them come out: the whole English colony of Coblenz including a school for young ladies, all adorably thin and flat, in exquisite dresses, pleated and gathered. And I find myself dreaming of flirtations on fashionable beaches—along the fringes of the resounding sea. (D:167-8)

One suspects that the same school for young ladies was the subject of a later note in his journal: 'A morning of sun on the Rhine, with a grass-cutting noise from the little lawns where nymphs play tennis' (F:241)—tennis being still a novelty at the time in Germany.

But the English nymphs were not his only reason for adoring Coblenz. Under his window lay a real treasure, the great wide river . . . a river seen in plunging view from as high as a Paris sixth floor. He would never forget those first sunny mornings when all was misty down there on the water, while from above the forms of the big black tugs could be dimly seen. (J:16-17) 'If only I could draw properly all the different kinds of rusty tow-boats and brave little tugs, faded tourist steamers and lighters and floats that pass beneath my windows!' (C:129) Despite this modest disclaimer he could draw all these types with great proficiency.[23]

> That tired mooing comes from a green and white boat with a black and white funnel. It is crammed with men and flagons, huge bottles called demijohns. A thin pipe fixed to the funnel shoots out white steam in a furious jet, while the big funnel itself breathes out black smoke in a big booming bass. And there goes the whistle from the bridge-of-boats which is preparing to let it pass.[24]

He grew so fond of the boats that the view without them was never the same. 'It's sad here,' he writes to Ephrussi one winter day. 'It's snowing, the Rhine's as flat as a pancake and, as a result, the boats are few and far between.' (E:101)

Much of his feeling for the Rhine he put into 'Les deux pigeons' ('The two pigeons),[25] apparently unconcerned that the place he was describing in that story was meant to be a sea-port. The river, in fact, was one of the few things he never tired of. 'My window offers me,' he wrote to Théo, 'the same view as ever in the same frame. But here's a charming note: the clear barking of dogs which reaches me from the other bank is as clear as a watercolour. Don't think of that as mere literature: it's an exact impression.' (E:141) Elsewhere he returned to the idea: a painting could have the same limpid clarity as sounds (he instanced an orchestra playing Wagner) which come to you across a full river such as the Rhine at Coblenz. (K:175) But he nonetheless recorded that one day a child in a Sunday suit, playing ducks and drakes under the Rhine Bridge, yodelled to the point of provocation and beyond. (F:241)

The view that he had of the opposite bank of the river was one he described many times: the dozen or so dirty-white villas strung out like toys along the water's edge; and the weedy row of poplars along the crest of the hill, which yet had a sort of poetry because only they could see down the other side.[26] One special thing at Coblenz was the moonlight: golden in July, misty in November. 'Tonight, full moon on the Rhine' is a triumphant summer note in his journal (F:241), as is: 'Moonlight, charmer of birds' nests' (F:246-7). An entry in one of the notebooks begins: 'A full moon made of old gold, motionless and round, like a child's balloon,' and ends: 'Even the pretty lamp-posts have that special colour-of-moonlight glow, as charming as old-fashioned country jewellery of no value.'[27]

When he tired of the view across the river—and the river itself—Laforgue withdrew into his immediate surroundings and described

the Château garden and shrubberies alive with birds. The Coblenz
sparrows, especially, found a sort of immortality in four lines of
the famous 'Complainte d'un certain dimanche' ('Lament for a
certain Sunday') (A:52):

> Les moineaux des vieux toits pépient à ma fenêtre,
> Ils me regardent dîner, sans faim, à la carte;
> Des âmes d'amis morts les habitent peut-être?
> Je leur jette du pain: comme blessés, ils partent!

[The sparrows of the old roofs twitter at my window, they
watch me as, without appetite, I dine à la carte; do souls of
my dead friends inhabit them perhaps? I throw them some
bread but, as if offended, they leave.]

In an unpublished fragment he describes one of the sparrows at
length:

At regular hours of the day I scatter bread on my window-sill
above the garden. . . . It's for the usual sparrows; I know them,
they know me. Yet they never come too near and, so long as
I'm there, they take endless precautions before coming to eat.
Among these sparrows there is one rather common one, with a
hard black beak and a mouth as wide as his head. He's always
there, long before the others, but always at a distance. When I
scatter the bread he at first waits, because he daren't be the
first to approach. Then he cheeps to call the others. When they
arrive he stays on cheeping, exciting them, showing them the
bread, perhaps even persuading them that he's already had his
fill with impunity. The others approach gradually one by one.
When they're all busy gobbling—and my sly one sees there really is
nothing to fear—he hurls himself into their midst and carries off
all the biggest pieces. He reminds me of some politicians.[28]

In another unpublished piece he speculates about where the sparrows go at night (out on the town perhaps?) because, as twilight
descends, he only sees bats, or the occasional swift looking like a
winged dart, black with a sliver of white and three friends in
vibrant tow, diving to break up the peaceful minuets of the midges.
On a melancholy Sunday evening he imagines that his hide-out is
the keep of a state prison and that he himself is the Man in the
Iron Mask. He listens to the surrounding noises: the whistle of a
railway engine, the shouting of men on the log rafts, the hollow
sound of the wagons crossing the three-span railway bridge made
up of cast iron sections.[29] High up above the park and its noises,
facing the river and sky, he feels of no more account than the
smoke from that cigarette he has just thrown away and which
expires on the edge of the roof. Without a word a servant enters,
bringing tea in a plump tea-pot of fine porcelain with silver strainer,

milk, buttered bread, petits fours. After he has savoured it he returns to smoke a cigarette at the window. Everything is now suffused in night, that net of many meshes. The shrubberies are asleep and the noises have stopped. All the more distinctly is heard the sound of darkness. Later—when he gets up at one, two or three in the morning—he notes the silver fury of the water against the central supports of the bridge.[30]

A characteristic sound of Coblenz is spelt out by Laforgue as 'Ga-Ga-Ga'. It is the cry of one of those interminable goods-trains that glide along the far bank of the Rhine and transfix him from head to foot with despair. (E:142) 'Ga-Ga-Ga' was responsible for his ringing alexandrine about the sadness of goods-trains in the rain: 'Que tristes sous la pluie les trains de marchandise' (A:115) which is perversely to be found in a prose-poem, the 'Grande Complainte de la Ville de Paris'. It is, of course, an 1880s up-to-date version of Vigny's 'Dieu que le son du cor est triste au fond des bois!' ('God, how sad the sound of the horn in the depth of the forest').

Ten in the evening. His clock dismally strikes the hour, which is taken up by grandfather clocks chiming their own distinguished notes down the corridors of the Château. Then come the bugles and drums up on the hill, in a moving Last Post for this little German town. Finally the churches, taking their time, first on one side, then on the other side of the river: this one pastoral, that one pompous—and two or three frankly degenerate. (J:20-1)

By now, almost incidentally, Laforgue's great gift will have become self-evident: he had not only a painter's eye but also an acute ear, ultra-sensitive to every sort of sound. At Baden-Baden in Messmer's Hôtel Garni (Room 19) he listens to the doors banging in the corridor, dogs howling at the moon, people gently coughing themselves to sleep, a dance going on all night and the fountain splashing in the courtyard. He wakes to the sound of gravel being raked, and notes the crisp sound when it is freshly disturbed by shoes. He listens to the washing up of plates and the polishing of floors. He distinguishes the wind in the pines which sounds like an express train, from the breeze that merely rustles the crystal stalactites of the chandeliers. He notes the nervous, involuntary swallowing of a sick visitor, the squeaking in the street outside of new shoes returning from mass, a horse-carriage on a distant road, a nearby bicycle-bell, a gate being shut. There is that eternal band playing English waltzes next door; and there are hunting horns, and pianos that play fugues and Chopin nocturnes. All around there are pines, shivering and creaking like old furniture, and in among them the chattering of birds: cawing crows, tireless blackbirds, deafening swifts. And the bells: the cracked tinkle of the one downstairs, calling guests to lunch, the elevation bell of a religious procession. That saddest bell of all, the one that sounds from a thousand little German railway stations. And countless bells in the valley, brought closer by the wind: it is almost a tangible relief when they stop.

The scene changes from Black Forest to Rhineland: a hundred and twenty miles north as the swallow flies. High up in the Château he hears a different set of sounds but just as accurately: the noises from across the water, the barking of dogs as clear as a watercolour, the shouts of children playing ducks-and-drakes, the mournful cries of goods-trains on the other bank. There is an altogether endless variety of sounds centred on the great river: the passing boats, hissing or booming their signals, the throb of engines and the plaintive bells of a steamer. The thrash of paddle-wheels, the hailing cries of rowers on one of the Rhine rafts. The gentle lap of waves against the bank, or their rage against the piers of the bridge. Hollow footsteps in the night; the even hollower ring of carriages crossing the iron bridge. Whistles from the station or from distant trains. The desolate sound of the wind. The lawnmower cutting the grass for tennis, English hymns in the chapel, the military band playing *Carmen* to please the Queen. The tiny whip-crack of a bat, the twittering of house-martins and the cheep of sparrows. Unknown birds darting, quarrelling, their faint prattling like the chock of glass on metal, the scrape of a file, the scratch of wood. The croaking of toads, the chiming of clocks, his own and others'. Church bells rustic and worldly, answering each other from different sides of the Rhine. A salute of kettledrums from the fort on the hill. And finally the sound of darkness.

And yet, although Laforgue was superlatively served by two of his senses—his artist's vision and his acute ear—it is a curious fact that he hardly ever records scents or smells. It is odd, for instance, that Amédée Pigeon, his predecessor as Reader, should continually refer to the smell of the lime-trees at Coblenz, and yet Laforgue never mentions it. 'Coblenz has its own particular smell, it is the scent of lime-tree flowers,' says Pigeon in his *L'Allemagne de M de Bismarck* (1885). And again in *Le Figaro* for 8 July 1885: 'The lime-trees of the Parade Platz litter the ground with their golden dust which smells so delicious.' For him it was the main characteristic of this little German town during the month of June. For Laforgue it did not exist. But then Laforgue . . . I was about to say that he never mentions a single smell of any kind, good or bad, either at Coblenz or at Baden-Baden . . . but that would not be correct: at Baden-Baden, in the midst of a million pine-trees, he does once mention the smell of—coffee.

'Have I spoken to you about Coblenz?' he asks Henry at the end of June 1882.

It's a town I adore. There are some extraordinary little streets with gabled houses, and a huge old bridge over the Moselle with shrubs growing out of its hulk. With its quaysides and the manoeuvring of the rafts and so on, it satisfies all the longings of someone like me who was born in a seaport. (D:171)

And to Sanda Mahali he says: 'I adore Coblenz, just as much as I hate Baden-Baden. The decor in which the Moselle throws itself into the Rhine is a sight for sad eyes.' In spite of which he admits that his eyes are still sad: 'I've told no woman that I love her, because to do so would be to tell a lie.' And what of Sanda herself?

You're always talking of mysterious sufferings. Why aren't you happy? You have a charming flat in a quiet district, you write poetry, you love roses, you appreciate Courbet, you sing. Why aren't you happy, dear muse and primadonna? Is it your dogs again?

She sends him a telegram, apparently asking for a sonnet. He obliges: 'Oh come, silken body that I adore, let's melt together . . . for the bow which plays scales upon our nerves is summoning today our bewitched atoms.' (D:173-5) After which he wonders if he has gone too far. 'I was afraid from your silence that the sonnet might have annoyed you. But alas, not a bit of it! When are we going to have a really good row?' (D:176) Then on 18 July: 'What do you mean about the thin girls I look at through my windows? What do you mean by windows? Is it an allusion to my dull, lacklustre eyes?' He gives her professional advice: 'Why, for heaven's sake, if you're a poet, do you talk about sirens and Circe? Talk about men for God's sake! . . . If I were a woman I'd write such love poems—variations on the "Song of Songs"—that Paris itself would be scandalized.' In the same letter, however, he slightly contradicts himself: 'I'm dreaming of a kind of poetry that says nothing, that is made up of pieces of disconnected dream. If you want to say anything, expose an argument or prove something, there's always prose.' (D:180-3) This is interesting because it recalls what he said about Baudelaire:

He was the first to break with the public. Poets always used to address themselves to the public, offering a repertory of the usual human interests. He was the first to say, 'My poetry will be for the initiated. . . . The public can keep out. And to scare them off it's no bad idea to affect the mask of the practical joker.' . . . He wrote short detached poems without a definite subject, unlike the others who fashioned their sonnets to tell a story poetically or make a point. His own poems are as vague and inconsequential as the flutter of a fan, as equivocal as make-up, so that the bourgeois who reads them asks: 'So what?' (K:115-16)

This, of course, is an excellent description of the poems Laforgue himself was beginning to write—and also of the reception which awaited them.

On 25 July the court moved on to Homburg, and Laforgue wrote to Henry (who was then in his native Haute-Saône):

Are you rolling in the grass in your sailcloth trousers? . . . I can't wait to see your sculptures. As for me I dream of etchings: elephants walking down the boulevard des Italiens in cross-hatched rain. . . . Here I have girl-friends. Do you flirt sometimes . . . often . . . a little? As you know there's no longer any gambling at Homburg, any more than there is at Baden-Baden, but there are lots of English women and parties and dresses, gentlemen with wrist-watches and girls in socks and Greenaway hats. As you know there are three sexes: men, women and English girls. I am taking notes on it. . . . You're the only person I send my poems to. It's a great pleasure to have one's little efforts appreciated. It's like an old roué hearing his mistress praised. . . . I've made two visits to Frankfurt to the house of Schopenhauer. The Empress teases me about that 'wicked man'. (D:184-7)

The next stop on the Court tour of Germany was the palace of Babelsberg. Situated on the Havel lake near Potsdam, it welcomed the Royal party once a year for three weeks in August. It was always the period just before Sedantag, the anniversary on 2 September of the vital battle of Sedan in the Franco-Prussian war. On that day there were parades in Berlin and all members of the Royal family and their retinues were required to be present. Needless to say it was not the Empress's favourite day of the year.

'Vicky' once described the château of Babelsberg in guide-book prose as 'situated on a wooded hill three miles from Potsdam with a splendid view of the great lake and all the country around.' Her mother Queen Victoria also described it, rather more cosily, as 'a real little Gothic gem, full of furniture and climbing plants and a large assortment of pretty little screens and lamps of every kind, as well as an enormous number of towers and turrets and steps.' Is there a suspicion of irony in the lines? With Queen Victoria it is always difficult to tell. Laforgue himself did not live in the palace but in a small cottage in the park, where he hoped to get some work done, although Berlin was only half an hour away. Whether he did have time for work we do not know, but he seems to have had some amorous adventure, recalled in the following line (reading April for August to disguise the date) of the 'Complainte de l'ange incurable' ('Lament of the incurable angel'): 'Où vont les gants d'avril, et les rames d'antan?' ('Where go April's gloves and the oars of yesteryear?') (A:67), a comment on Villon's more famous line: 'Mais où sont les neiges d'antan?' ('But where are the snows of yesteryear?').

In the 'Complainte à Notre-Dame des Soirs' ('Lament to Our Lady of the Evening') he recalls again the days on the Havel:

Mais les lacs éperdus des longs couchants défunts

Dorlotent mon voilier dans leurs plus riches rades . . . (A:38)

[But the desperate lakes with their slow dying sunsets cradle my sailboat in their matchless reaches . . .]

At the end of the poem are the words (which seem to be very personal): 'De *vrais* yeux m'ont dit: au revoir!' ('And *real* eyes signalled: let's meet again!') (A:39) The italics and exclamation mark are Laforgue's.

But the busy days at Babelsberg were disturbed by something other than the boating parties with what he calls his 'amies' ('girlfriends'). Three days after the arrival from Homburg—on 12 August 1882 to be exact—the Empress had a serious fall in the palace. She never recovered from it and was to spend the rest of her days in a wheel-chair. Even her state coach had to have its floor lowered, so that the chair could be moved in and out. The attendant who found

Prince Henry (20)   Crown Prince Frederick (52) and
Princess Victoria (16)   Crown Princess Victoria (42)
Princess Sophie (12)   Princess Charlotte (22),
Princess Margaret (10)   the Duke of Saxe-Meiningen
                                 and Feodora (3 years 9 months)

Prince William (24), the future Kaiser, with Princess Augusta Victoria (25), and their son William (9 months), the future 'Little Willy'

'The Silver Wedding at Berlin: The Imperial Crown Prince and Princess of Germany and their Family.'—Extra supplement to the *Illustrated London News*, 3 March 1883.

her lying helpless on the floor was the first Woman of the Wardrobe
Rosa Bachem, of whom we shall hear more later. One might have
thought the accident would have thrown a certain gloom over the
Court but Laforgue does not sound unduly perturbed in his letter
to Henry of 20 August. He is full of a scheme to collaborate with
Sanda Mahali in a three-part novel about lesbians:

> It will begin in a shady boarding school where they aren't too
> particular about the pupils' antecedents with the result that some
> of them are a bit strange. I've already got masses of personal
> notes. The second part is a correspondence between Aline in
> Rome and Jeanne in Paris. But here's the gimmick: the letters
> will be reproduced facsimile in two different handwritings,
> which will be analysed in the text—you'll see, it offers all sorts
> of possibilities. Then in the third part there's a seemingly insipid
> ending with everyone swearing faithfulness and the girls returning
> to their husbands—but finally it's their old vice they go back to.
> Amen. (D:192-3)

He is less than forthcoming, however, when he writes to the 'collaborator' herself six days later:

> Here I am at the Château of Babelsberg, a quarter of an hour
> from Potsdam and forty minutes from Berlin. I live on the edge
> of the Havel, a kind of enormous lake full of duckweed and
> frogs. My joy is to watch the kingfishers catching tiny silver
> fish; I meditate on the struggle for life. My little house is set in
> the middle of a huge park where I've already lost myself more
> than once. We also have (my girl-friends and I) a sort of miniature
> steamer and a boat with oars. I throw bread to passing swans.
> It's very late now and I'm listening to the frogs and toads. A
> boatload of people has just gone by singing the 'Watch on the
> Rhine'. . . . I've a tremendous idea for a novel, with a wonderful
> gimmick, but I won't say more for the moment. . . . I'm smoking
> cigarettes while murmuring lines of Spinoza and thinking of
> you. I'm thinking that you're not thinking I'm thinking of you,
> which is no reason for not thinking of me who am thinking of
> you. . . . I'll be in Paris in a week's time and shall stay a week
> before going on to Tarbes. I can hardly wait for your evening
> parties. I notice you offer me men friends but no women. All
> right, no women then, and so much the better—but no men
> either, that's fair! . . . And how's your book, oh red-robed blue-
> tit? . . . The moment I get to Paris I'll ring your bell frantically.
> (D:188-91)

'Promises, promises . . .' Sanda Mahali must have thought, as the
week slipped by without any frantic ringing of her bell. To add
insult to injury, Laforgue was lying low not a hunred yards away

in a lodging house at 99 boulevard Saint-Michel, and somehow or other Sanda seems to have got to know about it. Perhaps she simply saw him going in or coming out. In any case she appears to have written him a letter there, and then to have collected it and read-dressed it to Tarbes. These developments seem to have left Laforgue bewildered, and no wonder—but he passed them off in sublime fashion by saying they were nothing but the workings of Fate:

> Your bit of a letter caught up with me here at Tarbes. I wonder who could have collected it from my hotel and forwarded it. I was only in Paris a few days: don't be too angry. Besides, we'll meet again anyhow, I'll be passing through Paris on my way back to Germany. In this as in everything else Fate is to blame. Why don't you go and complain to her, I'm told she lives in the Office of Longitudes. (D:195)

Someone he had not neglected to go and see, however, was Henry's mistress Léonie Duhaut. Henry was still away in Eastern France but Léonie was installed in their new flat, which was in the same rue Berthollet where the Laforgues had lived (but at number 22 instead of number 5). It was no doubt Léonie who had fixed it up with a grand piano and a chandelier to give it a certain style. Did she know already that her time was almost up? When her relationship with Henry came to an end the following February it had lasted five years, a record for the careful Henry. For most of that time she had been held at arm's length and appreciated more as a secretary than a lover. Despite this she remained continuously loyal to her disappointing companion. Several of Henry's friends (including no doubt Laforgue) were smitten with this attractive girl, but she had eyes only for Henry, who in turn found her passion only embarrassing. It was a tragic situation and had a tragic end. Henry, in the meantime, would have been delighted for Laforgue to take her off his hands. At this period he wrote letters to the two of them together as 'Mes chers enfants' ('My dear children') and tells Léonie to shake Jules's hand affectionately. But Laforgue remained as ever the soul of discretion, and Léonie her faithful self.

Back in Tarbes Laforgue wrote a long overdue letter to Gustave Kahn, who had now been transferred from Algeria to Tunis. He begins by extolling the French provinces (including Tarbes) which he considers very much underrated. He then goes on: 'How wrong one is to want to write, and to print what one writes. My great desire now is to travel and to see things and enjoy them. I used to be a tragic Buddha but now I'm a dilettante one.' (C:41) To Sanda the message is a little different:

The only thing people live for here is gossip, which they peddle from street to street in an abominable accent. I'm leading a vegetable life, not a line of poetry or prose, not even the strength to observe what I see or note down what I hear. Ah, provincial life! . . . It was written that we should not meet on my first trip to Paris. When we meet it will be autumn, Henry will be there, the lamp will be lighted at five o'clock and there'll be a fire in the grate. (D:196)

And on 13 October:

What is this tragic letter? Have you lost your dog again or only a sonnet? If we didn't see each other in Paris, it's because it was written in the stars that we shouldn't see each other. . . . Strange, isn't it, that I don't know you at all, absolutely not at all. What sort of temperament have you? What sort of soul? What sort of brain? Have you got nerves? I've seen you only twice. Perhaps I'll never see you again. Have you studied how to grow pineapples? I'm just beginning. (D:197-8)

To Henry he complains:

The poet of the rue Denfert sent me a long tragic letter yesterday, reproaching me for my lukewarm friendship and slapdash letters. What have I done? I must go and ask her forgiveness. . . . I've embarked on a study in depth of the culture of pineapples; I want to be a millionaire at twenty-six. . . . Shall we go on a pilgrimage to your cell in the rue Séguier, where on certain nights inanimate objects are animated by the multipresent spirit of Baudelaire? Goodbye. A letter for the love of God (por l'amor de Dios).

With his emphasis on travel, his denial of writing and his threat to go into commerce, there are suggestions here that Laforgue might be about to emulate Rimbaud and exchange poetry for pineapples. The temptation—if such it was—was firmly resisted. Returning to Paris in the latter half of October he found time to dine with Delcassé (E:53) but resumed his hard-to-get minuet with the unfortunate Sanda:

26 October: Poet, don't be too hard on my permanent state of fugitivity. You'll forgive me when I tell you that I'm staying on in Paris till 15 November. . . . Soon you will receive the visit of the simple, so simple, young man in black. (unpublished)[31]

5 November: Really, really, what can you have been thinking of me these last ten days? I'm leaving Wednesday, can I come Tuesday and apologize for what you must certainly have taken for a discourtesy? I'll try to make amends. I've seen nobody these last ten days, nobody—and I regret it bitterly: it was insurmountable cowardice. Most probably you are the only one who will believe and forgive me. (M:279)

14 November: I'm back in Coblenz and you're in Paris.... What do you think of me? For a whole week I-who-am-so-simple did not wish to present myself to you-who-are-so-simple because... I had a silly sore on my lip! Is it all over between us? ... What are you thinking? Have you decided in your woman's heart never to see me again, and to send to the devil (whom he never should have left) the young man so simple and so all in black? (M:280-1)

To which Sanda Mahali presumably replied (*sotto voce*): You can say that again. As far as we know, this was the end of the affair that never began. It is pleasant to record, though, that Sanda bore him no ill will and always spoke of him in later days as a good and talented friend.

Nine days later, on 25 November, Laforgue announced to Charles Henry that he was working again, that he was writing poetry and intended to publish a volume entitled *Complaintes de la vie* or *Le Livre des Complaintes*: it was the official opening of a new phase in his life. Back in Berlin, he gave the same news to Ephrussi:

I'm working like mad. ... I work at night by the lamp, it's an infinitely voluptuous feeling. The whole house is asleep; just now and then a cab goes by under the Linden and moonlight bathes the fine snow of the Zeughausplatz. My pages of scribbles are piling up. At Coblenz, too, I worked pretty well, with the Rhine down below, studded with reflected lights. The result is that I've got a new little volume of verse, but I won't publish it any more than I did the first, since in a year's time it will seem as completely ridiculous as that one does today. ... They are still pleased with me at Court. ... It appears, however, that I have my off days, when my voice goes very high—and others when it's no more than a whisper. I invariably reply: well, that's life. (D:214-17)

At the time he wrote that letter he hadn't yet been back to see his friend Charles Bernstein, whom he had left in the spring contemplating his solitary Van Goyen. When he did so, at the beginning of 1883, he was in for a surprise: for the house was now resplendent with Impressionists—and the prime cause and inspiration of this sensational change was Laforgue himself. In those few weeks of February and March 1882 he had planted a seed in the austere mind of the specialist in Roman Law, and that sober gentleman had gone to his cousin Charles Ephrussi in Paris with a startling request: find me ten or twelve of the best Impressionists obtainable. The paintings had arrived in Berlin towards the end of the year, while Laforgue was still on the road, and they had been put on view in the Bernstein house to a select number of German artists. Among them was the formidable Adolf von Menzel himself, whom Laforgue admired, not only as an artist but also as an eccentric, a 'gnome as high as a cavalryman's boot' whom he had seen circulating among the guests at Court functions with his enormous sketchbook. (G:56) He liked especially what he called Menzel's minor manner ('la petite manière') as in the 'surprising' little gouache 'Coin de Rue à Berlin' (1863) from the *Album d'Enfant*, which showed a couple leaning on the sill of a lighted window at night.[32] He had also thoroughly approved when the Princess-Royal made a present of a Menzel to Ephrussi. (D:141) Imagine his amazement, then, when the Bernsteins told him of Menzel's reaction to his beloved Impressionists. 'Did you really pay good money for that trash?' the gnome had cried. And then, realizing that Félicie might take offence, he had confounded his gaffe with, 'Excuse me, Madam, but this stuff is really atrocious!' It was an extraordinary judgement, not least because Menzel, in his best work, had many of the Impressionists' virtues. But he was a volatile, choleric little man who was nothing if not tactless.

The marvellous paintings that Menzel failed to appreciate included no fewer than five Manets, three of them glorious flower studies only recently painted: 'Roses, tulips and white lilac in a crystal vase' (1881), 'Bouquet of peonies' (1882) and the splendid 'White lilac' (1882). In Rouart and Wildenstein's Manet catalogue of 1975 they are numbered 381, 426 and 427 respectively. Earlier Manet periods were represented by 'Departure of the Folkestone boat' (1869, number 147) and 'Fishing boat arriving wind astern' (1864, number 77). There were, in addition, two fine Monets: 'Summer: the poppy field' (1875) and 'Woodland path' (1878), which are listed as numbers 377 and 464 in Daniel Wildenstein's Monet catalogue of 1974. Then there was the Eva Gonzalès pastel of a child's head which had been exhibited in the Paris Salon of

1879, as well as unidentified paintings by Degas, Sisley, Morisot, Cassatt and de Nittis. It was the first time that a group of Impressionist paintings had ever been assembled in Germany, and a year later they were to form the nucleus of a famous Berlin exhibition. But most of the local artists consistently shared Menzel's viewpoint, even if they did not all quite share his manners: the whole affair was a flop—but it did have one good result. It fired Laforgue with an ever greater enthusiasm for the French painters and led directly to the writing of his brilliant exposition of Impressionist aesthetics. It is fairly clear, too, that it was Laforgue who leaked Menzel's fatal remark to Amédée Pigeon, who in due course printed it in the *Figaro*, thus helping to make poor Menzel foolish in French eyes. But he had asked for it.

In his next letter to Henry, Laforgue is already enquiring about Théodore Duret's book on the Impressionists ('It appeared four years ago, I think. . . . I used to see it chez Marpon under the Odéon') and he explains: 'I'm writing an article on Impressionism, which will eventually be translated and appear in a German magazine—on the occasion of which a friend of mine here in Berlin, who has ten or so Impressionists, will put on an exhibition.' (E:7-8) The exhibition would not materialise for another eight months (October 1883) but in the meantime Laforgue began to write the famous article, which seems never to have been published in German as planned—but the draft has come down to us and may be summarized as follows:

The Impressionist is a painter who can forget all those paintings that have accumulated in museums over the centuries. Similarly, he can forget the education in line, colour and perspective that he received at school. Through direct experience in the open air he has learnt to see again the natural way and to paint what he sees. Painters for too long have been saddled with illusions about drawing and perspective. In Impressionism shapes are no longer enclosed by a contour-line but rendered through the interplay of colour vibrations. Likewise, theoretical perspective is discarded in favour of a natural perspective obtained through contrasting colour vibrations.

The expression of living reality by means of the contour-line and theoretical perspective were childish illusions, for the eye can only know vibrations of light, just as the ear knows only vibrations of sound. After being held back for years, the eye is at last learning to recognize its own prismatic sensibility, the art of breaking down forms into their ever-changing colour vibrations. In a landscape bathed in light the Impressionist sees thousands of contrasting colour vibrations. Where the academic painter sees objects enclosed by lines, the Impressionist sees living contours without geometrical form but built up from a thousand irregular brush strokes which, seen from a distance, resemble life. Where the academic painter renders things which are positioned at varying distances from himself according to an arbitrary theory of drawing, the Impressionist's perspective is established by a thousand variations of tone and brushstroke, suggesting the very mobility of the air itself. The Impressionist sees and experiences nature as it is, that is to say uniquely in colour vibrations, and his effect is obtained by a thousand little dancing brushstrokes like threads of colour.

Each man, according to his moment in time, his race and social condition, his personal stage of development, is a keyboard on which the exterior world plays in a particular way. . . . My keyboard is perpetually changing and there is not another exactly like mine. All keyboards are legitimate.

Painting is concerned with the eye—and with the eye only.

This group of painters—the liveliest, boldest and most sincere there has ever been—asks the state to stop meddling in art, to sell the School of Rome, to close the Institute. Let there be no more medals for recompense. Let artists live in anarchy, which is life. (K:133-45)

It is interesting to observe how a discussion about the Impressionists had widened to take in all art (for example Laforgue's poetry) and finally life itself. This is because Laforgue sees no separation at all between these various concepts. The implication is that he wrote poetry as the Impressionists painted pictures because both shared the same basic philosophy of life. 'Let artists live in anarchy, which is life' is not finally a recommendation to a certain group of painters but the slogan by which Laforgue himself would henceforth live.

CHAPTER 5
Dilettante (1883)

LAFORGUE was now moving into the second year of his German cycle. Life resumed in Berlin, and the following letter to Eugène Ysaÿe gives the flavour:

Divine Eugène, My God yes, this is from me! . . . I've heard all about your successes and I come to congratulate you, to place at your feet all the enthusiasm that my poor grocer's soul can muster. Is that enough? . . . I've just seen Frau Hesse, who gave me your new address; but don't worry, I won't take advantage of it, and I won't be there too often to stop Théo working. He's playing tonight with Liebling at some house or other. . . . So Lindenlaub's still in Petersburg or Moscow? I saw a scrap of letter in which he called me a filthy Reader. The wretch! But let it pass. . . . This morning I met handsome Oscar and he looked well. What a character! They tell me you'll soon be back in Berlin. I can hardly wait for the day; we'll go and dine at Lantzsch's in Charlottenstrasse. . . . There's been heavy snow and the churches with domes look as if they're wearing cotton nightcaps. . . . I've seen a horrible photograph of you. Have you really become a monster? Is that why the Norwegian birthrate has fallen—did the mere sight of you cause an epidemic of abortions? Please tell me it isn't true. Adios, mein kind. I speak less German than ever, which really isn't enough. (M:282-3)

Liebling, the pianist, and Oscar Lewinsky, clerk and amateur musician, were just two of the bit players on Laforgue's Berlin scene. Others included another pianist, Büchheim, and Huster, son of a restaurant-owner, as well as the Maywald family who lived in the fashionable suburb of Charlottenburg and were always asking Théo and Laforgue to dine with them. They were really friends of Théo, who was soon to be installed in Kanonierstrasse to be near Laforgue. Laforgue wrote to Henry: 'I hope one day to present to you my young Rubinstein. Hardly eighteen years old but you'll adore him as I do. A dark chap with a wild sort of face, perhaps a bit taller than you with a mass of crinkly hair. I call him the Nubian.' (E:15-16) All Laforgue's Berlin friends figure in a desultory journal (usually referred to as the 1883 Agenda) which Laforgue left behind him in Berlin and which was later discovered and handed to the painter Jacques-Emile Blanche on one of his visits to the city. It is interesting mainly for its indiscretions: the normally careful Laforgue occasionally lets slip a detail on which we can embroider, perhaps not unrewardingly. At other times Laforgue keeps his secrets. On 1 January, for instance, we read:

> Bed at four after Charlottenburg champagne. At 8:30 to Mass at the Sankt Edwige Kirche with M. B. Coated tongue and bleary eyes. Icy cold. She on a bench; I by the door next to a beggar woman, my feet frozen on the paving stones. . . . Gambetta is dead. (F:216)

Who was M. B.? Was it Marie von Bunsen, who was at Court at this time and later wrote about Laforgue in her book on the Empress? We shall never know.

On 21 March he has an entry appropriate to the first day of spring:

> My beautiful stranger at the Opera. An eternal memory. My last thought on my death-bed will be for her. An ideal glimpsed and lost. I'm certain that she saw I adored her, and that she adored me for it. Where is she now? She's going to bed perhaps? She's dismantling her false locks while humming that obsessive overture from *Tannhäuser* (which the pilgrims sing later), that overture that was so dinned into me at Coblenz. All is mystery. She was alone. (F:218)

Other entries include: 'Nearly run over. Imagine being buried in Berlin!' (F:221) and 'What did I do on Friday? Did I perhaps have a total absence of life?' (F:222)

The Agenda gives us a fairly complete list of his amusements, including not only the names of the operas he saw, the dates of the concerts, and a selection of his favourite music-halls (like the Reichshallen and Walhalla in south Berlin) but also a record of such jaunts as 'to Friedrichstrasse with Théo'. He acts as translator and interpreter for the pianist Francis Planté whom a tour brings to Berlin. He falls in love (at a distance) with the leading dancer at the Opera. Antonietta dell'Era, a Sicilian from Medina. On 30 March he buys her photograph 'on points and smiling'. On 2 April he notes that she is still smiling. On 8 April he goes to see her in *Carmen* (which almost reconciles him to his hundredth *Carmen*); on 13 April in the *Queen of Sheba* and so on. A photograph shows

Antonietta as having massive hips; one suspects, though, that it was taken near the end of her long career (thirty years) at the Berlin Opera and that Laforgue's smiling photograph would show a thin girl, which was the only kind he liked. She was a year younger than her French admirer, and her reputation among balletomanes rests on her Sugar Plum Fairy in Tchaikovsky's *Nutcracker*, a role she created at the Maryinsky, St Petersburg, in 1892. If Laforgue had still been alive then, he would no doubt have smiled at the smiling photograph and been proud of her.

On 17 and 18 April Laforgue and Théo made a flying visit to Dresden, ostensibly to see the Rembrandts in the Zwinger. 'They make you want to lick the parquet that reflects them,' he tells Henry (E:17) and to his diary he confides: 'A stream of master-pieces, so beautiful you could weep!' (F:224) But the two friends did not behave at all like sedate art-lovers. For one thing their hats were so enormous that people in the street stopped and stared: technically the style is known as 'Rubens', the width of the brim equalling the wing-span of a condor. In their Rubenses they spent hours lurching about the Dresden streets, having hysterics and shocking the natives. Finally the two delinquents ended up ex-hausted at the railway station, just in time to catch the train back to Berlin in the evening twilight. Early next morning the Court left for Baden-Baden.

Now began a mysterious period in Laforgue's life, during which he appears to have had a highly charged love-affair with a lady called 'R'. Almost all we know about this idyll is contained in twenty-two cryptic notes of the Agenda. The first mention of 'R' is on 20 March when they are still in Berlin together, and the last is at Coblenz on 19 July:—

BERLIN, March

Tuesday 20: I let R read *the letter* taken from Eugène. (F:218)

Friday 30: A visit with R to the exhibitions at the Gurlitt and Jannsen galleries—I guess her instinctive antipathy. (F:219-20)

BERLIN, April

Saturday 14: I go to R's. 'Forget everything, except that I'm devoted to you.' (F:223)

Sunday 15: In the morning, a walk with R. (F:223)

Monday 16: After the Reading—to R's. An interminable scene. Iceberg and fire. (F:223)

Thursday 19: From Berlin to Baden-Baden. Dined with R. Cigars. R and Sch. And Sister Placida laughing—signs. Crazy. Twilight. The engine derails; we borrow one from the Mann-heim train. A little tenderness, a squeezing of hot hands with R. (F:227-8)

BADEN-BADEN, April

Saturday 21: Mad walk with R. The moanings of an ambitious slave. (F:225-6)

Sunday 22: Early walk to Lichtenthal. Then to mass with R and D. (F:226)

Monday 23: Scene with R! Plans for making money: an art gallery. (F:226)

Friday 27: Scene with R. (F:227)

BADEN-BADEN, May

Tuesday 1: With R. Tenderness. (F:228)

Sunday 27: Big scene with R. She was born to be a mother. (F:235)

BERLIN, May

Monday 28: In the carriage from the Potsdam station with R and Sister Placida (who loves me?). R pressed herself against me . . . and Placida (it seemed) gave me looks. (F:235)

Wednesday 30: Tendernesses with R. Explosion. (F:236)

Thursday 31: Exhausted. Tendernesses. (F:236)

BERLIN, June

Friday 1: Exhausted. Tendernesses. (F:236)

Sunday 3: 'I am no longer worthy of your kisses.'–'Tell me everything then.' Sch. had cried. She's unhappy. (F:236)

Monday 4: The Charlottenburg Salon with R. (F:236)

Wednesday 6: R's reaction to my appearance. (F:238)

[This entry refers to an early morning scene at Potsdam station when Laforgue, after a night out in Berlin, joined the Royal party for the journey to Coblenz. The French text 'R devant ma mine' has been elucidated as meaning that R welcomed the bloated and dishevelled reveller with a look of dismay and indignation. Similarly the following entry, 'Scène de l'indigne,' is an allusion to Laforgue's subsequent abject apology.]

COBLENZ, June

Friday 8: The scene of the unworthy one. (F:238)

[Undated entry]: A period of pointed politeness on both sides. [F:243]

COBLENZ, July

Thursday 19: As usual . . . croquet with B or scene with R. Then a coach ride for the four of us, or more croquet. (F:247)

At which point the affair petered out, and 'R' is never mentioned again. In future, whenever the letter R crops up, it can be seen to refer to other Rs: for example the Paris editor Remacle, a friend of Henry's called Regina, Laforgue's schoolfriends Rieffel and Riemer, the pianist Rubinstein, etc.

Not unnaturally, in the case of someone so discreet as Laforgue, the whole question of 'R' has mesmerized critics and commentators, who have allowed their imaginations the fullest rein. One of the most amusing candidates has been Princess Catherine Radziwill, the supposed author of the scandalous *Berlin Society* who did indeed come to Berlin at the end of 1882 and whose articles (if they were hers) began to appear in the *Nouvelle Revue* in September 1883. Catherine was an eccentric twenty-five-year-old mother of four—unhappily married—who could be cast for a role in almost any kind of scenario. Unfortunately there is no proof that she travelled with the Court; indeed there is positive proof to the contrary: on 27 May 1883, for instance, she was in Moscow for the Tsar's coronation—so it would have been difficult for her to have had the 'big scene' described by Laforgue or to 'press herself against him' in the carriage the following day.

Various writers have described differently the colour of R's eyes, how she did her hair, what she wore and everything about her. Some think she was one of the temporary ladies in waiting fresh from her naïf château; others have seen her as the Mysterious Lady of the *Complaintes* and the Femme Fatale of Symbolism. One of them has even suggested she must have been a lesbian, which is carrying insight to great depths. The only thing they all agree on is that they do not know who she was.

It is fortunate, therefore, that when G. Jean-Aubry was editing the Agenda, he was able to consult Théodore Lindenlaub, who had not only known Laforgue personally in Germany but was a first-rate journalist, accustomed to observing the world coolly and impartially for his paper *Le Temps*. Jean-Aubry asked him to examine the Agenda and try to explain some of the more cryptic entries. The result is contained in a letter dated 28 July 1921 which Jean-Aubry's widow Mme Paule Jean-Aubry kindly placed at my disposal: it is invaluable, being all we have in the way of evidence.

When Lindenlaub reached the entry for Tuesday 20 March he wrote: 'Now appears the initial R. I will look in the Gotha for 1883 under the heading Household of the Queen.' But Lindenlaub discovered what subsequent researchers have also discovered: that the Gotha did not go into such minor details. In the space he had left blank for some sensational revelation he was therefore obliged to pencil in: '(Two days later: Have checked with the Gotha for the years 1883-1884 but it does not help us with our problem.)' Lindenlaub, however, as a resourceful journalist, did not leave it at that. 'I seem to remember,' he said,

one allusion, and only one, to a girl in the Queen's retinue whom L described to me, without naming her, as distinguished, analytical, ultra-sensitive, even turbulent. Those aren't exactly the terms he used, but they do convey fairly exactly the unknown girl's psychology. She was apparently the daughter of a mayor of Cologne (or was it Coblenz??). They lived through a long story of sentimental complications, all very idealistic, truly noble and childishly dramatic. L talked about it just that once. One day, it seems, she said to him: 'We're two unhappy people.' It all sounds like a new chapter to add to Goethe's *Elective Affinities*. With the help of the West and East German archives it was not too difficult to discover that the Empress Augusta did indeed have a lady in waiting whose father had been mayor of both Cologne and Coblenz and whose Christian name began with the letter R. She was Rosa Bachem, second daughter of Alexander Bachem (1806-1878) who, after being mayor of Coblenz for ten years (1847-1857), became mayor of Cologne for a further twelve (1863-1875). German mayors at this time were extremely competent and well-paid officials, somewhat resembling a French Prefect in grade. Normally appointed for twelve years, they usually came from a legal background and were often excellent linguists as well. Rosa herself had been at Court, as first Woman of the Wardrobe, since 1875—but perhaps the most interesting fact about her was that she was twenty years older than Laforgue. She was, in fact, exactly the same age as Crown Princess 'Vicky' and, as we have seen, when not writing about very young girls, Laforgue was quite susceptible to older ones. The difference in age, moreover, might explain the way R seems to dominate and mother him, and the constant scenes.

Dr Anne Holmes, who came to the same conclusion independently in her unpublished doctoral dissertation ('The Poetic Development of Jules Laforgue', Cambridge, 1956) has written perceptively in a letter to the author (1 March 1972):

I can remember my dismay at finding that the only possibility I had was aged forty-two. Today it doesn't seem to me impossible that Laforgue might have carried on a flirtation with Mme Bachem for all her forty-two years! . . . It is a pity one knows so little, though I would guess that, practically speaking, there probably was very little to know. . . . I see it all as very much in the imagination. . . . I feel he rather likes the sound of all those references to R, and is to some extent building the thing up, almost pleased that someone is having scenes with him because it makes him feel grown up.

One can, of course, approach the problem from another angle, taking as one's point of departure the poems which he was writing at the time. The 'Complainte d'un certain dimanche' records a parting, and it is dated in the copy given to his sister: Coblenz, July 1883. Since this is precisely the time when the references to

R come to an end in the Agenda, it has been widely assumed that the parting referred to in the poem was the departure of R:—

> Elle est partie hier. Suis-je pas triste d'elle?
> Mais c'est vrai! Voilà donc le fond de mon chagrin!
> Oh! ma vie est aux plis de ta jupe fidèle!
> Son mouchoir me flottait sur le Rhin. . . . (A:52)

[She left yesterday. Am I not sad for her? But of course! So that's the cause of my depression! Oh my life is faithful to the pleats of your skirt! Her handkerchief floated towards me on the Rhine. . . .]

But the woman who threw her handkerchief to him from the Rhine steamer need not have been R; and there is no need to suppose that R left Coblenz at this time, just because she disappears from the diary. It is as likely that the stormy little affair, if you can call it that, had blown itself out, and that Laforgue and Rosa were left only with the slight embarrassment of having to go on meeting at Court for the next three years.

But if the lady of the *Complaintes* was not R, who was she? Fortunately there is another poem which offers a clue. In the 'Complainte de la lune en province' ('Lament for the moon in the provinces'), which again is obligingly dated: Cassel, July 1884 (exactly one year later), we read:—

> Lune heureuse! ainsi tu vois
> A cette heure, le convoi
> De son voyage de noce!
> Ils sont partis pour l'Ecosse.
> Quel panneau si, cet hiver,
> Elle eût pris au mot mes vers. (A:61-2)

[Happy moon! for you can see at this moment the train taking her off on honeymoon! They've left for Scotland. What a disaster if last winter she'd taken my poems seriously.]

Again thanks to German sources (and notably to Charlotte Countess von Klinckowstroem) we know that one of the Court ladies did in fact get married in July 1884, and she did go to Scotland for her honeymoon. This was the young 'temporary' maid of honour Carola von Vitzthum von Eckstädt, who was at both Baden-Baden and Coblenz in 1883 and whose name appears four times in Laforgue's Agenda. Aged eighteen, she was about to wed her cousin, the cavalry officer Captain Adolf von Bülow, ADC to Prince William (the future Kaiser). The ceremony took place near Hamburg on 1 July 1884 and has been described in his *Memoirs* (volume four) by Prince von Bülow, later German Chancellor and brother of the bridegroom. According to the unpublished *Memoirs* of the bride's father, Count Otto Vitzthum, the couple did go to Scotland for their honeymoon. It is possible that the poem Laforgue showed her (and which she fortunately did not take seriously) was the 'Complainte d'un certain dimanche' and that the lady who dropped her handkerchief into the Rhine was therefore Carola and not Rosa.

Whatever the roles of these two ladies in the life of Laforgue, they are very much shadows today. On the one hand there is the forty-year-old attendant to the Empress, a lady of strong personality with whom Laforgue had indulged in discussions, walks and endless scenes, together with brief moments of tenderness and hand-squeezing. 'R pressed herself against me,' he writes at one point; but at another: 'She was born to be a mother.' She dominates and often irritates him. He is none the less proud to write day after day in his Agenda: 'Scene with R. . . . Big scene with R. . . . Endless scene. . . . Mad walk together!' For after all, something is happening to him at last. 'Now I'm someone to reckon with,' as he is to write in 'Légende' ('Ah! voici que l'on compte enfin avec Moi!') (A:301). No one's a child any longer when a woman of forty bothers to have rows with him.

On the other hand we have the extremely young Countess who finally intrigues him because of her great reserve. This is a woman who was, according to her brother-in-law Prince von Bülow, 'a great beauty with magnificent though sad eyes, child-like, slender, full of charm' (*Memoirs*, volume four, pages 36 and 553) and whom Laforgue described as 'a strange girl . . . thin and silent' ('l'étrange backfisch' [F:242], 'toujours perche et muette comme le poisson· de ce nom' [F:240]). When she leaves he is almost surprised to find himself missing her: 'Am I not sad for her? But of course!' At the same time this deliciously thin Countess with the sad eyes was engaged to Prince William's ADC, so one can well understand Laforgue's saying some months afterwards: 'What a disaster if she'd taken those lines seriously!' In the event there is no suggestion that Laforgue's love for the Countess at Court was other than . . . courtly.

So much for the Countess and the Wardrobe Woman. The whole story (as much and as little as is known of it) is told in this list of arrivals at the Hotel Messmer, Baden-Baden, on 19 April 1883 (which was discovered for us in a local news-sheet, the *Badeblatt*, by the town archivist Mme Margot Fuss):—

Verzeichniss
der vom 18. bis 20. April angekommenen Fremden.

Im W. Messmer'schen Hause.

Ihre Majestät die Deutsche Kaiserin und Königin von Preussen.

Brandenburg, Gräfin von, Hofdame Ihrer
  Majestät der Kaiserin.
Vitzthum, Gräfin von, Hofdame Ihrer
  Majestät der Kaiserin.
Oehnhausen, Graf von, Kammerherr Ihrer
  Majestät der Kaiserin.
Knesebeck, von dem, Cabinetssecretär
  Ihrer Majestät der Kaiserin.
Velten, Dr., Geheimerath und Leibarzt
  Ihrer Majestät der Kaiserin.
Neindorff, Frl. von, Kammerfrau Ihrer
  Majestät der Kaiserin.
Schöler, Frl. von, Kammerfrau Ihrer
  Majestät der Kaiserin.
Bachem, Frl., und
Dominicus, Frl., Garderobefrauen Ihrer
  Majestät der Kaiserin.
  Nebst Dienerschaft, 33 Pers., Berlin.
Artelt, Hofrath, Berlin.
Placida, Schwester, Berlin.
Laforque, Paris.

In similar lists Laforgue appears variously as Professor Laforgue, Prof Laforgue, Prof Laforque (*sic*) as well as the simple Laforque (*sic*). No doubt he enjoyed the irony of the professorial title being awarded to one who had failed his 'bac' at least two and possibly three times.

It was during this visit to Baden-Baden that he started his story
'Le Miracle des Roses', the first part of which gives a not unsympa-
thetic portrait of the place (considering the rigour of his real
feelings):

Never, never, never could that little town ever understand!—its
uncivilized town council was elected by rapacious hillbillies (who
were not in the least comic opera despite their costume).

Ah, why isn't everything comic opera? Why doesn't everything
go round to the tune of that English waltz 'Myosotis'[33] which
we used to hear at the Casino that year?—with me feeling desperate, as you can well imagine, in some corner or other. A waltz
so decently melancholy, speaking so irrevocably of the last fine
days of summer. (That waltz! If only I could find a word to im-
pregnate you with its essence before letting you into my story!)

Hail to you, oh gloves that were never rejuvenated by benzine!
Oh the brilliant and melancholy hither and thither of all those
lives! And all you beautiful women who will age and wear black
lace by the fireside, never understanding the conduct of your
lively and muscular sons, to whom you gave birth with such
chaste melancholy.

Little town, little town of my heart.

The sick no longer move around the Pump Room with grad-
uated glass in hand. The waters now are for bathing in: a dip at
twenty-five degrees followed by a walk and siesta. Intended
mainly for the neuropaths, especially women and other delicate
creatures.

You can see them wandering about, the good neuropaths,
dragging a leg which will never waltz again, even to the fragile
and prim measures of 'Myosotis'—or pushed about in a little
cart upholstered in faded leather. You can see one of them suddenly leave his seat at a concert in the Casino with a strange noise
of automatic swallowing—or swing around on the Promenade
with a hand to his neck, as if some practical joker had just
slashed him with a razor. You can see them at the corners of
woods, their faces convulsed with weird contractions, flinging
small pieces of torn letters into the antediluvian ravines. They
are the neuropaths, children of a too brilliant century. They are
everywhere.

To this place, as to all places, the good sun, friend of snakes
and cemeteries and waxen dolls, attracts a few consumptives,
that slow-footed race so dear to the dilettante.

Once upon a time people used to gamble in the Casino (Oh
brilliant and irresponsible epochs, how my mad heart weeps for
you!) but now they gamble no more (Oh shade of Prince Canino,

1 (a) and (b) Charles and Pauline, the poet's parents.

(c) Laforgue aged eleven in his *lycée* uniform, photographed by M. Blanchard of Tarbes on 29 January 1872.

2 (a) and (b) above, Laforgue's elder brother, the easy-going Emile, and his sister Marie with her family.

(c) Laforgue in 1885 at the Prussian court – a sketch by the Croatian painter Franz Skarbina (1849-1910).

3 Gustave Moreau's famous painting of 'Galatea'
which Laforgue saw at the Paris Salon of 1880.

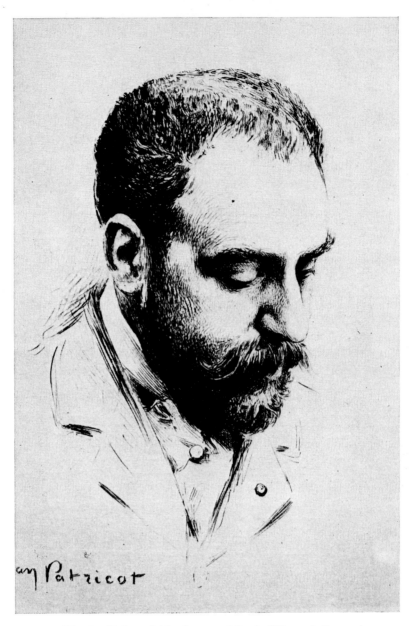

4 Charles Ephrussi (the lesser original of Proust's Swann)
became Laforgue's lifelong friend and protector.

5 Two more of Laforgue's patrons: (a) above, Paul Bourget in the days when he was an elegant and sharp young man, and (b) Théophile Delcassé, one-time junior assistant at the Tarbes *lycée* and later French Foreign Minister.

6 Prince William (later the Kaiser) was on back-slapping terms with Laforgue, who complained wryly, 'That chap's mad on uniforms – it runs in the family.'

7 The German Empress Augusta saw herself as
a French great lady of the *ancien régime*.

8 Crown Princess 'Vicky' was a favourite with Laforgue for two good
reasons: she was an art-lover and she was English.

9 Berlin: Princess Vicky's palace in the middle, with Laforgue's on the right. The three windows at lamp-post level are those of his apartment.

10 Eugène Ysaÿe (with his friend Théodore Lindenlaub) had just been discovered by Rubinstein and was at the start of a memorable career.

11 (c) opposite, Laforgue and his friends were frequent visitors to the Berlin tingeltangels, lowlife dives of the period.

11 (a) Adolf von Menzel   (b) Léo Trézenik

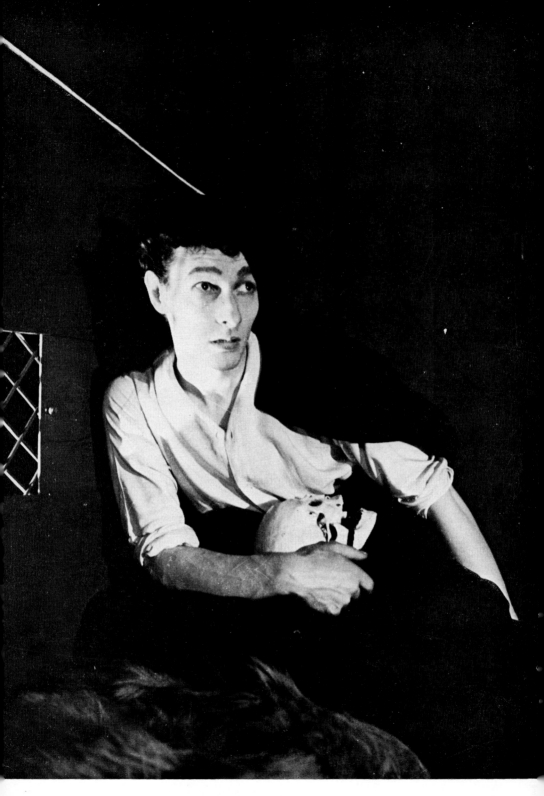

12 Jean-Louis Barrault as Laforgue's Hamlet:
one of his earliest and most successful creations.

13 (a) Laforgue had little good to say of Baden-Baden, where his hotel adjoined the Kurgarten. (b) But he never stopped praising the vast château of Coblenz with its fine view of the Rhine.

14 (a) Brilliant man of letters and faithful friend, Teodor de Wyzewa devised ways to help Laforgue in the last weeks of his life.

Two more friends of the last years, as seen by Toulouse-Lautrec: 14 (b)
opposite, Félix Fénéon is the check-coated gentleman in the lower right-
hand corner, watching La Goulue. 15 above, Edouard Dujardin on the
right is escorting Jane Avril.

16 Leah's tomb in the cemetery of her native Teignmouth. The photograph inset (a) shows her aged 21 in January 1883.

ever accompanied by his faithful Leporello, what unappreciated gravedigger serves you now?) The rooms are deserted, except for their useless attendants in blue cloth and metal buttons. The Reading Room—since newspapers are still allowed—invariably contains one of those neuropaths (to chase you away) whose involuntary deglutination makes *Le Temps* drop from your hands. The old gaming-room now only has Dutch Tops and Jockey Billiards, with cases of prizes for children's lotteries and the paraphernalia of draughts and chess. Another room is used to store the ancient grand piano. (Those incurably romantic ballades of Chopin have buried another generation and the new girl who plays them today really *loves*: she thinks that love was never known until she appeared on the scene, was never known until the arrival of her distinguished and misunderstood heart; and she is full of sorrow, oh ballades, for your sorrowful cadences.) But as for this particular old-fashioned piano, nobody lifts any more its cloth of faded flowers, though on fine summer evenings the breezes still practise harmonica-style arpeggios on the crystal stalactites of the chandelier—a chandelier which shone down on so many plump shoulders dancing to the guilty tunes of Offenbach.

And from the terrace of the old guilty Casino you can see a healthy green lawn for playing lawn-tennis, where modern youth in the full meaning of the term—muscular, straight from the shower-bath and accountable to History—gives vent to its animal spirits with arms bare and torso proud, while the free and educated girls, limping elegantly in their flat shoes, hold their heads high in the face of Man and the Open Air (instead of cultivating their immortal souls and thinking of death, as befits good Christians).

Beyond this truly modern lawn of youth the first hills begin, with the Greek chapel and its gilded domes, and the vaults to which they finally relegate all that is mortal of the princely line of Stourdzas.

Farther down, at the Villa X, there sulks a fairly illiterate and deposed Catholic queen, of whom people take less and less notice but who goes on thinking that it is she who brings prosperity to the town.

And beyond all this the real hills: pretty views touched here and there with romantic castles and cottages you could eat.

And over the whole mad little town, with its circle of hills, there reigns the infinite sky—but here, it seems, one prefers not to see it, since not one of these delicate creatures ever goes out without putting up a parasol between herself and God.

The Fêtes Committee have a magic touch: whether it's Venetian Nights or Balloonists Ascending (he is always called Karl Securius), children's roundabouts or seances of spiritualism and anti-spiritualism. And everything goes to the strains of the honest local orchestra, whom nothing on earth could stop from appearing at the Pump Room every morning at half-past seven for their overture to the day; and again in the afternoon under the acacias of the Promenade (Oh the solos of the little harpist in black who makes herself pale with powder and raises her eyes to the roof of the bandstand, all in the hope that she'll be carried off by some exotic neuropath with a soul as quivering as her own instrument!) and once more finally in the evening, by courtesy of the famous electric light (Oh the march from *Aïda* on the cornet as it wafts up to the indubitably fabulous stars!)

And so, in short, what we have here is a small luxury resort, a hive of distinguished activity at the bottom of a valley. All these wandering couples have a rich, if unknown, past; and there are no proletarians in sight (Ah if only capitals could be like elegant watering places!). The only underlings on view, in fact, are luxury ones like grooms and coachmen, white-clad chefs standing by night at the doors of their establishments, drovers of donkeys and men who herd special cows for consumptives. Every language and every human type is represented here.

And at twilight, listening to the band, when you yawn a bit and raise your eyes to the eternal circle of well-kept hills, with all those people walking round with their sharp pale smiles, you really have quite desperately the feeling that you're in a luxury prison, with a green yard, and that all these sick people—sick because of their picturesque ideas and past—have been sent here as exiles from the serious capitals where progress is marching on.

In the evenings they used to dine on the terrace and I could see, quite near me, the table of the Princess T (a big dark creature, awkward and overripe) who thought she was witty (what a mistake!) sitting with her friends who thought the same (another mistake!). But I preferred to watch the fountain spring up towards the planet Venus, which had just that moment appeared on the horizon—while rockets (awakening echoes in the valley) themselves rose like fountains and fell in the form of stars. And as for the real stars they remained as indubitably fabulous in their deportment towards fountains and rockets as they had to the march from *Aïda*, which was still being brazened forth nostalgically by that 'thinking reed' of a cornet. Believe me, they were ineffable, those evenings. You who were there and failed to attract to yourself an unknown fiancée, like lightning to a

conductor, don't bother to search any more, for the only one
you'd ever find now would be second-best, a poor substitute.

Oh little town, you were my only love. . . . (B:67-71)

If the 'fairly illiterate' ex-Queen of Naples ever read the above
piece, she may not have been over-pleased. But at least she would
be consoled in her later years, when Proust made her lend an arm
to the shattered Charlus. 'I have never met Monsieur Proust,' she
said after reading the book, 'but I feel he understands me perfectly:
that is exactly what I would have done in the circumstances.'
Monsieur Laforgue, perhaps, did not understand her.

While at Baden-Baden in 1883 Laforgue wrote a couple of letters
to his sister:

14 May: I read, smoke, work and wander about the Black Forest.
But the landscapes here, though unique in the world, make me
sick. They're prettier than nature, they're like paintings by
Gustave Doré, truly they are! I've decided to copy some verses
for you. . . . They may seem a bit odd; I've abandoned my rue
Berthollet style, my philosophical poems: I think it's stupid
now to put on a big voice and play at eloquence. Today I'm
more sceptical and get carried away less easily, and also I have a
more exact and humorous control of language. I write little
poems of fantasy with only one aim: to be original at all costs.
I have the firm intention of publishing a very small book, but
well presented with good typography, a worthy casket for my
literary gems, called *Quelques Complaintes de la Vie*. . . . I've
already got twenty; another dozen and I'll take the manuscript
God knows where. I regret only one thing: a few naturalistic
lines have got through the net and seem somehow necessary, but
in general I'm veering away from enthusiasm and naturalism
(only as a poet, of course; novels are different). . . . Life is raw,

we all know that, but in poetry for God's sake let's keep it elegant as pinks. We can still say absolutely everything (and it's precisely the filthiness of life that gives a melancholy humour to certain lines) but let's say these things with a certain style. A poem shouldn't be a literal transcription of life (like a page from a novel). A poem should be drowned in dream. . . . In this respect my *Complaintes* are not yet quite right. I'll retouch them. I'll drown them a bit more. (E:19-22)

21 May: I've just dined in a hotel and heard nothing but French spoken. I'm in Strasbourg. I'm writing in a café full of sunlight. I had nothing to do in Baden-Baden today . . . so I came here. I'm delighted to be in Strasbourg for a day. What a place for observing! You know that it has been a part of the German empire since the Treaty of Frankfurt ended the war of 1870, so it's all very interesting. You'd think you were in France. The signs, for instance, are in French. And everywhere you hear our gentle language spoken—except, alas, by the youngest children playing in the gutters: something that touched me to the heart. Instead of the cigar-sellers of Germany, here it's the old bureau de tabac with the red sign. In the cathedral someone offered me his services as a guide and, when I declined in French, he gave me this little image (which I send you). He spoke to me with tears in his voice and I forked out a franc. As I came into town a child was crying by the entrance to a shop. A girl came up and asked, 'Pourquoi que tu pleures, René?' I can't tell you how that simple phrase went straight to my heart; the best way to keep the French patriotic is to send them abroad. Everywhere you see top-hats and scruffy shoes, and you know you're in France, where the cigarettes, as well as the hair and beards, are black or dark brown. I have in front of me a couple of Alsace papers. They're divided down the middle: half in German, half in French. But if I'm at all in doubt I only have to look up and see the great boots and pointed helmets drilling outside. (E:23-5)

For some reason known only to the Empress—perhaps the annual review of the Berlin garrison?—it was the custom for the court to spend a week in Berlin, sandwiched between the spring visits to Baden-Baden and Coblenz. Although the exact reason escapes us, there must surely have been one, since this arrangement added considerably to the rail travel, and the Empress was never too keen on travel after her accident. The Berlin week of 1883 was notable for a marathon night-out (the night of 5-6 June) during which Laforgue took in an art exhibition, dinner at a restaurant, coffee

with the Maywalds at Charlottenburg, a couple of tingeltangels, a
brothel or two, the Café Bauer, a philosophical walk along the
banks of the Spree, followed by a two-hour discussion in Théo's
flat. Finally he retired to the palace at seven in the morning, but
only to pack hurriedly and rush to the Potsdamer Bahnhof just
in time to catch the train for Coblenz. Here in detail is the night
in question as recorded by Laforgue with all its ambiguities:

> *Tuesday 5*: To the Salon with Théo—three hours of notes—dined
> badly on restaurant terrace—coffee with Maywalds—La Lidschen
> [the Maywald's daughter-in-law] is desirable—we come home—
> at eight Lewinsky—'The Academy of Music'—the old man whose
> stomach vibrated all by itself—The first girl seemed weary of
> life—the one who asked me for pineapple salad and looked like
> Marguerite—the last one with the mad voice—then to the tingel-
> tangel in Hauvogteiplatz—a Jewess with black armpits—a blonde
> made of wood—the red-faced English girl, unbelievable—'Yours,
> yours, yours'—collecting pfennigs—at midnight with Lewinsky
> to the tram and borrowed ten marks from him—A crazy four-
> some ['partie carrée insensée'] —a contest (beginning with ear-
> rings for small change)—incredibly stubborn—Friedrichstrasse
> 159, c/o Elsa, third floor—to the Café Bauer at two o'clock—a
> philosophical ramble along the Spree, desolate in the light of
> dawn with enormous barges—unbelievable—back to his place at
> 4.30—talk till 6.30—the palace at 7—packed and washed and to
> Potsdam station—the Emperor joins us—I go with Dr Velten—
> R's reaction to my appearance—slept or tried to—wonderful
> weather—arrived Coblenz 9.30 night—Countess Hacke waiting
> for us on the steps—supper with Velten—my room on the Rhine
> —slept—(!) (F:237-8)

'The Academy of Music', according to Lindenlaub, was a pretty
low-class dive, but the tingeltangel in Hausvogteiplatz was lower
still.[34] As for what Lindenlaub calls the 'ten-mark programme of
variegated noctambulism', he declines to elucidate further, leaving
it to M. Jean-Aubry's imagination.

On the fairly slender evidence available it looks as if Laforgue's
night-out in Berlin drew the curtain on his relationship with Rosa
Bachem. Perhaps he intended it to. The day after their arrival at
Coblenz Laforgue plays the role of 'unworthy one' to Rosa's
'pure angel' (an allusion to Donizetti's opera *La Favorite*)—
after which nothing more is heard of R except for a reference
to 'a period of pointed politeness on both sides' and the final
note suggesting that a 'row with R' has become no more or less
important than 'croquet with B', both being purely routine
matters. The affair was over. At the end of the year, when he

refers to her one last time in the Agenda, she will merely be
'Bachem'. (F:257)

To supplement the occasional glances exchanged with his muse
the Countess of Vitzthum Laforgue had other girl-friends at Coblenz, whom we meet in rapid succession. 'Little Countess Blumen-
thal who's become quite pretty' is on the boat coming back from
Cologne on 11 June (F:239) and she turns up again for an outing
on 6 August (F:251). Countess Elsa is in love with a polar explorer
and of the two young Furstenbergs 'the little one is especially
piquante'. (F:245) Bebelchen (or little Barbara), with whom he
walked in the moonlight at Baden-Baden (F:233), becomes a
regular croquet partner at Coblenz (F:241, 247, 252). Maria and
Valerie von Schöler, with whom he had drunk a glass of milk on
the heights above Baden-Baden (F:234) could possibly be related
to the second Woman of the Bedchamber, in which case Cécile
de Schöler might belong to a French branch of the family. He had
nearly missed the train to say goodbye to 'la petite Cécile' at
Baden-Baden (F:235). He needn't have worried: all the Schölers
turn up again at Coblenz.

So, temporarily at least, Laforgue found himself with an embarrassment of riches, but his friend Charles Henry was without a
girl-friend altogether and—far more important—without a secretary.
Léonie Duhaut had finally walked out after surprising him with
Marie Krysinska, a Polish Jewish poet nicknamed 'La Reine de
Pologne'. This sounds suspiciously like a staged provocation to get
rid of poor Léonie, since Krysinska was interested not in Henry but
in his friend the artist Georges Bellenger, whom she subsequently
married. Laforgue thought little enough of her as a poet and probably rather less after her behaviour towards Léonie, but he admired
her future husband, the illustrator of Zola. Ironically enough,
Krysinska was later to be set up publicly as one of the inventors
of *vers libre*, by which time the real inventor (Laforgue) was dead.

Though Laforgue admired many French painters, he chose to
correspond with a German one, Max Klinger, whom he had met at
Bernstein's and who lived near him in Berlin, in the Mittelstrasse.
At this time Klinger was just off to Paris, probably at the instiga-
tion of Laforgue himself, who wrote to him from Coblenz:

11 June: What a terrible job being an art critic! The profession has been dishonoured by so many ignorant fools, and artists are often right to despise us. For my part I do assure you that I tackle the job seriously: not so much by reading books and hunting around old museums, as in trying to see the world clearly—and by observing as a simple human being (a prehistoric one if you like) the Rhine, the sky, fields and crowds and streets. I have studied life far more in the streets, flats and theatres of Paris than in the libraries. I am convinced that I have the artist's eye; I am hostile to all artistic prejudices and sincerely wish to inform public opinion. If I didn't believe all that, I wouldn't write. You are going to Paris and I am happy for your sake. . . . You are going to see the lovely landscapes of the Seine, Notre-Dame in the sunset and so on. . . . You will see how sublime the dress-coats are in Paris. And women's hats. Go and spend an afternoon in the Louvre and Bon Marché department stores. . . . Your pessimism will become blacker still amid the sad splendours of that monstrous city. You will read a lot. Your drawing will become freer and more emphatic, your eyes more wide-ranging and sharper. With your native imagination you will conquer Paris. And you will find that the Paris press can be admirable when it discovers a truly original artist. (E:28-31)

15 September: You found the Luxembourg a disappointment? Go back and try again. . . . Love Paris, I implore you, and especially the suburban landscapes like the Bièvre. Have courage, work hard and Paris will acclaim you as king. (E:50)

Also from Coblenz he wrote to Ephrussi:

14 June: It is written in the stars that you won't write to me, so it has to be from the Empress that I learn the news. So you showed the Princess Royal round the Paris Salon and she asked you (or you asked her) for news of me. Well, here it is: I spent last week in Berlin and wore myself out at the Salon in Charlottenburg. I've worked up my notes, so can I send you the thing as usual? (E:32)

3 July: I got my Salon back. *Alas poor!* [*sic*] I've now redone it. . . . I've sacrificed exactly thirty-nine names. The ones left in are absolutely necessary if the Old Museum of Berlin, complete with Schinkel frescos, is not to collapse on my head, oh horror! . . . I've been spending whole afternoons on the heights of Baden-Baden, driving myself silly with the sun and all that green greenery. . . . Have you the courage to work in this weather?—which is so hot even the infusoria in inkwells are bursting into bloom! (E:34-6)

There were letters, too, for Henry:

14 July: Spent a day and a half in Cologne and four in Munich, where I saw Bellenger in front of the Rubens pictures in the Pinacothèque.... Now back in Coblenz with the Rhine under my window ... smoking my pipes and polishing my *Complaintes*. (E:37-9)

27 July: I'm not surprised they didn't reply to you from Berlin. What a bunch of boorish layabouts that lot are! I've spent two years acquiring the conviction that they really are the most actively inartistic people on earth. God, if only I could write my Berlin Salon for a less timid outfit than the *Gazette* [*des Beaux-Arts*]. Even so, I managed to get some things off my chest. (E:40-2)

2 August: Delighted you're going to be in Paris. I'll make a bee-line for the rue Berthollet. . . . Are you sometimes at home? Not often, I imagine. The evenings perhaps, since you're not tempted out by the circus and theatres. . . . My *Complaintes* now seem a small and passing fancy. What's not eternal is short, and what's not all-inclusive is narrow. All the same they're the best thing I've done. . . . We'll have a lot to talk about in your salon. You'll let me bring my pipe, won't you? (E:43-5)

Holiday time was here again. Laforgue went to Paris, via Belgium, where he spent a couple of days with Eugène Ysaÿe and Théodore Lindenlaub. In Paris he clocked in at the usual place, 99 boulevard Saint-Michel, but there was no problem this year about seeing (or avoiding) Sanda Mahali. She was no longer in his thoughts. On the day after his arrival he went to the attractive new Eden Theatre with his old school friend Victor Riemer. The big hit there, which had been running since the beginning of the year, was the ballet *Excelsior*, portraying the victory of Light, symbol of scientific progress, over the forces of darkness and obscurantism, with the legendary Cecchetti in one of the major roles. The charming Bérénice (or 'Petite-Secousse'), heroine of the Maurice Barrès novel *Le Jardin de Bérénice*, formed part, it will be remembered, of the Excelsior troupe, which excelled in dancing the Can-Can to the Marseillaise. Almost every day Laforgue saw Henry but he only stayed six days in all, before leaving for Tarbes, and when he got there he wrote:

What are you doing? All those days in Paris you seemed vaguely to be doing nothing. You should get started on your novel. Between ourselves that's something I look forward to with the most sincere and singular curiosity. For your age you have an impressive past, be it in science, books or life. Begin a novel, give us some of that rich material extracted from your innermost self and even farther down than that. You've already thought about it and now you must do it. You know very well that it's the only thing that matters. . . . (E:48)

Laforgue himself was now working on 'Le Miracle des Roses', which he had begun at Baden-Baden and which was to become the first completed story of his *Moralités Légendaires*. Happening to attend a bullfight at Saint-Sebastian, he immediately incorporated it into the story. He was also working hard on the *Complaintes* and the same thing occurred. Chancing to visit the cemetery at Ivry on All Saints' Day, he at once commandeered the scene for one of his new poems, the beautiful and mysterious 'Complainte de l'ange incurable'. That same day in Paris (1 November) he noted in the Agenda: 'Twilight in the Luxembourg', a note which was extended into the following very characteristic mood-piece:

A chilly twilight. The leaves, irremediably burnt with rust, seem to be huddled together in heaps to keep warm. In delicate outline one can see the arbours stripped bare by the mean winds and eternal squalls of rain. At the horizon the sky is pale gold, with red splashes invading areas of dull lilac and cloudy violet: forming a wide band against which are picked out the calm outlines of the roofs with their chimneys, and the towers of Saint-Sulpice. Higher up, the sky is an anaemic yellow, which dissolves into a milky veil, finally becoming the pale blue sky itself, with here and there wisps of purplish, deep-red and dark-brown cloud. All is calm, except that, beyond those tree-trunks and between the two indented roofs, there is a pink spot which marks the agony of the defeated sun.

The pond, shimmering with tender gold and reflecting broken images of trees, is quivering with a thousand small movements constantly renewed. In the middle, in the bowl held by three cherubs, the fountain is dead.

The whole place is filled almost imperceptibly with the confused sound of streets and traffic, the crack of a whip, a tramway horn, the bark of a dog, an impression of distant city life. The hour strikes on the palace clock. How strange the sky has become, in just a few minutes, over there to the left—like a great field of golden wheat on which a storm is beating down, those slanting lines being caused by clouds on the horizon that have been torn to shreds by a sudden wilful gust of wind. A factory chimney slowly pumps out purplish gobs of smoke which rise, spread out and dissolve. These are the final curiosities, the last playful games of the majestic sunset. But behind us night is falling, hurrying down, covering everything, including the pale statues. And now the gas begins to sputter. And ah yes my goodness, quite a bitter little wind springs up. 'Closing, closing, we're closing.' A sudden impression of autumn: the approach of unescapable winter with its sad Sundays. (K:27-8)

A surprise had awaited Laforgue when he came back to Paris from Tarbes: his friend Charles Henry had a new companion, a bright girl from Poland with an Italian name, Regina Candiani. During the weeks of October Regina and Laforgue were able to see quite a lot of each other, and they at once became friends. On his return to Germany he continually asked about her. Already from Baden-Baden on 5 November he proclaimed: 'Place me at the feet of Mme Candiani with all the civilities of her abominable and powerful servitor JULES LAFORGUE.' (E:56)

But there was a certain mystery about the way he rejoined the Court that year. It was the only time he ever visited Baden-Baden in the autumn. Why did he hurry back instead of waiting till the Empress had reached Coblenz? The clue lies perhaps in a letter to his sister on 28 October, asking for two copies of the *Nouvelle Revue* left at their home in Tarbes by his school friend Pérès. (D:202) It is probable that these were the copies (for 15 September and 15 October 1883) containing the first articles in the scandalous new series by Catherine Radziwill on Berlin Society. When Amédée Pigeon had begun his own series in the *Figaro* eighteen months before, Laforgue had rushed around the Court proclaiming his innocence. Did he intend to do the same this time? It is not impossible. In fact his letter to Pigeon of 1 November, which is referred to in the Agenda (F:256) but has since disappeared, may well have been on this very topic. 'What has this Radziwill woman been up to?' one can imagine the present Reader asking the previous Reader. (Answer: exactly what the previous Reader was up to last year, and the present Reader will be up to in his own good time.)

When he arrived at Baden-Baden on the night of 3 November, Laforgue recorded that the only windows in the Hotel Messmer still lit up were those of 'Neindorf and Bachem' (F:257), while down below he could vaguely see Sister Placida, 'a white figure arranging cushions'. Next day he heard that same bell that rang in the afternoons of May, when Bachem was still 'R' and there were no dead leaves. He 'passes the brush of euphuism' over the strange 'Complainte de l'ange incurable' but it was time to move on to Coblenz. At the station young Dr Schliep, the local physician, quoted from the late Russian minister Gortchakoff: 'A man is as old as his . . . '. (F:257) The word is left out, but Gortchakoff's fate is well known. It was at Baden-Baden earlier in the year that he had died in the arms of a prostitute and, to avoid scandal, his body had been removed from the hotel in a linen basket, covered in dirty linen. It is a bleak story and the days are drawing in. . . . The closing lines of 'Complainte de l'ange incurable' remind us:

Tant il est vrai que la saison dite d'automne
N'est aux coeurs mal fichus rien moins que folichonne. (A:68)
[So true it is that the season called autumn for shaky hearts is anything but merry.]

He now spent a period of twenty days 'shut up and cloistered' in the Château of Coblenz, during which time he 'thought and worked intensely'. (E:60) He tells Ephrussi:

I reread all the various theories of aesthetics in a state of mind unknown to me since I was eighteen in the Bibliothèque Nationale. I withdrew into myself and, in the course of a single night, from ten o'clock to four in the morning. . . . I wrote ten pages setting out the metaphysical principles of my new aesthetic: an aesthetic which is perfectly in harmony with Hartmann's 'Unconscious' as well as with the works of Darwin and Helmholtz. (E:60)

As he himself suggested, the so-called aesthetic was more a statement of fundamental beliefs than a mere aesthetic, and as such it was of vital importance to the life of Laforgue if not to the history of philosophy. Indeed it has been roundly criticized and even ridiculed by all sorts of writers who failed to perceive its salient point, which was that it worked for him. It gave him something to hold on to when everything else, including Christianity and Buddhism, had failed. And as such it provided the essential underpinning for all his subsequent work, which was also his best work. It gave unity to everything he did, creative or critical.

The theory of the 'Unconscious' which he finally worked out owed as much to Laforgue himself as to Hartmann. Hartmann would probably have disowned it. It has, of course, nothing to do with Freud, either, and the very word 'Unconscious' is misleading; he might just as well have used the word 'God', which has the advantage of being shorter. But it was a God without strings attached, which Laforgue could adapt to his own purposes, and that was what mattered.

His new belief was a deliverance, offering him a wonderful relief from former anxieties, as Léon Guichard has explained.[35] Put another way, the natural strength of his organism had freed his mind from the need to worry. After all, he was only twenty-three so he might as well live. He came to believe in a transcendental god who (so long as you sensed him) would reciprocate by being your guardian angel; would protect you in life while giving valuable inspiration for your work.

There is no doubt that Laforgue, for most of the time, felt protected. 'I live in the arms of the Unconscious, which will look after me,' he wrote to Henry. (E:96) And to Kahn:

My faith, as you know, is the philosophy of the Unconscious. It means everything to me: it explains everything and answers to all my needs. In the street, with people at a party, or with just one person, when a phrase, when anything catches my interest, I try resolving it by means of the infallible Unconscious. (C:59)

Even more important were the implications for his work:

Today everything points to (and leads to) the exclusive rule of Reason, Logic and Consciousness. . . . We're heading for dessication: a race of rationalistic skeletons in spectacles. Let us return, my friends, to the wide waters of the Unconscious. (J:64) . . . Let us abandon ourselves to the great force that is present everywhere. . . . A guardian angel is detailed for each one of us from the great angel of history. . . . The unique force which guides me, gives me ideas I never knew before and rescues me from the world of reflection, reasoning, calculation and premeditation to cast me loose on the waters of the Unconscious. (K:16-17) . . . The Unconscious blows where it listeth; let it do just that and our arts will follow. (K:154) . . . Its principle is the anarchy of life: let it lead us where it may, let us delight in the limitless treasures of our senses and bedeck our dreams with flowers

during the short time that is left to us. (K:207-8)
It was all summed up in the splendid battle-cry which he adapted
from the Marseillaise and which the Surrealists were to borrow:
'Aux armes, citoyens, il n'y a plus de RAISON' (A:294) ['To
arms, citizens, REASON is dead'.]

   In the letter to Ephrussi announcing his new faith, there was
other important news: he had just been to Germany's first Impressionist exhibition at the Gurlitt gallery. Naturally he went with the
Bernsteins and naturally the nucleus of the show was the little group
of paintings that Bernstein had bought in Paris with Ephrussi's
help. These had been added to, however, by the Impressionists'
famous impresario Paul Durand-Ruel. The prevailing economic
climate in France at the time was poor, and Durand-Ruel had had
to look abroad. He had just had a big show in London, at the Bond
Street gallery of Dowdeswell and Dowdeswell. The Berlin show
was peanuts in comparison but at least it was a milestone for
Germany (though Menzel and his friends preferred to call it a
millstone).
   Durand-Ruel had brought over from London the great Manet
figure painting of 1873 'Le chemin de fer' (number 207 in
Rouart and Wildenstein's 1975 catalogue). Also perhaps the Degas
'Course de gentlemen' (begun in 1860 and finished in 1880)
though this is less certain. These were the two most important
paintings in the London show, priced at £400 each, which was
high for those days. From somewhere else he had picked up Mary
Cassatt's 'La tasse de thé' of 1879 (number 65 in the Breeskin
catalogue). There was a Pissarro 'Pontoise', probably the 'Marché
Saint-Martin' that Laforgue has described elsewhere in one of the
fragments (J:72-3), together with a nude by Renoir and a sea-
scape by Boudin. These were judged to be important enough to
bolster up the Bernstein nucleus, but Laforgue was only mildly
impressed by them. It is difficult to be sure if all the Bernsteins
were on view—certainly his two marvellous Monets were there and
at least some of the Manets. Also a Sisley and a Morisot and the

Eva Gonzalès 'Tête d'enfant'. Whether the exhibition did anything to change German attitudes is another matter. The director of the National Gallery, von Tschudi, was eventually forced to resign (by William II) for the crime of acquiring Impressionists. Not, be it understood, for 'paying out good money for this trash' (in the words of Menzel) but simply for accepting them as gifts.[36]

Writing to Gustave Kahn, Laforgue had said: 'Berlin is busy laughing its head off at a little show of Impressionists that for my part I have always adored, ever since I've known them in fact.' (C:46) In the letter to Ephrussi he says:

> M and Mme Bernstein are the most artistic people here. . . . We've just been to see the Gurlitt Impressionists: very interesting but nothing special. Pissarro is certainly a solid chap, but there's no Caillebotte. The Degas jockeys are marvellous with that mellow tapestry look, but no dancers. As for Renoir, I always feel the same: he's subtle, soft and shimmering as a pastel; his female nudes are strong and clever and curious; but I don't like that smooth porcelain effect. I've written a fairly long magazine article: an explanation, both physiological and aesthetic, of the Impressionist formula. M Bernstein plans to translate it for a review. I gave it to him yesterday. (E59-60)

The article in question was, of course, the one he had begun nearly a year before.

To Henry he reported: 'My Berlin life gets going again: snow, beer, music and sluggishness. I've done an article explaining Impressionism to the people here—who'll then say that Impressionism, being crazy, must have been invented in Germany by Fechner.' (D:212) And to Lindenlaub:

> Théo is still in his little slum. . . . He gets up at noon, washes and starts work. He composes pieces to impress me, but I'm not impressed. Then we play draughts and I win. . . . Since last summer he hasn't grown any more, but his horrible leather coat has gone a new shade of dirty brown. At Gurlitt's we saw a show of Impressionists which bewildered and charmed him. . . . Otherwise snow, mud, filthy verminous droshkies, and skies that make you go Ugh![37]

But the most unusual letter he wrote at this time was to an unknown woman who is usually taken to be Sanda Mahali. Yet it was over a year since he last wrote to that lady, and the break had seemed to be pretty final. The letter in fact could be addressed to almost any exasperated female of his acquaintance. She has charged him with being a Joseph: a man who fails properly to respond to a lady's amorous intimations. It sounds very much as if Laforgue has been up to his old game of starting something and then getting too bored to finish it. But who was the lady? Was it perhaps Henry's new Polish companion Regina Candiani? Did he start teasing her, and did the teasing misfire? In any case his letter (whoever the recipient) is vintage Laforgue:

You!!—I got your jesuitical lines. What's all this couch-talk? Why don't you make yourself clear? Why such reticence? You speak of my affections being more than fraternal and less than amorous, but with whom? What do you mean by Joseph? I am an artist. A French poet. A troubadour. And at your service as such. But let me assure you I don't drink beer at Kroll's or anywhere else, and that my cheeks are not shining and swollen, but on the contrary pale and hollow, especially the left one where they took out two teeth. Neither have I got big vicious eyes, but medium-sized blue ones, gentle with an exceeding gentleness. On top of all which, you're an odd creature, aren't you! And now, to talk of other things, I do not know what's been translated of Heyse's work in the *Revue des Deux Mondes*, because I do not happen to have the back-numbers available to me here; Henry on the other hand can find them in the first library he cares to enter. For the rest I'll reply to you tomorrow, since today's Sunday when my bookshop is shut (geschlossen, do you understand). I kiss nothing of yours—neither the tips of your fingers nor anything else and beg not to remain your JULES LAFORGUE. (E:63-4)

CHAPTER 6
Publication (1884-1885)

NOW began the long business of getting his first book published. But apart from the *Complaintes* he was campaigning on behalf of the sculptor Henry Cros, whose Paris studio he had visited during the summer. 'Exquisite waxes,' he had noted in the Agenda—for Cros (brother of the more famous Charles Cros, poet and inventor) was at this time modelling in wax in the manner of the little Degas dancer of 1881. Laforgue had commissioned one of his pieces for Bernstein, and on 8 January 1884 he wrote to Henry:

Tomorrow I'll show the wax to her future owner. I'll arrive very late in the evening and I'll enter the salon with the wax under my arm. She is quite simply delicious. The expression is incredibly subtle and he has caught it in a fleeting moment of time. Ah the pretty little sphinx! I like the feather, and the introduction of gold in the hatband, and the collar again scored with gold. And that delightfully rumpled way the lace falls. As yet I've only seen this child by artificial light—I've received her this minute and it's eight in the evening. Will the ground-colour change in daylight? In this light at the moment it is quite perfect. Except perhaps for the shawl, which seems to be the ordinary wax-colour, reddy-brown siena, and I would have liked it more unusual (though it may be so in daylight). But what would you say to a Scottish shawl in black and white check, wouldn't that be the thing? In any case she's a little marvel and I say *merde* to anyone who doesn't fall in love with her. . . . Are you going to see the Manets? Did you get my *Complaintes*? When you have a moment, could you deal with them as you think fit? Let's publish quickly (at author's expense, of course) and get it over with. Would April be possible? Tell Cros we're going to show both his waxes round the corner at Gurlitt's, which is the equivalent of the Goupil gallery. (E:68-70)

As things turned out, April was decidedly not possible, either that year or the next. In fact, the *Complaintes*—at author's expense—were not to be published till 25 August 1885. Incidentally, the Manets to which Laforgue refers in this letter were the contents of the artist's studio, when on view at the Beaux-Arts prior to auction, Manet having died the year before.

Laforgue wrote to Kahn on 10 January 1884:

I'm just as much an exile as you are. I've only one girl-friend here, it's a wax by Cros. Talking of which I've just received another, less sublime but a smart little Parisienne none the less. . . . Yes, I'm just as exiled as you are; I can't go and see the Manets on the quai Malaquais any more than you can. My God, it's time for my reading. Never a dull moment. (C:51-2)

He wrote to Henry on 20 January:

Her shawl is carmine and the ground-colour bronze, so all is well in the most coquettish of all possible worlds. I made my entry into the salon just as I promised, and both waxes were a great success. The wife of the gentleman thinks the Parisienne is adorable—the gentleman likes her too but prefers mine; he's got his eyes on her and obviously wants her instead. We chatted about it as one does in a salon—but this morning he sends both of them back to me without a word. I'll see him on Tuesday and then I'll know what it's all about. In any case if he doesn't want her (out of spite because he wants mine) after having ordered her—even though he's the most artistic man in Berlin, the owner of a dozen Impressionists, and one of the richest too —well, if Cros agrees, I'll keep her for my own exquisite delight and pay when I can.

As for my poor book I think [Lemerre's] price is terrifying. The fact is that, for various reasons, I'm living at the moment on my next quarter's pay and the best I could manage would be 300 francs in July and the remaining 700 not before 1 January. But anyway do you like the idea of these lavish productions on de luxe paper? Wouldn't it be better to go to that sublime Léon Vanier on the quayside just before you get to Notre-Dame —Léon Vanier who prints Verlaine on that lovely grocer's paper? We'd ask him for an edition with as few copies as possible, third class (as with funerals) and we'd offer him 300 francs in all, payable in July. Lemerre must be drunk with the success of all those gift books with coloured illustrations, otherwise he wouldn't take such diabolical liberties with a modest rhymer like me. Thanks for all the trouble, though. You're lucky, you know, to be seeing the Manets. If I had any money I'd ask for a fortnight's leave. (E:71-3)

He wrote again to Kahn in February:

It's me again—but worn out. Here is yesterday's score. Three hours at the Opera: an idiotic ballet, all tights and no soul, six cigars and a dozen cigarettes . . . plus a visit to the dentist and three less teeth. . . . Having nothing else to say, I offer you my 'Complainte du soir des comices agricoles'. To appreciate it properly you should sing the refrain to an old tune for hunting horns that I heard during my provincial childhood. It was played then by the horsemen of an Anglo-American circus who paraded round town in the afternoon to announce the evening's prog- ramme. The single word 'Mystery' should be written in Gothic, or better still in Uncial letters. Do you realize that we shall be seeing each other in November? What are you going to do? Install yourself far from the Chat Noir and get down to some work? Your sole reward to pop round to Henry's in the evening for coffee or tea and cigarettes? That's the state of grace I invoke for you, and in the meantime what about a huge great sonnet? (C:53-7)

On 28 February he wrote to Kahn:

Let me confess that all this week I've been in an absolute 'troubadour' state. I'm just back from strolling under the Linden in a spring overcoat. Last night till two I was observing the dresses and shoulders of blondes by the hundred at the annual artists' ball. Same thing tonight at the Château. Shoulders and eyes advancing with that intoxicating look of spring itself. I'm worn out, sickening for love—and poor. Five years ago in Paris I wrote poems proclaiming that I had plumbed the depths of Illusion itself—and what an illusion that was! Je suis aimant ('loving', as they say in English) but not in a mood for poetry. I find myself desiring a nice little private income because I want to live, and working isn't living. All the same I have much to be thankful for: good health for one thing, without its being offen- sively good! . . . and then my friend Ysaÿe played Chopin to me all morning. Life seems to me infinitely and minutely precious. And I cry out for my private income in the accents of the 'Song of Songs'. Blessed be Thou, O Lord, who shalt give me my private income. (C:58-61)

Meanwhile Vanier had offered reasonable terms for the *Complaintes* and Laforgue wrote to Henry on 13 March:

Thanks for all your trouble with the book (which now at a distance is beginning to seem false and naive, but never mind). I've just written to Vanier who must surely be an intelligent chap to have published Verlaine (after his troubles) in *Paris Moderne*. I've told him the manuscript is complete as it stands. The gentleman who turned down the wax sculpture confirms that it was because he wanted mine. He was quite wrong about that, though not normally boorish at all; in fact he's an artist and is really keen on having a wax by Cros come what may. . . . In a month or so Cros will be having a visit from two people who admire him and will certainly want to buy something: one is the cleverest painter in Germany, Skarbina (who isn't German at all but Croatian or Hungarian), and the other his inseparable friend the Empress's dentist M Dumont, a marvellous chap from Brussels, the best type of Belgian, who's a collector and also has memories (for instance of Poe in Washington, whom he used to pick up off the pavements outside pubs). You really must campaign for Cros. He could make plenty of money without lowering his standards at all; he has only to look at life in the streets and start doing studies of tarts and soldiers and babies and jockeys and dancers. Not to mention old-clothes men and even townscapes in bas-relief. There are so many attractive things to do; heaven knows why they haven't all been done before. Well, let him get started then, and I promise you I'm a good propagandist: I do my stuff in the clients' own houses. (E:74-6)

Again to Henry in 23 May (from Baden-Baden):

I place myself once and for all at the feet of Regina, so that she may deign to excuse all the imaginary wrongs I've done her. I also place at her feet the idea of translating something by Kraszewski, whom the recent trial has made fashionable (unless, of course, with your habit of never having a paper in the house, you don't know what trial I'm talking about). So you've appointed yourself guardian angel of my *Complaintes* and I'll receive the proofs here: let's hope Vanier, in the depths of his countryside, doesn't forget all about me. It's extremely hot here and we eat four meals a day, which means smoking four pipes and eight cigarettes. One tends to become decrepit and blow like a seal. . . . I'm starting my old trick again of closing my eyes and summoning up the different parts of Paris: the shops at the Panthéon, the omnibus station at Odéon and so on. I mean to save money seriously, so that this year I can stay on in Paris without the economical detour to Tarbes. If I can hang on till

November, Kahn will be back and that'll be nice. Of course the poor chap will be waylaid by women again, passionate ones who only live by night. We might arrange for him to catch an unpleasant disease: that would keep him quiet for a couple of months. (E:83-6)

Two days later a trusting Laforgue wrote to Vanier, exclaiming his delight that the book was to be out by June. Little did he know that Vanier himself would not even choose a printer till the following December. But although they were not to be published for another eighteen months, most of the *Complaintes* had by this time been written, so it is appropriate to talk about them. Behind the title with its reference to the old hurdy-gurdy dirges—of which Kurt Weill's MacHeath song from *Die Dreigroschenoper* is a latter-day example—there lies an entirely new kind of poetry.

Laforgue claimed that he got his first inspiration from a street fête which was held on 20 September 1880 to celebrate the inauguration of the Lion of Belfort, the famous statue in the Place Denfert-Rochereau. That may well be, but the original flavour has survived only in a very few pieces, such as the 'Complainte de l'oubli des morts' ('Lament for forgetfulness of the dead') which begins:

> Mesdames et Messieurs,
> Vous dont la mère est morte,
> C'est le bon fossoyeur
> Qui gratte à votre porte.
>   Les Morts
>   C'est sous terre;
>   Ça n'en sort
>   Guère.   (A:104)

[Ladies and gentlemen, all you whose mother is dead, here comes the good gravedigger to scratch at your door. The dead are under ground; they don't come out much.]

This has something of the feeling of a genuine Complainte, like the ritual beginning of a blues. The words were printed on a kind of scroll, which was turned over by the showman verse by verse. But, if Laforgue used the word in the title of his book and in the title of each poem, it was only to gain a spurious unity—for he turned the book into something quite different: something highly personal and sophisticated. It was a psychological poetry in which all the complexities of modern life were expressed in free association, as on the analyst's couch. The poem emerged from the interaction of reality and dream in the form of strange dialogues between various of the poet's personae. But this revolutionary and essentially serious poetry was conveyed not with solemnity but through irony and humour. Laforgue had come to the conclusion that truth was better expressed through comedy than tragedy. It was something he had learnt the hard way through the total failure of his earlier manner. And at the same time, as he told his sister in the letter already quoted, he had acquired a new lightness of touch with which he handled comedy. The sudden change of method was almost like someone acquiring a sense of humour overnight. By distancing himself from life and looking at all things henceforth with an amused and detached air, he acquired a new literary approach which was as rewarding as the other had been sterile. The early poems, in which he had taken squarely on his shoulders all the woes of the world, had proved merely depressing. But now, with his new irony and understatement, together with a very personal blend of the ordinary and extraordinary, he had a telling instrument at his disposal on which he could play original and moving tunes.

The dexterity with which he had made the change was not altogether surprising, for Laforgue had a natural gift for handling words. Even Jacques Rivière, who was not one of his greatest admirers, has conceded him this 'extraordinary power of expression, an incomparable richness of vocabulary.' One particularly dazzling trick was the way he juxtaposed everyday words and ideas with prestigious ones—juggling the concrete and the abstract so that each set off the other. Lofty words and ideas might gain a new poetry and resonance from being placed next to everyday ones; or, alternatively, the effect might be to highlight their pomposity and introduce an ironic note. This special contribution by Laforgue to modern poetry was well defined by F. S. Flint in the June 1913 issue (page 228) of *Poetry and Drama* as the 'sudden juxtaposition of the sublime with the commonplace, by which the one is made to criticize the other ironically.' In subsequent years the effect has been so completely appropriated by poets, lyric writers, copy-writers and ordinary people that, when we see it in Laforgue, we tend to forget how extraordinarily original it was in the 1880s.

Nor did he neglect the simpler interactions between the sublime and the commonplace, as when modern vulgarity is illumined by ancient grandeur. He never forgot Baudelaire's supreme achievement in celebrating everyday Paris in noble alexandrines, so that a poem about urban despair ('Le cygne') could begin with the words 'Andromache, je pense à vous . . .' and the sordid itself be touched with glory. (K:117-18)

He did not make the revolution in one go, however, and the *Complaintes* is far from being a perfect book. It is marred especially by a mass of liturgical imagery which, though playfully perverse in intention, becomes tedious in execution. (At the last count, the book contains over ninety images drawn from the Catholic Mass.) At other times his current philosophical ideas make an unwelcome appearance, in their raw state, killing the poetry stone dead. Often, too, there is a freeze-up into cerebral obscurity: from the extremes of naivety he goes to the extremes of artifice, and the strain shows. The technique, too, is not always satisfactory: he is seen to be trying every possible variation of liberated (but not free) verse in an effort to break down old conventions; but often when he bursts out of his straitjacket he destroys the poem. One thing at least, however, will be evident to any reader of the *Complaintes*: the *vers libre* of Laforgue, as it evolved at the end of his life, was a completely natural and inevitable development, the extension and goal of all his previous work; and the first signs are to be seen here.

The early readers of the *Complaintes*, without appreciating their real originality, were startled by all sorts of things: for instance, when they came on couplets like this, having nothing to do (it seemed) with the rest of the poem:

> 'Oh! j'ai peur, nous avons perdu la route;
> Paul, ce bois est mal famé! Chut, écoute . . .'   (A:50)

['Oh, I'm scared, we've lost our way; this wood's dangerous! Paul, listen . . .']

('Complainte de l'orgue de Barbarie' ['The hurdy-gurdy'])

And if interpolations like the following made some sense in themselves they were completely baffling in the context of the poem:

> —Ah! vous m'avez trop, trop vanné,
> Bals de diamants, hanches roses;
> Et bien sûr, je n'étais pas né
>   Pour ces choses.
>
> —Elles, coudes nus dans les fruits,
> Riant, changeant de doigts leurs bagues;
> Comme nos plages et nos nuits
>   Leur sont vagues!
>
> —Berthe aux sages yeux de lilas,
> Qui priais Dieu que je revinsse,

> Que fais-tu, mariée là-bas,
>   En province?   (A:99-100)

[Ah, you've worn me out too, too much, dances and diamonds and pink-clad hips; and you know very well I wasn't born for such things. / The girls, elbow-deep in fruit, laughing, slipping their rings on and off; how shadowy must seem to them our beaches and our nights! / Bertha of the wise lilac eyes, who prayed God for me to come back, what are you doing, married down there, in the country?]

('Complainte des grands pins dans une villa abandonnée')
Who was speaking, the readers wanted to know, and why? Similarly, in the poem about the girls practising piano in the rue Madame ('Complainte des pianos qu'on entend dans les quartiers aisés' ['Lament for the pianos heard in well-to-do districts']), there seemed to be so many different voices:

> Dans le bal incessant de nos étranges rues;
> Ah, pensionnats, théâtres, journaux, romans!
>
> Allez, stériles ritournelles,
> La vie est vraie et criminelle.   (A:47)

[In the non-stop dance of our strange streets; boarding schools, theatres, newspapers, novels! Listen, you stale old refrains, life is real and criminal.]

Those 'many different voices'—the multiple selves of Laforgue and others—today seem to produce a magical synthesis, but then they seemed a mere cacophony. And whose leg was the poet pulling when he wrote in 'Complainte de l'automne monotone' ('Lament for the monotonous autumn'):

> Allons, fumons une pipette de tabac,
> En feuilletant un de ces si vieux almanachs,
> En rêvant de la petite qui unirait
> Aux charmes de l'oeillet ceux du chardonneret.   (A:66)

[Come, let us smoke an ounce of tobacco, and leaf through one of those ancient almanacks, while dreaming of the girl who shall combine the charms of the pink and those of the goldfinch.]

Or, in the 'Complainte de l'ange incurable':

> Où vont les gants d'avril et les rames d'antan?
> L'âme des hérons fous sanglote sur l'étang.
>
> Le hoche-queue pépie aux écluses gelées;
> L'amante va, fouettée aux plaintes des allées.   (A:67)

[Where go April's gloves and the oars of yesteryear? The soul of mad herons cries across the pond. / The wagtail pipes by the frozen lock; the love-lost girl is driven down screaming paths.]

Or these examples from 'Complainte du pauvre chevalier-errant'

('Lament for the poor knight-errant') and 'Complainte des nostalgies préhistoriques' ('Lament for prehistoric nostalgias'):

> Jupes de quinze ans, aurores de femmes,
> Qui veut, enfin, les palais de mon âme?   (A:73)

[Teen-age skirts, dawn women, which of you would like the palaces of my soul?]

> La nuit bruine sur les villes:
> Se raser le masque, s'orner
> D'un frac deuil, avec art dîner,
> Puis parmi des vierges débiles,
> Prendre un air imbécile.   (A:70)

['Night falls on the town: we shave our mask, don a funereal coat, dine artistically, and then, among sickly virgins, take an idiotic stance.]

'All modern life in that last stanza,' commented Aldous Huxley in a letter written in August 1915. All modern life, indeed, is in Laforgue. And all these quotations, which seemed so crazy to his contemporaries, are no longer so. But the full force of his revolution was still to come. The *Complaintes* were only a beginning.

During the summer of 1884 he had written a couple of letters to Max Klinger. 'How are you and how's your famous genius? Feeling pretty sick as usual, I expect, which is all to the good.' He had been with Bernstein to see Klinger's murals in the Villa Alpers at Steglitz (a suburb of Berlin) and he approved of them. He urged Klinger to read Huysmans's new book *A Rebours* (*Against the Grain*) and to illustrate Poe; also to learn modern French (rather than Voltaire's or Béranger's).

In the same letter he announced an article he had written for the *Gazette* on Menzel (E:77) but when it appeared Klinger was shocked by a reference to Menzel's 'Prussian hands'. Laforgue pleaded (in a letter now lost) that the unfortunate phrase was added by the editor, which was certainly true since he explained as much to Henry: 'The editor, a certain Gonse, asked my permission to arrange it a little because it was above the subscribers' heads. I should have refused . . .' (E:90-1) 'Honestly, you'll please me by not reading it. It just isn't me. You can't imagine what that gentleman has saddled me with in the way of style, psychology, intelligence and even plain fact.' (E:92-3)

As a slight variation to the normal programme, the Court this year spent ten days on the island of Mainau in Lake Constance. To Henry Laforgue wrote:

I'm on an island. I eat—off royal porcelain—the masterpieces of two French cooks. I've nothing to do. I receive my three papers and spend four hours on the lake in a rowing-boat. There are even a couple of gondolas. I row and row, and smoke pipes while watching the fishermen cast their nets. I amuse myself by chasing floating branches, and go to bed early, worn out. . . . It's one o'clock now and I'm neither washed nor dressed. In half an hour I'll go to Constance. I'm still living the same empty life and it's time I did something else. While you're feeling happy and complete, installed in an existence of your own, I live like a parcel. I could and should have saved money in these past three years; then I could have left this place, gone back to Paris and floated around for a year or so till something turned up. But there you are, I live in the arms of the Unconscious, which will look after me. I'm absolutely flogging myself to cover this paper, on the principle that it's writing paper and has to fulfil its destiny! (E:94-6)

As he intended, he was able this year to cut out the 'economical' stay in Tarbes and concentrate his entire holiday on the capital. How he managed it financially is a bit of a miracle. It must have become evident by now that Laforgue was somewhat extravagant by nature (I have one of the tailor's bills to prove it) and, though his salary was more than adequate, he was never able to save. Everything went on books, art albums, clothes, etc., so that each quarter's pay, when it came along, had to cover the debts of the previous quarter. He was now to spend three whole months in Paris and it would be interesting to know who paid the bills or at least whom he stayed with (apart from Henry). There are no letters for the period and no diary—but there is a notebook, the Carnet of 1884-1885,[38] which at least gives a few clues.

Mention of a certain corner of the Luxembourg and the Lahure printing works, as well as the horse-bus that went down the rue Vavin, places us firmly in the district of the rue Madame, which had already been the scene of his 'Complainte des pianos' written the year before. These and other topographical clues in the first section of the Carnet headed 'La province de Paris' ('Provincial

Paris') seem to pinpoint his lodgings at or near the strange Pension Orfila, an establishment for men only where, a few years later, Strindberg tried to make gold in his room and feared he was going mad. This was halfway down the rue d'Assas, near the entry of the rue Madame. The young employees of the Lahure printing works turn up in another of his fragments, shoving sand down each other's necks (J:12) and the pianos of the rue Madame are heard again in the following street stroll:

> Walking in a capital city on the day after rain. Looking at the women's faces and trying to perceive the everydayness of their existence and of their destiny. A smart girls'-school goes by, and I watch them pass. Oh what delicious orgies of insipidity: a mood of melancholy mass-produced until it becomes monotony. What is the name of this well-to-do provincial street? At one solidly curtained window a piano is playing (in time with a metronome) that eternal Chopin waltz as threadbare as love itself. What poignant pleasures! What excellent fatalism! I light up a cigar. And now plane trees, a housemaid cleaning windows and a passing tram. Look, though! From under an arch comes an open carriage containing two ladies in black putting on their gloves. A little girl who limps is clutching an orange. And all the windows are like sightless eyes. One imagines the boredom of the dining room with its polished copper suspension lamp; the painstaking awfulness of the salon; the immutability of the bedroom. At a window high up: a canary cage. At another window, in the roof, a young man leans out contentedly as if he has just paid the rent. Two nurses meet and chat while their charges, during this forced pause, look away over their shoulders, fascinated by a stray dog. (K:30-1)

With fragments of this kind Laforgue seems almost to have invented a new art form. He wrote hundreds of them, all of the same length and all combining in one neat package the author's mood of the moment with its correlative in the outside world. Eliot certainly read some of them before writing the 'Preludes' and 'Prufrock'.

In another rue Madame fragment he watches workmen in billowing blue trousers re-paving the street; laying the numbered cobble-stones in a bed of clean yellow sand, while a hurdy-gurdy plays and a lonely cabhorse stands and waits. (J:11-12) But it is interesting to note how often his eyes are raised to the rooftops. Apart from the canary and the young man at his window, he mentions dishcloths at a skylight, a melon ripening on a garret window-sill. His own room, too, must have been under the roof (just as in Baden-Baden and Coblenz) for the view he describes of the rue Madame is often a plunging one. It is true, of course, that poor people in Paris always have plunging views, like the cheaper seats in theatres.

He observes that rows of windows are shuttered because the occupants have gone off for the summer holidays, while others have slim red cushions thrown over the hand-rail to lean on in the warm summer evenings. All the residents seem to be distinguished architects, and even the concierges are powerful people to be reckoned with. The nursemaids come from the best Catholic agencies and wear solid shoes. The old ladies in mourning carry umbrellas that are careful not to be too smart. The shiny two-horse van from the Bon Marché department store has an 'academic' coachman and is delivering good solid linen. The girls carrying rolls of music look as if they live in a city which has never heard of prostitution. As for the local policeman, he has nothing to do and that, too, is sad. Still looking down from his lofty perch, Laforgue observes the red and yellow election posters on the railings at the corner of the Luxembourg, and the blue enamel plate bearing the street-name.[39]

Also written at this time and precisely in this district (his sister's copy is marked: 'rue Madame, August 1884'), the 'Grande Complainte de la Ville de Paris' was his only 'prose poem', which he preferred to call 'prose blanche' and which the Surrealists have hailed as a precursor of their own experiments.

At the end of what one might call his rue Madame period, Laforgue jotted down in the Carnet this short but intriguing note: 'He regretted having had her in 1884 rather than in 1878, when girls' clothes were so much more attractive.' If the subject of this laconic entry was by any chance Léonie Duhaut, it was that lady's definitively final appearance: by the end of the year she had married a painter on porcelain so jealous that he made her destroy every letter Laforgue had ever sent her.

But August ended and it was time to leave the rue Madame and join Charles Henry in a cottage he had rented at Chevreuse, southwest of Paris. It was a primitive little place and on the first night they went round burning spiders' webs in the corners of the ceilings. Laforgue noted the sky of 'full-mourning violet' (his 'local colour') and, in the darkness that followed, two flickering spots of diamond light; while a row of poplars across the way looked impressive enough to be cypress trees. (J:13, K:31) Regina Candiani was also there, and Charles Henry later described (to Jean-Aubry) the merciless way Laforgue used to tease her. He also paints (in that unpublished interview) a relaxed picture of Laforgue in espadrilles, competing in a game to see who could kick highest against the wall, and then going to get water at the Goutte d'Or or helping to

cook. Sometimes they were joined in their open-air life by Henry
Cros, who happily inspired the poet by singing popular songs from
his art student days, a couple of which Laforgue put into the
Complaintes with new words. 'Quand le bonhomm' revint du bois'
('When the man came back from the wood') became the 'Complainte du pauv' jeune homme' ('Lament of the poor young man');
and 'Qu'allais-tu faire à la fontaine?' ('What did you go to the
fountain for') acquired a new lease of life as the 'Complainte de
l'époux outragé' ('Lament of the outraged husband'). Neither
Complainte was especially remarkable, but they were a little
nearer to the original popular-song idea.

At last the holiday was over and Laforgue had to leave for
Coblenz. Before he left he wrote two desperate letters to his publisher: the first on 30 October saying: 'Allow me to remind you
(with anguish!) that by Tuesday I shall no longer be in Paris.' On
5 November, the eve of his departure, he left a final missive, written
in an unusual handwriting—was he drunk or just hopping mad? It
was couched in the third person and addressed to a deliberately
mis-spelt 'M Vannier'. Neither letter seems to have elicited a reply.

Back in Coblenz he fell ill and passed the time with *War and
Peace*, which had just been translated. 'One of the most astonishing
things I've ever read,' he told Ephrussi. (E:100) He also read with
pleasure a less famous book called *A Gentleman of Leisure* by the
American writer Edgar Fawcett. It contains the following passage
which could not have failed to interest Laforgue:

> 'Mr Large is our great coming poet,' said Mr Binghampton . . .
> 'His poems are perfectly splendid,' said Mrs Brown.... 'I reckon
> I don't understand them all, though, they're too grand. Some of
> 'em almost take away a body's breath . . . they're like a tempest.'
> Mr Large cleared his throat . . . 'I'm a pioneer, sir.... I recognize
> there is a great work before me, and I am going to do it if I
> can, in a manful, earnest, honest way.'
> 'Mr Large is writing the poetry of the future,' said Mr Bing-
> hampton.
> Mr Large again cleared his throat. 'The poetry of the future,
> sir, is but a name given to that healthy impulse which would
> sweep away the rhyming pettiness, the sickly and hectic affec-
> tation, the absurd metrical restrainments of the past.'
> 'Mr Large, you see, tumbles over all the old idols,' said Mr
> Binghampton. 'He doesn't believe in the past at all, do you, Mr
> Large?'
> 'I abhor the past,' said Mr Large.
> 'Isn't it horrible!' said Mr Binghampton in the ear of Wain-
> wright.

'What are his writings like?' inquired Wainwright.

'He calls them democratic chants. They are about boundless prairies and brotherly love and the grand coming amelioration of humanity. . . . His book is called *Earth-clods and Star-beams*.' This caricature must have been Laforgue's first introduction to Walt Whitman, several of whose poems he was subsequently to translate with decidedly odd results.

The Court now returned to Berlin and Laforgue resumed, not only his love affair with music but also his correspondence with Gustave Kahn, who was now back in Paris. 'In the last fortnight,' he told Kahn, 'I've heard *Die Walküre*, four piano concertos, Liszt, Essipoff, *Carmen*, a Schumann quintet and a quartet by Brahms, who you know, of course, has just published a new symphony.' (C:63) More in anger than in sorrow he wrote again to Vanier:

LÉON VANIER, par Coll-Toc.

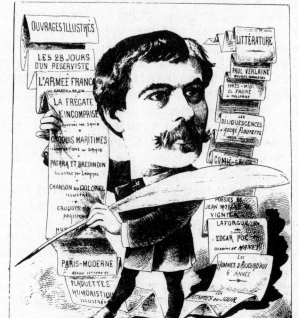

Le Père des Décadents.

'Now that I am removed from Paris and France, I hope you won't think of me as distant, lost, mythical and for ever negligible.' (M:85) Does Vanier feel a sudden pang of remorse on reading these lines? Whatever the reason, something happens!

The printing of the *Complaintes* was a farce from beginning to end, in which the two main characters were the publisher Léon Vanier, who ran a bookshop at 19 quai Saint-Michel, opposite Notre-Dame, and his no less bizarre printer Léo Trézenik, whose printing works were half a mile away at 16 boulevard Saint-Germain. These two amusingly hard-bitten professionals—rascals with a love of literature—took our innocent hero for the first ride of his career.

Vanier had published some of the best avant garde work of the period—often at the author's expense, as in this case—and his shop was also something of a literary salon. He was a jovial man with a habit of rubbing his hands together with glee, as if he'd just heard some wonderful news. (Unkind tongues suggested it was the news of another big sucker landed.) He and Trézenik had worked in harmony for some time; each knew what the other was up to and when not to trust him.

Trézenik also ran a periodical called *Lutèce* (the Roman name for Paris) in which he could give free publicity to Vanier's authors, while at the same time acquiring free copy for himself. His real name was Léon Epinette but, just as he liked to wear a Breton hat on his impressive head, so too he preferred to be known by a Breton name. Thus Epinette became Trézenik, both meaning (most appropriately) 'little thorn'. Sometimes Trézenik wrote rude letters to his own paper about the books he had himself printed—and then replied to them under the pseudonym of L-G Mostrailles. He had an endless number of pseudonyms, so that in his circle it was impossible to know who was real and who was Trézenik. In a previous existence he had even been Pierre Infernal of the Club des Hydropathes.

The two Léons' most successful recent enterprise had been *Les Poètes Maudits* (*The Doomed Poets*), Verlaine's vigorous discovery and defence of Corbière, Rimbaud and Mallarmé, which had originally appeared in *Lutèce* between August and December 1883 before being assembled as a book in April 1884.

After doing nothing at all about the *Complaintes* for nine months (from March to December 1884) Vanier decided for some reason that the time had come to set the wheels in motion. Trézenik submitted an estimate, 520 copies of the 148 page book at 20 francs an eight-page section. But he asked for a fairly quick turn-round of proofs and this for a particular and important reason: Trézenik had all sorts of qualities but his main trouble as a printer was that he hadn't enough type. Added to that, he was a printer who could never say no, which meant that he always had too many books in hand at any one time. At this time he had just enough type free to set sixteen pages of the *Complaintes*. After he had set them,

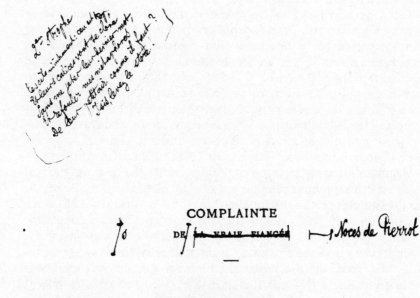

COMPLAINTE
DE ~~LA VRAIE FIANCÉE~~ — Noces de Pierrot
—

Où te flatter pour boire dieu,
M~~on éphémè~~re corybante?
Je ~~pompe~~ mon âme en tes yeux,
Je ~~bois~~ ta beauté pénitente,
Où donc es-tu? Moi si pieux,
Que tu ~~es~~ lente, lente!

Tes cils m'insinuent : ç'en est trop
Et ~~son~~ calice ~~entre encore,~~
Sans me jeter ~~son petit sanglot~~
~~Et moi, je vais te voir te clore~~
~~Sans t'arracher ton~~ dernier mot
Isis, levez le store!

~~Ah!~~ cette fois, c'est pour de bon
Trop ~~longtemps~~, quittant la partie

11

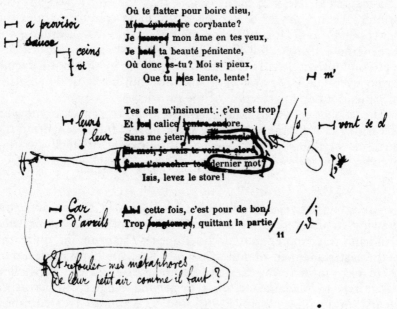

Proof of *Les Complaintes* corrected by Laforgue

and Laforgue had passed them, it was necessary to print them at once, so that the type could be distributed—that is, freed for use in composing the next sixteen pages.

This operation had to be repeated nine times, allowing three weeks each time for setting, proof-reading and printing. Thus the printing period for a relatively slim volume added up to no less than seven months; and as the tortuous operation proceeded in short bursts from December 1884 to July 1885 Laforgue seems to have been quite oblivious to the bizarre nature of the enterprise. Even scholars have solemnly studied the first edition text without accepting the awful truth: if *Yeux* is printed *Jeux*, and grave accents replace circumflexes and a blue cover suddenly changes to green, there is no need to look farther than Trézenik's terrible outfit.

Meanwhile Laforgue raged at Vanier but failed to guess the real cause of 'this inexplicable slowness'. He likened his publisher to Fabius Cunctator, the procrastinating Roman consul (E:125) when all the time the real villain was the printer. 'What a long time it takes to publish a volume of poems!' he sighed forlornly.

Unperturbed, as the printing went painfully forward, Trézenik published seven of the poems in his own *Lutèce*. Laforgue was completely puzzled about this; not displeased but curious how it had happened. He still didn't know that the editor was also the printer. When a reader of *Lutèce* wrote in to complain about the new poetry, 'L-G Mostrailles' swung into action with a thunderous leader and Laforgue fell for it like a bird, submitting a brilliant reply on his own behalf. This, too, was printed by the cool Trézenik —who even made Mostrailles thank the Imprimerie de Lutèce for the splendour and perfection of the printing.

The further course of events, however, shows us a Laforgue who is learning fast. By the end of the affair he had fully recognized the methods of the two Léons—even to the extent of finally writing his own press reviews.

The affair between Charles Henry and Regina Candiani was now drawing to its close after a bare fifteen months. No doubt Mme Candiani was unprepared to be Henry's factotum in quite the enthusiastic manner of Mlle Duhaut. Even in Laforgue's letters there were intimations that all was not well at 22 rue Berthollet. 'Greetings to Madame, if she's in a good temper,' he wrote to Henry on 15 November. (E:98) And to Kahn on 16 December: 'My respects to Mme de Caudrain. I dare not risk a more familiar formula, not knowing what the weather will be like on the day you see her.' (C:66)

Now, at the beginning of 1885, things were moving to a climax. In an unpublished part of his 1 January 1885 letter to Henry (E:106) he asked: 'How goes Madame (alias Regina nostra)?' while in another censored piece from the 8 January letter (E:108) he said mysteriously: 'I'm returning to you a telegram about which I understand nothing whatever except for its registration number, with the times and places of departure and arrival.'

On 18 January he asked Kahn: 'Is one allowed to write to Henry at home, 22 rue Berthollet?' (C:81) And again on 25 January: 'How has Henry arranged his domestic existence?' (C:87) On 29 January mystery intrudes again: 'I did indeed get a breathless message from the rue Berthollet about 10 January. It said that Kahn was a traitor. In reply I gave my word that I didn't know what it meant (which was the truth).' (C:76) Regina is never mentioned again but it is not impossible that Laforgue continued to see her from time to time. The 'R' who plays the piano for him at rue Papillon in November 1885 could well be Regina—her daughter has confirmed to us that she did indeed play the piano—and there are other references to 'R' in the same fragment. (J:18-19) Of Russian origin, Regina was in her mid-twenties at this time and had only recently arrived in France. Though by temperament a mystic, she played a leading part in the Women's Movement of her day, as well as translating Tolstoy and Turgenev: all qualities calculated to appeal to Laforgue. She had many contacts with the Nihilist party, and was also an ardent cyclist.

After the break Henry decided to leave rue Berthollet, and already by 1 May it seems he had his eye on a new flat. In Laforgue's letter of that date he wrote: 'Congratulations on the quai d'Anjou. I can see it from here: you couldn't have chosen better—old walls with water close at hand, and aristocratic to boot!' (E:119) But most of the letters at the beginning of 1885 are concerned with the printing of the *Complaintes*. Much time was wasted—by Laforgue on this occasion—in discussing Vanier's trademark, a kind of female acrobat prancing across an open book on which are inscribed the letters 'LV'. 'La petite baladeuse' ('The little prancer'), as they called her, was generally thought by Laforgue and his friends to be unworthy of the new poetry, but nobody could think of a suitable  substitute. Since the journalist Lindenlaub was now back in Berlin for the Congo Conference, he and Laforgue took the opportunity to make a selection of Menzel drawings for an exhibition in Paris later that year. 'What do you think of Lindenlaub?' Laforgue asked Henry. 'He's not much at a first impression, but afterwards one begins to realize that he knows a thing or two and has had interesting experiences. He's a welcome and lively addition to any group of friends smoking together.' (E:110-111) As always, Laforgue confides in Henry about his sex life or lack of it.

> My heart is empty with all the emptiness of provincial exile, and in these cases, as you know, the feminine question installs itself, even more insoluble than the Eastern Question. The best I can do about it here is the odd platonic contemplation combined with risky physiological derivatives. (E:108)

For the celebration of Bismarck's seventieth birthday (1 April) he told Henry that his room would be invaded by all sorts of people, but only for the sake of his windows, which gave on to the Linden where the processions pass. (E:113) By the beginning of May he was envying Kahn, who had been touched by spring: 'He's just written me a very funny letter: he sounds a bit tipsy, I think he's up to something. Kahn and the month of May, what a couple!' (E:120)

The return of Kahn from North Africa was, of course, the best thing that had happened to Laforgue for some time. Their correspondence now leapt to life again, for Kahn was an excellent letter-writer—much more than Henry who 'always has his head in the clouds through being too tall.' (C:84) With Kahn he discussed poetry at length and explained why he wanted to start the *Complaintes* with a compilation from the old *Sanglot* poems.

> It's a patchwork of all my old stuff, noisy and pathetic and autobiographical. I sacrificed a big volume of those old philosophical poems because they were obviously no good—but at least they represent a stage in my career and I want to tell that small group of people to whom I'll send the book that, before being a dilettante and a pierrot, I sojourned in the cosmic. (C:79)
>
> I saw *Tristan* three times last year. It's one of those Berlin pleasures you're always telling me to make the most of—that and two or three quaysides along the Spree, Saturday night at the Aquarium, a few canvases in the Old Museum, and a couple of cafés-chantants. And now I shake your hand but not too energetically, so as not to disturb my white tie. (C:84)
>
> I could bellow with boredom—as happens every year at this time, when spring coincides with income tax and I'm left in a penniless state waiting for my April quarter's pay. Then there's all this aimless strolling around, living in exile far from the Paris spring, with music everywhere and the scents of last year still clinging to one's spring overcoat . . . this accursed season which gives you

the feeling that everything's beginning again, and one hasn't yet come to terms with one's elusive self. (C:70-1)

All I can think of is the pleasure of returning to Paris and going off for a glorious month with you and Henry at Chevreuse or somewhere, reading and listening and working and smoking and talking together, a game of shuttlecock between our three temperaments. (C:72)

Paris is the only possible town. I know Berlin and Munich and Frankfurt; as for St Petersburg, Vienna and London I can imagine them. (C:94)

Tell me what you think of [the pianist] von Bülow. He's very cold, with a dash of madness, but impeccable.... For many he's a god, especially for those who prefer that sort of strange, febrile impeccability to the genial and frank fervour of a Rubinstein. (C:103)

Are you coming to Baden-Baden? You might not be too bored, even though there's nothing to do. It's the fifth time I've been there and all I can see in it now is a summer hospital for provincials with modest private incomes. (C:109)

Tell Henry to stop worrying about my novel: it has a subject and two characters, and a little bit of decor; but it also has, and above all, the rest. (C:110)

So you're going to see some Claude Monets: he's certainly the most solid and reliable of the Impressionists, if not the sharpest. I remember Manet's gesture of absolute conviction when telling me that for seascapes Monet was the only painter in the world. (C:114)

Laforgue was given an unexpected extra holiday in the summer of 1885. On 18 June the Empress left Baden-Baden for Coblenz but she did not take her French Reader with her. At the time she was extremely worried about the health of the Emperor, and knew that most of her spare time would have to be spent at Ems, where he was recuperating. Laforgue made quick arrangements for a visit to Paris but, on his way there, stopped off at Strasbourg to meet Gustave Kahn (who was heading for Bohemia to examine some Casanova manuscripts). They arranged to meet at the Broglie and, after a visit to the Cathedral, they found a café under the arcades of the Place Gutenberg where they were able to talk and read the *Figaro*. Afterwards they ate in a cellar restaurant to the strains of some extremely sentimental music, and next day went their respective ways. But Laforgue's subsequent three weeks in Paris are best described in the letter he wrote to Kahn on 6 August:

I'm now in Homburg, a resort near Frankfurt, full of English people and attractive dresses, and cluttered with lawn tennis. I left Paris on 17 July and after a few days at Coblenz here I am. We leave again on 15 August, the eve of my twenty-fifth birthday (listen to me, harping on my age like René Ghil!) and then it's the castle of Babelsberg, which is near Potsdam, which is near Berlin. Which is a way of telling you I'll spend most of my evenings in Berlin and can already see us together there, under the Linden, at the Café Bauer and my place and so on.

Trust you to go to Bohemia of all places in the world! I'm sure you'll dine out on it for weeks when you get back to the rue Gay-Lussac . . . but I forgot: the district's changed, it's the quai d'Anjou now! In fact I helped him move. You should have seen that monstrous table hanging in the air. He's magnificently well installed . . . and I've got my eye on his belvedere, which is still empty. We had breakfast every morning at a nearby café 'Au Franc Pinot', where they thought we were a couple of pretty odd customers. Henry was ogled every morning by an old rag-and-bone woman who kept stoking up with glasses of wine and glaucous-looking segments of cucumber. Had she perhaps had a son (or even a daughter) or maybe a lover resembling our friend? Or did he merely remind her of an engraving in some old novel? Either way she couldn't keep her eyes off him.

When I first arrived in Paris I found him in bed with a fever, which lasted a week and then got better. We went to the Sorbonne in the evenings and ate happily at the Boulant or the Brasserie du Rhin. I saw no other locals, not even Moréas or Vignier, but I did see Ephrussi and the *Gazette* people . . . and I visited the Salon with Ary Renan and J-E Blanche, who had some nice pastels on show there. Renan was just back from Palestine.

Bourget's in Ireland. Lemerre have published his *Vie Inquiète* [*Troubled Life*] with an engraved portrait in front. I saw a lot of Pigeon; we went to the Alsaciens-Lorrains together. He's a delightful chap and the best possible company in this low world of parasites. Also visited the rue de Sèze gallery—will tell you all about that over an ice-cream on the balcony of the Café Bauer. The two Ysaÿes (the violinist has been on the jury at the Conservatoire) are now both in Paris, installed up at Montmartre since 1 July. Two big ground-floor rooms at the back of a court-yard in the rue Papillon. The pianist and I collected Henry at Chevreuse one day, and we all went on an outing to Cernay. You'll be hearing in due course the tale of the dog. As for my *Complaintes* Vanier had me going there every day without exception. Finally they appeared on 25 July in blue and green.

I think I'm having a review (knocked together by myself) in the *République Française*. And Pigeon's going to have a try on his side. But you know how hopeless I am: *Le Temps* has a big article today on the Decadents and I'm not even mentioned. . . . What pleases me, though, is that I'm not nearly so disgusted by my *Complaintes*, now they're in print, as I expected to be. I'm carrying on with my stories and have just finished *Hamlet*. . . . As for you, I don't doubt you're bringing me lots to see. . . . So many hotel tables have passed beneath your pen, with so many tempting horizons and so much solitude. . . . In the meantime it's agreed then, we meet in Berlin. (C:120-5)

On his return to Germany from Paris Laforgue spent ten days at Coblenz, and on the second day he wrote a fragment to an unknown girl. It is typical of all similar fragments describing women. This one is different only to the extent that it is tied to a definite place, and also to a certain hour on a certain day of a certain month in a certain year—which puts a tight rein on starry-eyed biographers who have tended to attach these fragments to specific women on the most flimsy evidence.

Sunday evening, ten o'clock, 19 July 1885—How pure she is, how completely in a class by herself! Nothing about her could possibly put me off. And I observe her with more composure than last year, the composure that grows as my dilettantism recedes. Oh for a kiss in the corner of that mouth, as she smiles with those lively eyes, so deep and good. It wouldn't satisfy me completely, of course, but such a smile would keep my whole life spellbound. I love her as I love my life. I would forget everything to go off with her hand in hand. It's not a happy or optimistic smile, but the smile of a wise angel who, when she's in society, wants to spread a little happiness. She even takes on a slightly provincial air, as of a twenty-year-old eccentric recluse. But that smile, so open, noble and true, absolves everything. How sweet her neck is! What a treasure her shoulders must be! Is all that really mortal and will it age? I'm about to descend into pits of analysis and fundamental problems, but her smile saves me. . . . (K:56-7)

But who is she? Who was she? No one will ever know. It is certain that, in the atmosphere of the Court, with the little maids of honour flitting in and out the way they did, Laforgue had his head turned many times 'et je n'étais pas né pour ces choses' ('I wasn't born for such things').

As we have seen, critics and commentators often claim to

'identify' these pen portraits of girls, pointing out how clearly they resemble such and such a lady—only to find that they were executed long before the lady in question appeared on the scene. But in a way this is the whole point and need not be disconcerting, for Laforgue did what everyone does: he went on falling in love with the same girl for ever. It is not always even possible to distinguish his real women from imaginary ones, since they are all alike. When he describes a typical English girl, for instance, it is not necessarily some 'Miss' he met at Homburg or even his wife-to-be. It could merely be both at the same time and yet neither: it could merely be his ideal.

Laforgue was very conscious of having lost his friend Théo Ysaÿe. Germany was going to be less fun in future. 'Dear old Théo,' he wrote from Coblenz in the latter part of July:

I came back through Belgium and saw all those piles of coal dust with upturned wheelbarrows on top and the girls with manners like uncouth boys, and the towns a sea of black tiles, and I thought: there at any rate are you, happy and in Paris. So work, smoke, remember me, and write to me . . . and keep for Paris an unbounded love. (E:142-3)

On his way back from Bohemia, Gustave Kahn arrived in Berlin on 1 September and was shown the sights by Laforgue. The most important of these sights, he remembered later[40], were on opposite sides of the Unter den Linden: the Aquarium and the Café Bauer.

The Aquarium especially, on the north side where no one walked, was one of those places—the quai Saint-Michel in Paris was another—that Laforgue called his 'rêvoirs'. The combination of 'rêve' and 'revoir' was meant to designate a dream-place which could and should be seen again and again. And certainly Laforgue went to dream regularly at the Aquarium among his friends the denizens of the deep, who became far more real to him than the denizens of Berlin. Many times he was to write about them, notably in his *Moralités Légendaires* story called 'Salome'. The Café Bauer, on the other hand, was not so much a 'rêvoir' as a port of call, where he could go to read the world's papers and periodicals, while drinking a coffee on the first-floor interior balcony. Kahn remembered turning over the pages of *The Graphic* there, with one fascinated eye on the multitude below.

Afterwards they went to see the clowns at the Concordia music-hall and to Laforgue's flat in the Palace of the Princesses, which Kahn was the only person ever to describe:

It was a vast olive-green room—study and salon combined—with black woodwork and sombre hangings. Connected to it were an entrance hall and a bedroom. On the wall: his portrait by Skarbina. A spacious table and a big divan. On the bookshelves: the complete works of Shakespeare in handy little volumes the size of a pocket hymn-book. Also Tennyson, Browning, Charles Keene, du Maurier, Kate Greenaway, Caldecott, Walter Crane. He was forever reading and looking at English books. I remember that in the train back to Paris he pointed out the Belgian girls, explaining that they were nicer than the Germans because more like the English.

Kahn noted that even during the Sedantag celebrations Laforgue's apartment remained comparatively quiet—obviously an ideal place for work.

One morning we were walking under the Linden when a little lieutenant of the Hussars, resplendent in a blue uniform with silver trimmings, came and slapped Laforgue on the back with a hearty 'Wie geht's?' There was some talk about the weather and the previous night's performance at the Opera. When he'd gone Laforgue said to me: 'That young man's mad on uniforms. It runs in the family.'

In his book on Berlin Laforgue describes the same young man at Court functions: 'He looks to right and left with a false vivacity, distributing handshakes with laughter too jovial to be true.' (G:59) On that occasion he was wearing the more familiar scarlet of the Red Hussars. Neither of the two Frenchmen realized just how soon the hearty young man in love with uniforms would be Kaiser Wilhelm II.

Reviews of the *Complaintes* began slowly to appear, and the one that gave Laforgue most pleasure reached him late in September when he was at Tarbes. Sandwiched between reviews of a new translation of Horace and the Leather and Shoe Industry *Year Book*, it was buried in an obscure Lyons periodical called *Le Zigzag* above the signature of Léo d'Orfer. Laforgue at once wrote to Vanier:

Who is Léo d'Orfer and where can he be found? Even in my dreams I never imagined such an intelligent article. The passage where he says I've gathered together 'songs of the streets and of the woods, of the bedroom and the church, public speeches and gossip of the town, people and solitude, earth and air' is amazingly perceptive. Who is he? (M:113)

Léo d'Orfer (real name: Pouget) was a young man of Laforgue's own age, who was to have a lively career in journalism, helping Barrès with *Les Taches d'encre*, moving to *Le Scapin* and then founding *La Vogue*. It was for him, for one of his questionnaires, that Mallarmé produced his famous definition of poetry: 'To express, in human language reduced to its essential rhythm, the mysterious sense of existence—which gives meaning to our life and is our only spiritual task.' At this time M d'Orfer was as unknown as Laforgue himself, yet he was able to pinpoint Laforgue's original-ity in words almost identical to those used thirty years later by F. S. Flint. 'It is a kind of poetry,' said Léo d'Orfer, 'in which all the prosaic and ordinary things of life are juxtaposed with superb flights of lyricism—and the two groups interact.' (M:205-6) And he ended his article with the following words: 'I would wager that this intensely original book based on banal thoughts and everyday speech—these new poems that are made with bits of old poems— will not be copied in a hurry.' And indeed it was nearly thirty years before T. S. Eliot paid these poems the compliment of imitating them.

In the whole artificial controversy cooked up by Trézenik in *Lutèce*, the ineffable 'L-G Mostrailles' had at least raised one interesting point, a distinction between Laforgue and Corbière: 'Corbière couldn't care less about anything. He joked about every-thing. . . . Laforgue also pokes fun at things but with bitterness. You feel he has a faith, and he believes in his mission.' (M:199) In his reply Laforgue was quick to agree: 'I live by an absolute philosophy and not in fits and starts. . . . I'm a good soul who amuses himself as best he can, but who has a faith and believes in his mission, just as you say.' (E:137-8) Kahn's comment was: 'How compare a wry, agitated joker like Corbière with a man of deep feelings like Laforgue, who lives sincerely according to his beliefs and is sensitive to everything artistic. It's as if you likened Harlequin to Pierrot.'[41]

And talking of Pierrots, one of the surprising things to happen in 1885 was that Laforgue, while still waiting in a state of deep depression for the *Complaintes* to be published, had suddenly started work on a new book of poems. In six weeks he finished *L'Imitation de Notre-Dame la Lune* (*The Imitation of Our Lady the Moon*) and this time he made no mistake: he hustled Vanier into publishing it before the end of the year and only partly at author's expense. Dedicated to Kahn, it appeared on 12 November, less than three months after the *Complaintes*. Its heroes are a race of sad clowns called pierrots, who resemble Laforgue himself as if they were brothers:

> Ils ont comme chaton de bague
> Le scarbée égyptien.
> A leur boutonnière fait bien
> Le pissenlit des terrains vagues. (A:145)

[They wear, set into their rings, the egyptian scarab. In their buttonholes they sport the dandelion of vacant lots.]

Laforgue had long worn the first and hankered after the second. They recall, these white-faced creatures, the Deburau of Jean-Louis Barrault in *Les Enfants du Paradis*:

> Je hais les trémolos, les phrases nationales;
> Bref, le violet gros deuil est ma couleur locale. (A:151)

[I hate ringing pronouncements and patriotic phrases; in short, full-mourning violet is my local colour.]

Sorrowfully, the clowns see right through any girl who bothers to approach them:

> Je songeais: oui, divins, ces yeux! mais rien n'existe
> Derrière! Son âme est affaire d'oculiste. (A:151)

[I thought: yes, divine, those eyes! but nothing exists behind them! Her soul's a matter for the oculist.]

And if, by mishap, they get too involved, they can always execute a pirouette à la Laforgue:

> M'est avis qu'il est l'heure
> De renaître moqueur. (A:156)

[Methinks the time has come to take life less seriously again.]

At the end of the book he makes a promise:

> Oh! j'ai été frappé de CETTE VIE A MOI,
> L'autre dimanche, m'en allant par une plaine!
> Oh! laissez-moi seulement reprendre haleine,
> Et vous aurez un livre enfin de bonne foi. (A:177)

[Oh, I was struck by this life of mine, the other Sunday as I strode across a plain. Just let me get my breath back, and you'll eventually have an honest book.]

It was a promise he kept.

Laforgue returned to Germany that year with a heavy heart, and from Coblenz wrote to Théo (8 November, unpublished):

My dear Toto . . . I got back here four days late, which caused a certain coldness. All very amusing, I'll tell you all about it one day. . . . I'm waiting for them to make the slightest complaint and I'll be off by the next train. . . . I saw your brother (just before I left) with the virginal Reichelt, who looked bewildered by Paris, and the cynical, impotent Lindenlaub. Actually I saw quite a lot of your brother, so I know all about your misfortunes, both as a tenant and as a man possessing a stomach. In fact we came to your rescue in a sort of way.[42]

The new book, which he privately called *Les Lunes*, was welcomed by 'Mostrailles' with a characteristic squib in *Lutèce*:

Vanier has just published a new book by Laforgue, from which I quote two alexandrines, one of which has only eleven syllables:

Oh! laissez-moi seulement reprendre haleine,

Et vous aurez un livre enfin de bonne foi.

It could hardly be proclaimed more clearly that both *Les Complaintes* and *L'Imitation de Notre-Dame la Lune* were practical jokes. Well, I don't complain about that. What I do complain about is that Laforgue thanked me publicly for my article on the *Complaintes* (and *Lutèce* very graciously printed his letter) but in private he tells anyone who cares to listen that the article was no good . . . so I'll just let M. Laforgue 'get his breath back' and I'll review that 'honest book' when and if he writes it. (M:216-17)

In the first of three letters from Coblenz Laforgue told Kahn (10 November):

I hope you're still seeing Ysaÿe (Théo comes from Théophile, just between ourselves). You are probably beginning to gauge the quality and quantity of his possibilities outside music. It was more or less left to me to cram a little knowledge into him, which I did in a fairly haphazard way. As to the basic things he's never learnt, I suppose he will pick them up somehow. You're no doubt aware that he's a bit of a strange case; on the other hand you'll admit he's open-minded. I'm saying all this so that perhaps you will talk to him, when it's a question of things he's never learnt, and take trouble to dot the 'i's. You understand me, don't you? He's a chap who sometimes needs to live with a Larousse. . . .

So you envy me the Rhine. Well, I envy you the chalk and blackboards of the Sorbonne. Which of us is right? . . . I've just written to Mallarmé to thank him for his letter. Ah, if only you could come to Berlin this winter, just for a little. We return on the evening of the 30th, but what shall I do there? Seriously, do you realize it will be the first time in my life (like you in your Tunis, I suppose) when I've spent a year completely alone. I might emerge from it an old man or something. I might suddenly dry up. I'm not joking, one's not a Breton for nothing.... I spend the days in my room without a thing to do. The view's not bad and I have a few books, but it's ridiculous eating elaborate food all alone and then putting on a white tie at five o'clock, exactly at the twilight hour which speaks of liberty. I'm sure that when I'm free at last in Paris I shall react with a spate of ghastly bohemianism. Write to me . . . send me piquant news items of our little world. You know I can't rely on letters from Henry or the pianist. I'd like to finish this letter with some enormity expressing the enormous vagueness of my mind.... I can hardly stop myself spitting on the paper. Luckily I have a spittoon. (C:126-30)

A week later, on 17 November, he wrote:

So you're going to spend a week at Meudon. You'd work much better (exoticism and music) in Berlin. But so be it. At least you won't have those unbelievable walks between the quai d'Anjou and the boulevard de Courcelles. Get your book in order and send me excerpts as you go along. . . . Now listen to this: I see you as a very considerable oriental gentleman ... the touchstone of your orientality is for me your whole attitude towards women . . . so it's natural that when I pick up your book I want to find out first of all how you deal with the woman question. Well then, exhibit your pride and accentuate the note: let's have the whole voluptuous repertory in which you so excel. And at the same time tell us about the obstacles that our modern towns put in the path of you oriental gentlemen. . . . Continue the good work and don't spoil the purity of your origins with a lot of European claptrap. . . . The tedious Greek gods should be mentioned only to make fun of them (as you do so well). Catholicism and mystical rhetoric (which again you know all about) can be a useful adjunct to your vocabulary, nothing more. Above all, let's have no sin and remorse . . . which isn't you at all. . . . We'll soon be back in Berlin. I'll give you news of the Reichs-seraglio and the Concordia (where the troupe of clowns we saw is still on the bill). (C:131-5)

The following week, on 23 November, he wrote from Cologne, where he had gone to hear Brahms conduct his recently finished Fourth Symphony at the Salle Gürzenich:

I leave it to this beautiful writing paper with the nostalgic heading to tell you where I am. . . . For two days I've been wandering in the streets and through the suburbs and along the Rhine (and inside the cage of that interminable bridge that leads to Dietz) without speaking to a living soul—except perhaps for a word at the hotel, another to the tobacconist and a third when buying a concert ticket. Absolutely alone: have you ever known the feeling, even during your four years in Africa? It's then that I wallow in blackness and am more nihilist than life itself. It's then I set forth with my pipe and go marching through the suburbs and along the riverside, preaching the gospel to myself in harsh and pathetic parables. I expect you know the mood. Tonight I heard Brahms conduct his latest symphony—after which I wandered about full of huge and complicated plans for Italian sonnets and things. And in the process I got a magnificent headache which I can feel in all four corners of my head. I'm not the slightest bit hungry. I'm not really sure what I'm doing here below —or, more to the point, what I'm going to do. The cathedral looked immense and sinister when I passed it. The two towers were overwhelming. (C:136-8)

Back in Berlin, about mid-December, he wrote:

Excuse the long silence . . . my twelve-page article for the *Gazette* has been a millstone round my neck for the last ten days, with its necessity for traditional form and stilted French. To give myself a treat I hope to go to Hamburg for the New Year and perhaps even farther (whence I will write you, no doubt, some sublime letter). . . . The merest titbit of news about my book will be most welcome. I know you're above such trivialities, but I'm not. . . . I'm having to read *Tartarin sur les Alpes*; you can't imagine anything more grotesque, heavy and boring. Your comments on Tolstoy confirm me in my opinion of your art and of your life: you will never enter the kingdom of heaven. I've just heard *Die Walküre* the day after *Siegfried*. Since the first line of this letter I've yawned twelve times. . . . All I'm capable of is the reflex action of filling a pipe. . . . Not being able to stay in my room, I go for endless walks—sometimes with a stick, sometimes with an umbrella. Your JULES LAFORGUE, a being without reasonable reason for being. (C:139-42)

The letter—and the year 1885—end with a drawing. It shows a man walking away from a lighthouse labelled 'Lighthouse of Bitterness'—but the man's leg is chained to the lighthouse by a ball-and-chain labelled 'Desire', while from his mouth issues the word 'Spleen'. Underneath Laforgue has written: 'This allegory will explain everything.'

CHAPTER 7
Apotheosis (1886)

THIS was the most important year of Laforgue's short life. 1880 had been a year in which he made friends. 1883 had also been a year of meetings ('R' and the Countess Vitzthum) as well as the year of the *Complaintes*. But 1886 was the year of apotheosis, when he produced everything by which he has since been best remembered.

He began it with a visit to Elsinore, to put the finishing touches to his Hamlet story. The significance he attached to this visit is clear from the letter he wrote to Gustave Kahn. This was the 'sublime letter' he had promised:

It's from Elsinore, the land of Hamlet, that I write you! I'd intended to go to Hamburg but, as it turns out, I'll only stop there on the way back. Instead, I pushed on to this famous island. I spent a horrible New Year's Day: icy wind, mud, seagulls and a Mass of the Reformed Church. . . . I even mingled with tourists to see a procession of local dignitaries, suitably uniformed, entering and leaving a palace—a palace which is the home of the married Parisian, Marie d'Orléans.

For Copenhagen, please read Kjøbenhavn. There are seven hours of sea between Kiel and Korsor. Coming here, I did them between midnight and six, and what a crossing! Going back, I'll travel by day from ten in the morning till five. Why aren't you with me? Ah, how that cold and dirty wind from the ocean blew to pieces my poor prose poems! And in the streets those adorable anonymous faces! And all the strange pathetic business of being in these windy, storm-tossed islands on the first day of 1886—a year which we may not survive. But whatever happens, we shall have cried to the wind some relatively immortal truths. . . .

Not having posted this letter in Copenhagen, I continued to traipse around with it in Hamburg—and here I am back in Berlin.

Between times (as the good Belgians say) I spent an artistic day at sea: stormy weather with occasional slanting sunlight; gulls, rain, no horizon and a frightful seasickness, which up till then I'd never believed in. Horrible, horrible, horrible, as they say in Elsinore—whence I come, Monsieur. Then I had two good January days in Hamburg, around the port, where I watched the arrival of a steamship flying the flag of Montevideo (blue stripes on a white ground, with a golden sun in the corner). I lived in the sailors' quarter, got indigestion from tropical fruit, bananas and suchlike, and discovered all sorts of low dives: negresses, Norwegian and English singers, shooting galleries, weighing machines, exotic zoos, freaks, etc. . . . (especially the etcetera). Back in Berlin, and still at liberty, I prolonged my exhausted nostalgia in the local dive you know too well. Congratulations on the new flat. I hope you grow to love it and live in it seriously, and create there to your heart's content. Let me know how you arrange it. (C:143-9)

The next letter is written to Kahn's new address, 4 rue Laugier:

Your belongings sound funny and simple. I'm sure that for a few sous you could find, on the right bank, not far from the Belle Jardinière, two little satisfying plants. But if you're wedded to plaster casts I recommend the shop in the rue Guénégaud, there's nowhere like it. . . . I heard the Essipoff woman [playing the piano] last night and observed her closely till two in the morning in a salon. . . . Every morning at 7.30 I catch the train to go and skate on the Neuer-See [in the Tiergarten]. I will now draw for you one of my skates. . . . Thanks for the Italian artic-oletto. . . . I think that de Goncourt is pretty naive to imagine that Tolstoy cares a jot about him. Can you think of two more different temperaments? I'd wager everything dear to me that Tolstoy, supposing he didn't throw them away after the first chapter, would despise the works of Edmond de Goncourt. Nothing more disgusts that noble and primitive savage than the fussy analysis of eighteenth-century art treasures. (C:150-2)

Then on 30 January in a letter to the Ysaÿe brothers came the bombshell:

Did I tell you that I'm marvellously in love with a young English girl, my professor of English, and that I might very well become engaged? It would be a beautiful and positive act. What adorable novels I'd write then! As it is I can't write a line, not even a false one.

The paragraph is buried in the middle of a longish letter, which ends as follows:

I still wander around with Lewinsky, who's bent on emancipating

himself in a big way, or rather he's sowing his last wild oats in a
kind of frenetic and concentrated rage. (I was with him last night
at the famous Subscription Ball, where Théo and I went last
year.) So that's life: I'm bored, accomplishing nothing solid and
getting older. So try to come and surprise me in Berlin. It would
be a nice, romantic thing to do. (M:288-9)

There is no doubt that the throwaway paragraph in the middle is
the most important part of the letter and will have been judged so
by the two recipients. For someone as discreet as Laforgue it is the
equivalent of having the banns read out in church. The girl he had
so instantly fallen in love with was living alone in Berlin, studying
painting and giving English lessons. Her name was Leah Lee. Though
fragile in appearance she was headstrong enough to have stormed
out of her father's life because he'd gone off with the governess.
In looks she was striking and conformed uncannily to Laforgue's
ideal. He had once told Théo he would marry a slender English
schoolteacher. And here was Miss Lee teaching him English and
thin enough to satisfy his most exacting requirements. Besides that
she had red hair with a milky complexion, big dark eyes and a long
slender neck. Laforgue was overwhelmed. As the Tuesday and Saturday lessons proceeded in her lodgings at 57 Königrätzerstrasse
(now Stresemannstrasse) he began to bring her articles he'd written
in the *Gazette*, as well as etchings and books and opera tickets . . .
and gradually, very gradually, his friends were allowed to know
what was happening, beginning with Kahn:

You can't imagine the sort of life—totally different from anything I've ever known—that I'm leading this winter. I don't write a
line. I don't read a book. But I do a little English. I'm smoking
less than last year, half as much, but enjoying it more. I wander
off quite a lot, something I never did before because I clung to
the pianist who was a real stay-at-home. Every day I spend two
or three hours on the ice. I've learnt to do Dutch turns and
figure-8888 and I always come back looking stupid and glowing.
Besides which I've been going to a series of balls, where I observe
life in the manner of Gaspard Hauser. And I talk for hours with
beings who are absolutely strange to me: young girls. Do you
know them? I'm still astonished even now. They disconcert me
much more than Naturalistic novels ever did. . . . And what about
your plans for the summer? Are you by any chance thinking of
going to London this summer? And when shall we be able to
snatch Henry from his giant oak table and point him in all
sorts of unsuitable directions? I have to go now but I would
first like to state that at this precise hour (8.30) I should like
to be smoking a pipe with you and Henry. In support of which
proposition I sign myself JULES LAFORGUE, honest French
poet. (C:153-6)

His remark about being disconcerted by the young ladies of Berlin
was no exaggeration. An unpublished note[43] dating from about
this time reads: 'Talk about Dante's Hell! It was nothing compared
to the spectacle of Miss Lee with her friend!' He decided there was
only one solution—and he wrote to Kahn about it in February:

Every morning I almost write to you. I stop myself each time,
worried by your silence, and apprehensive of all the things that
could have made you change your address. But now you tell me
that nothing of the sort's occurred, you're simply 'bored, tired
and ill'—despite the magnificent life-style suggested by your visit
to the Grand Comptoir des Halles with Barrès at five in the
morning. As for me, I'm also 'bored, tired and ill'. The real nub
of all this is that we aren't married. I hope Henry soon will be,
despite all his previous experiments. After all, how can you be
made happy by an illegitimate wife, who doesn't feel at home?
I'm sure you'll come round to it before long, and that'll be the
day when you'll be happy and fulfilled from top to toe. Myself
I'm thinking about it seriously all the time, and no jokes or
romantic illusions are going to turn me off it. He who laughs
last, etc. I don't give you three months alone in the rue Laugier
before you come to it, too—and then you'll feel the full beauty
of the discovery. Henry ought to know that there are quite a few
charming girls in the world ready to be excellent companions

for whoever can catch them. And that's the first trump in our game if we're to stand up to the bourgeois. Think about it in all human sincerity and tell me, yes or no, am I becoming senile?

Dances of the Court and of the Diplomatic Corps, of the Artists and of the Corps de Ballet in fancy dress; nights spent alone in railway trains and afternoons among the remnants of bachelordom—everything I see—and everything I can imagine, looking on the bright side, even in Paris—binds me heart and soul to the idea of a charming simple marriage. (I'll let you know how it all turns out.)

It would be a friendly act if you told anyone claiming to have read me in the *Gazette* and its supplements that the articles in question are only vaguely mine. . . . But who cares? I'm above all that thanks to my new conjugal preoccupations, from which I get new strength, like Antaeus did from contact with Mother Earth. (C:157-60)

And, refreshed by Mother Earth, he returned to the attack in his very next letter:

Your letter is good fun but proves nothing . . . it's stupid and idiotic to lead the life we do, if you're so built (as I am) that you can't spend even half a day alone. It's asking for a miserably sterile old age with a softening of the spinal cord. Last year I used to work at Ysaÿe's; this year I do nothing. No matter how it blows and rains and snows, I can't stay at home for twenty minutes—unless it is to snooze on the couch. I cannot and will not eat alone. I cannot go alone to the circus, a museum or an exhibition. So it's all very sad. And for travelling it's the same. When I really start living my life I shall need a home, and a companion to keep me there, or to draw me back there when I've wandered off. And the companion might just as well bring all that side of life we lack, and be a woman. . . . In that direction, as far as my poor self is concerned, lie health and literature. At the time of my last letter (which must have made it sound unbearable) I was—but am not really any more—completely in love with an absurd and astonishing little person who is English and before whom you would instantly lower your eyes. I had a letter from the pianist . . . he's weaving dreams round the Swedish girls he's met or been applauded by. And what spelling too! (C:161-3)

He wrote to Kahn again on 21 March:

First big day of the thaw. Yesterday I did my last 8888 on the ice. Goodbye to that till next year. Today it's warm and I feel a bit crazy. With the last of the cold weather, the dreaded marriage bug has stopped bugging me. But now with the outbreak of spring (no less dreaded) I have developed a great pity for the men of this continent and dream of sudden journeys. I'm afraid that's how it is: by dint of culture I have brought my personality to its present pitch, which is to be a poor weathercock for the four seasons. By the same post as your bouncy letter I got one from the pianist: still in Sweden, this evening they're playing at Malmö. He complains about the local cigarette-paper being like blotting-paper. . . . He's also preoccupied with the local women. So you think I must look a sorry sight under the Linden. Not at all. In fact, I've never lived so naturally, which for me at least has the charm of novelty. It's the first year for six years that I haven't gone whole weeks without any appetite; it's the first year for years I've eaten evenly every day as a matter of course. And, after living by courtesy of the Unconscious, I now have no consciousness at all: I write nothing, read nothing, have no thoughts or projects about art—and it all seems quite natural. To sum up (in case you're interested): I've skated, smoked, eaten, been to Copenhagen and Elsinore, danced for a fortnight, conversed with exemplary young ladies, heard the *Walküre* and *Siegfried* at least ten times, puffed through the countryside in the little local train and . . . what else? Nothing. One of the stranger effects of my new life is that—without noticing it—I find I've been chaste since 31 December (Hamburg) and that, too, seems natural. In short I've become a ruminant without pretensions. (C:164-7)

Two events now occurred: at the end of March a couple of music-loving travellers came to Berlin . . . and on 11 April *La Vogue* magazine was founded in Paris (no connection with any other magazine of that name.)

Edouard Dujardin and Teodor de Wyzewa were musical Parisians. Between them they ran the *Revue Wagnérienne*. Dujardin (the director) was a bit of a dandy, addicted to red waistcoats, pale khaki suits and a monocle. Wyzewa, his assistant, was altogether more scruffy. Both of them were to play an influential part in

Laforgue's life as editors—but Wyzewa also became his most intimate friend.

Teodor de Wyzewa may not have been a smart dresser but he had none the less a striking and attractive appearance, with his feverish eyes darting glances at the world between a low-cut fringe and drooping moustache. He was often likened to Oblomov, a reference to his apparent laziness; but he could be galvanized at a moment's notice into hectic activity, during which he would improvise some brilliant article on the corner of a café table in five minutes. A fine translator of Tolstoy, Emily Brontë and Jane Austen, he was also a friend and mentor of music-hall star Jane Avril. He was a lively and versatile man with a great affection for Laforgue (of which his daughter Isabelle has given us touching proof).

Although the object of the visit was to hear *Siegfried* at Dresden on 30 March, Dujardin and Wyzewa spent almost the entire three days with Laforgue in Berlin. Wyzewa has described 'the slim young man with a round face'[44] who came to meet them at the Café Bauer. They talked till dawn and, a few hours later, met at the Museum. Dujardin was later to claim that, already in March of 1886, Laforgue was expounding his theory of *vers libre* which he had evolved (according to Dujardin) to achieve a more exact expression of his thoughts. 'While I talked of musical expression,' said Dujardin, 'Laforgue made it clear all along that his main concern was psychological.'[45] Dujardin was continually alert to new techniques. He himself was credited by James Joyce with having invented the stream of consciousness method. Though critics have consistently accused him of having a faulty memory, it is not impossible that he was right in recalling Laforgue's words of March 1886, and that the seeds of *vers libre* were already germinating.

As for *La Vogue*, it was founded by that same Léo d'Orfer whose review of the *Complaintes* had so delighted Laforgue. But, for reasons which have never been satisfactorily explained, there was a palace revolution and d'Orfer was quickly ousted from his position by Laforgue's other friend Gustave Kahn. Under the editorship of Kahn *La Vogue* became one of the most influential little magazines of the century, publishing in the course of the year (from 11 April to 27 December) almost all Laforgue's best work—and Rimbaud's *Les Illuminations*, too, for good measure. Kahn used to say that he had sixty-four faithful readers, by which he presumably meant subscribers. Whatever the readership figure, it had little to do with *La Vogue*'s real influence. For Laforgue it was a deciding factor in his career, encouraging him to write enthusiastically at a time when he was at the top of his form. Léo d'Orfer, who never seems to have borne anyone a grudge, made the interesting comment that part of *La Vogue*'s success was due to Charles Henry, when he chose the title lettering from a rare Italian book of 1515 by Sigismund de Fantis of Ferrara.

Though normally as reluctant as Hamlet to make a decision (K:19) Laforgue now felt himself being impelled unquestionably in one direction. The visitors from Paris, the founding of the new magazine, his new love (and spring itself) all suggested that his real place was in the French capital. The time had come to make a move. On 17 April he wrote to Kahn:

Very impressed by the magazine . . . what can I send you? I've nothing. My stories need to be revised. Here is the only poem I've written since *Les Lunes*, it's the Preface to my next book. The draft was written in my Copenhagen hotel on the evening I returned from Elsinore, on New Year's Day. . . . If you feel it's no good you can at least console yourself by caressing the beautiful Japanese vellum on which it's written. . . . Now, listen: here's some big news and it's serious too. I have just spent my last winter in Germany. As soon as I arrive in Paris I'm going to write and tell them I'm not coming back. I've got a family excuse, and a successor all lined up, to soften the blow.

And so I settle in Paris. I arrive with at least 2,000 francs and all my suits and linen in good order. You know I can live on nothing. I shall be able to work for ten months without needing to worry. What do you say? In any case, anything's better than another winter in Berlin, looking at the same faces. My mind's made up ab-so-lute-ly. . . . I ought to start packing up my books and belongings now, and send them on by the slow goods service. Perhaps you could store them for me for the time being? I've no idea where the rue Laugier is situated or what the prices are like, but I'd certainly like to be your neighbour. Can you give me any details? Take all this very seriously, won't you, because (first) I'd rather be chopped up for mincemeat than not come to Paris, and (secondly) 2,000 francs will be coming with me, all my debts having been paid. Please become a bourgeois, just for the moment, and if you can think of any objection, let me hear it. Did I tell you that a fortnight ago after a concert I met Dujardin and Wyzewa, who spent some time here and at Dresden (*Siegfried*)? All good wishes to the mathematician who (because he no longer writes me) is coming to seem a serene and distant figure. (C:168-72)

A similar letter (unpublished) was sent to Théo, together with a consignment of 'papier de chez Adamovitch'—but whether this was cigarette paper, music paper or Paul Adam's latest novel remains a mystery.

In fact he now announced to all and sundry—perhaps to burn his bridges—that he was leaving Berlin irrevocably at the first opportunity. To Lindenlaub he wrote three letters in rapid succession:

The Empress absolutely 'adores' your colour plates, but don't mention it in your terrible correspondence column.... Can I offer you some choice aphorisms in the style of the following: 'The only certain thing about life is that it gets twenty-four hours shorter every day.' . . . My Berlin life is just the same as ever: I still dine with Lewinsky at the Grappe d'Or at ten minutes to eight. Then I go and smoke his cigars, while dreaming of my posthumous fame, on his bottle-green couch at 5 Spittelmarkt. The house has a lift . . . but only for merchandise. When I take my holidays this year I've decided to make the big break.... I'm going to arrive in Paris with enough to live on for a year.... The whole thing's decided once and for all. . . . I've had enough. The prospect of spending another year between Oberwallstrasse, the Renz circus, the Café Bauer, the Brandenburg Gate and the mounted policeman opposite my window—and those miserable dog-cart and the Guard House across the way, and the footmen with side-burns and coffee-coloured gaiters—the sheer horror of it all might make me join the Mormons or have myself castrated for the Sistine choir. So it's my last winter. I'll arrive in Paris, I'll rent some studio, high up, one of those studios the painters don't want any more. . . . I'll buy some sheets and a divan bed, a huge table, some kitchen equipment. I'll prepare my own eggs and rice and coffee. With three or four vegetables and some olives, that will be adequate nourishment for a gentleman of my standing. While living in this simple fashion I shall take Vanier a new volume of verse (very serious and instructive) and a novel in support of marriage (based on the charms of legitimacy). . . . If the worse comes to the worst and poverty creeps up on me, I'll take a cab and ring at the door of Georges Ohnet, to offer myself as his secretary, quite seriously. Actually I'd rather rot in a cellar as a printer than spend another winter here. Five years' contemplation of the same heads is too much for a chap who isn't sure his own is screwed on properly. . . . My plans for escape are progressing: I've even got a successor who's all ready to start (a certain Rivière whom you met at the Café Bauer). . . . All these last weeks Lewinsky has been entertaining big manu-facturers, one after the other, from Crefeld and Barmen, so naturally I join them (champagne dinners at Dressel's) for their own sakes as well as economy's![46]

The same message went to his brother Emile, who had been in Paris since January, staying with their aunt in the Batignolles:

This time, when I get to Paris, I'll stay there. I've already begun sending my things. I'm going to live in the rue Laugier. As soon as possible I'll publish a book called *Berlin dans la rue* (*Berlin Life*) which I could never have done if I'd accepted a Court pension. It's useless for me to stay here any longer. . . . I'm borrowing more money than I save. And there's no point in putting off leaving till I'm dead, however soon that may be. . . . It won't be entirely easy to earn a living in Paris, but I can at least expect the Berlin book to bring in something. Anything rather than another winter in Berlin. I waste my time in pointless ways; and through boredom I nearly got married, which is something I haven't yet the right to do. . . . By the way I've had some news from Tarbes: Marie's been very ill, near to death in fact. One of those terrible illnesses which sometimes precede a first pregnancy. But she's all right now. (E:148-9)

The long-suffering Marie Laforgue had married a local architect the year before. It was not the first time she had been proposed to, but her first suitor had changed his mind after learning he would have to adopt the whole Laforgue brood. The architect Gustave Labat was an easy-going man who could take such responsibilities in his stride. They settled down at 25 rue des Grands-Fossés (now rue Maréchal-Foch) and, as if suitably to celebrate their marriage, Gustave there and then designed the municipal theatre, which still stands today (as the Imperial Cinema) bearing the memorable date 1885. Their first child, Juliette, named after Uncle Jules, was born on 3 June 1886. When last heard of, Juliette was alive and well and living in (or near) Nice.

In a slightly earlier letter to Emile, Laforgue had given his elder brother a monumental dressing-down. Emile had come to Paris, it seemed, after living it up in Tarbes (if such a thing is possible). And for his own misconduct he had blamed Marie; her bad temper, he more or less claimed, had driven him out of the house. The letter (unpublished) has been partly censored by the family, but what follows is the gist of it:

I accept that living with Marie isn't always easy [wrote Jules] but we all know perfectly well she has a heart of gold. If her nerves are sometimes frayed it comes from bottling up a series of daily martyrdoms throughout her entire youth. With someone of Marie's natural temperament I'm only surprised she didn't go mad. That's why I shall always remain devoted to her and if she has children I'll try to give them a hundredfold what she gave us. That seems reasonable. . . .

Now, you told me yourself that you lived it up at Tarbes and disappeared for days and nights at a time. Indeed it was clear to me during the last holidays that you hadn't done any work for years. Since it is best to be frank about these things, allow me to tell you (and I have some experience of artists) that you don't know how to draw and you don't know how to paint. . . . You must at all costs improve your technique. Go into the streets. You're living in a wonderful part of Paris for that. Go into the squares and the railway stations, every day, for hours, and draw, simply and laboriously, without any tricks or shading, everything you see—especially the things you didn't expect to see. Do that every day, do you understand, every day.[47]

To Kahn on 23 April he wrote:
It's ten o'clock. I've just got up. I feel crushed, broken, and why? This will give you a good idea of what's so revolting about my life here. Yesterday I had a late dinner date and, while hanging around for it, I took the edge off my appetite with cakes, coffees and cigars. Then I went to the dinner and stuffed myself and champagned myself for two hours. After which I took some ladies to a terrible exhibition by the charlatan Verechtchaguine. Today I can't do a thing, I'd like to run away and roll in the grass. But no, I've got to take a train and go and eat another meal, this time with some bourgeois who haven't even got daughters. It'll be the same thing tomorrow night after my Reading; and on Sunday there's a charity matinee at Mme Artot's, very starchy. On Monday I'll rest. . . . You can see, can't you, that a poor chap like me can't begin to cope with such a life. And then there are all those people you have to refuse, who reproach you politely and whom you then have to avoid in all the public places one visits: exhibitions, theatres, and so on. No, I will not spend another winter in Berlin. Once arrived in Paris I'm going to stay put; there'll be nothing doing even if they try to tempt me with the Grand Cordon of the Legion of Honour.

You can imagine how I jumped for joy at the suggestion that we live together. It would be a delightful and practical arrangement—but is your place big enough? Near the Bois too! It really is tempting! Well then, if you're sure it will be all right (and if necessary we could always find something bigger, with a studio, for example) I hasten to accept. It's a great idea to share the rent and thus let the race of landlords pay for our cigars, etchings and porcelain. Besides which, living together means working together. Dujardin told me he couldn't bear working in solitude: he lives up at the Place Blanche with Wyzewa. Yes, it would be both comforting and stimulating: I shall go on dreaming about

it till it happens. We could fix the place up nicely with my bits
and pieces.

At this point Laforgue gives a list of his 'bits and pieces', which
possibly gave Kahn pause for thought. They begin with his little
bronze elephant by the animal sculptor A-L Barye and include a
large assortment of pots and pans, a Hindu fish, the two girls in
wax by Cros, a Louis XV tea service given him by the Empress,
twenty-five art albums, a whole library of books, numerous
etchings and photographs, two portraits of himself by Skarbina, a
pipe on wheels and a monkey's skull. (C:173-6)

The letters that summer talked, not only of monkey's skulls and
pipes on wheels, but everything under the sun: 'When we're living
together I'll persuade you to bellow a bit, you know what I mean,
so that people will say, "That Kahn, they ought to lock him up.
He's a man without principles who undermines the foundations
of modern life." ' (C:177) 'My Aquarium piece is dedicated to
you. Remember our visit to the spasmodic bubbles, it's a shared
memory?' (C:180) 'Ysaÿe's staying another week in Norway: a
sentimental adventure, virginity, etc.' (C:184) 'My new book of
poems will have a shiny white cover, just like *Les Lunes*. It's my
livery!' (C:188)

In the general excitement, in fact, he had begun writing poetry
again—at breakneck pace. He had written *Les Lunes* in six weeks;
now he took six weeks to write the *Fleurs*, a much longer book.
The complete title, *Des Fleurs de Bonne Volonté* (*Some Flowers
of Goodwill*) is a respectful nod towards Baudelaire and his
Les Fleurs du Mal, on which Laforgue has left a perceptive series
of notes. Of all the poets he admired—Heine, Charles Cros, Verlaine,
Rimbaud, Mallarmé—Baudelaire was inevitably the Master, to be
revered throughout his entire life. If the black girl Jeanne Duval
inspired some of Baudelaire's most beautiful *Fleurs*, the *Fleurs* of
Laforgue owe everything to the English girl Leah Lee—and no two
women could possibly be less alike. Laforgue's book was written
on a tightrope of indecision as to whether he would or would not
ask Leah Lee to marry him. It is no accident that the work contains

a dozen English epigraphs from *Hamlet*. His conflicting emotions were so great that at one point he is said to have used his position at Court to retrieve from the Imperial postal services a written proposal to Leah Lee which he subsequently thought better of.[48] The poems are in some ways instead of a diary: an intimate record of his changes of mind from day to day. One of the best is the Preface or 'Avertisement', already mentioned, which was written in his Copenhagen bedroom on New Year's Day:

> Mon père (un dur par timidité)
> Est mort avec un profil sévère;
> J'ai presque pas connu ma mère,
> Et donc vers vingt ans je suis resté.
>
> Alors j'ai fait d'la littérature;
> Mais le Démon de la Vérité
> Sifflotait tout l'temps à mes côtés:
> 'Pauvre! as-tu fini tes écritures . . .'
>
> Or, pas le coeur de me marier,
> Etant, moi, au fond, trop méprisable!
> Et elles, pas assez intraitables!!
> Mais tout l'temps là à s'extasier! . . .
>
> C'est pourquoi je vivotte, vivotte,
> Bonne girouette aux trente-six saisons,
> Trop nombreux pour dire oui ou non . . .
> —Jeunes gens! que je vous serv' d'Ilote!   (A:193)

[My father, a shy hard man, died with a grim look; I'd hardly known my mother, so there I was at twenty. / I had a go at literature, but the Demon of Truth kept urging me to give up my scribbling. / Not keen to get married, being such a hopeless case! And the girls too quick to compromise!! Despite all their false raptures! . . . / So I'm just killing time, blown in all directions, with no answers to anything...—A sad example to Youth!]
In the poems that follow there are new plans (*Fleurs* 27) for the redemption of '. . . sa petite soeur humaine,/Qui fait tant de peine . . .' ('his little human sister, who's such a problem to everyone'). In *Fleur* 42 it's:

> Oh! parcourons le plus de gammes!
> Car il n'y a pas autre chose.

[Let's enjoy everything we can together! For there's nothing else.]
In *Fleur* 31:

> Tu te pâmes, moi je me vautre.
> Consolons-nous les uns les autres.   (A:237)

[You swoon and I pounce. Let us console one another.]

And in the 23rd:

> Rien . . . ne vaut deux sous de jupe,
> Deux sous d'yeux.   (A:224)

[Nothing's . . . worth two penn'orth of skirt, two penn'orth of eyes.]

There is a sparklingly clear memory (*Fleur* 55) of those winter mornings on the Neuer-See in the Tiergarten:

> Des Bassins
> Noirs d'essaims
> D'acrobates
> Disparates
> Qui patinent
> En sourdine . . .
>
> Ah! vous savez ces choses
> Tout aussi bien que moi;
> Je ne vois pas pourquoi
> On veut que j'en recause.   (A:274)

[The lake is black with a swarm of disparate acrobats and the whisper of their skates . . . / But you know all this as well as I do; so why should I need to say it again?]

Leah makes a brief appearance at the end of *Fleur* 26: 'Deux yeux café, voilà tous ses papiers' (A:229) ('Distinguishing feature: two eyes black as coffee'); and marriage itself is not forgotten: 'L'amour dit légitime est seul solvable!' (A:253) ('Legitimate love is the only kind that works!') The same poem (*Fleur* 41) ends hopefully:

> O mon seul débouché! O mon vatout nubile!
> A nous nos deux vies! Voici notre île.   (A:253)

[You're my only way-out, my nubile last throw! This is our life: an island for two.]

And, not least, the book contains Alain-Fournier's favourite, *Fleur* 16. As William Jay Smith has said, Laforgue is a Romantic and, in a sense, 'quite as close to Keats as he is to Eliot. It was Laforgue's mastery of feeling that Alain-Fournier appreciated and his friend Jacques Rivière did not.'[49] This simple little poem, 'Dimanches', was inspired by the Rhine and the English schoolgirls at Coblenz:

> Le ciel pleut sans but, sans que rien l'émeuve,
> Il pleut, il pleut, bergère! sur le fleuve . . .
>
> Le fleuve a son repos dominical;
> Pas un chaland, en amont, en aval.

Les Vêpres carillonnent sur la ville,
Les berges sont désertes, sans idylles.

Passe un pensionnat (ô pauvres chairs!)
Plusieurs ont déjà leurs manchons d'hiver.

Une qui n'a ni manchon, ni fourrures
Fait, tout en gris, une pauvre figure.

Et la voilà qui s'échappe des rangs,
Et court! ô mon Dieu, qu'est-ce qu'il lui prend?

Et elle va se jeter dans le fleuve.
Pas un batelier, pas un chien Terr'-Neuve.

Le crépuscule vient; le petit port
Allume ses feux. (Ah! connu, l'décor!)

La pluie continue à mouiller le fleuve,
Le ciel pleut sans but, sans que rien l'émeuve.   (A:215)
[The sky rains without rhyme or reason, your river's full to the
brim, shepherdess . . . / And it's having one of its Sundays off;
not a boat in sight either way. / Vespers are ringing all over
town, and the banks are quite bereft of lovers. / But now a
crocodile of schoolgirls comes in view, several already have
their winter muffs. / One, who has neither muff nor fur, looks
such a grey and sorry little thing / and look, she's broken ranks
and run away, she's going to . . . oh my God, she must be mad!
/ She's thrown herself right into the river and there's no
Newfoundland dog to pull her out. / Twilight falls over the
little port, lights go on in their familiar way. / The water just
gets wetter and wetter, and the sky rains without rhyme or
reason.]
But the *Fleurs*, as completed by Laforgue in early June 1886, were
never to be published in his lifetime, and their ultimate fate made
literary history.

This year the Empress was late leaving Berlin for Baden-Baden,
and it may be imagined that Laforgue was well pleased, for he was
thoroughly immersed in his affair with Leah Lee. Indeed, when
the Empress finally left on 15 May he seems to have made an
excuse to stay on: he had to see the centenary exhibition of the
Berlin Fine Arts Academy (a likely story) which didn't open till

23 May. Rough notes in the back of the old 1883 Agenda suggest that his last lesson with Leah Lee was on 22 May—and he did not finally leave Berlin till 26 May. A note to Kahn on 20 May had ended: 'I've got a heap of small worries here—or, rather, one big one.' (C:185) He and Leah were to be parted for three months, and he still hadn't made up his mind.

From a literary standpoint at least, his indecision seemed almost to inspire him. After the hectic blossoming of the *Fleurs* he turned his attention to the book of stories called *Moralités Légendaires*. The title first appeared tentatively in a letter to Kahn from Baden-Baden on 3 June (C:189); with the letter he sent one of the stories, 'Salome', for publication in *La Vogue*. He had just received May issues of the magazine containing the first instalments of Rimbaud's *Les Illuminations*, and was more enthusiastic than ever about Kahn's new venture. The next six months proved to be the most productive of his whole life. He was represented in no fewer than eighteen issues of *La Vogue*, which published five of the six *Moralités* and ten of his twelve *Derniers Vers* (the last poems he ever wrote). By the end of 1886 the hitherto unknown Laforgue had become a name to be reckoned with in Paris literary circles. If ever a writer was made by one magazine, Laforgue was, and credit must go to *La Vogue* and Gustave Kahn.

The *Moralités Légendaires* were a series of new looks at legendary themes which juxtaposed contemporary everyday life with ancient grandeur—and so, in a sense, were based on that old Laforguian trick. Once again it is a trick that has lost some of its impact, simply because it set such a long-running fashion. What has not been blunted is the charm of his heroines, all but one of whom were based on Leah Lee. The exception is the Kate of 'Hamlet', a minor character entirely subservient to the real hero of that tale, who is Laforgue himself:

Of medium height, having shot up rather suddenly, Hamlet displays a long childish head, held not too high, with chestnut hair advancing to a point on a thoroughly noble brow, and then falling back, straight and feeble, separated by a superbly simple parting on the right, to hide two sweet girlish ears. Clean-shaven without being too smooth, artificially pale yet youthful, he has two blue-grey eyes, surprised and candid, sometimes cold, sometimes warmed by insomnia. But luckily these same romantically timid eyes shine forth as limpid and unclouded orbs of thought; for, otherwise, Hamlet, with his habit of looking down as if trying to sense reality's invisible wellspring, might be taken for a monk rather than the Crown Prince of Denmark. He has a sensual nose and an innocent mouth, the

latter normally used for breathing but capable of switching itself
quickly from the amorous half-closed to a disturbing chicken's
rictus, and from a sulk with both corners weighed down by the
cares of modern life to the irresistibly slit grin of a jolly little
boy of fourteen. The chin, alas, is not very prominent; neither is
the lower jaw very determined, except on days of intense boredom
when it protrudes, and the eyes recede, beneath a defeated fore-
head—and the whole mask sags, ageing by a good twenty years.
Actually he's only thirty. Hamlet has feminine feet; his hands
are solid and a bit twisted and tensed. He wears a ring with a
green enamel Egyptian scarab on the forefinger of his left hand.
He is never seen in anything but black, and he goes on his way
with a measured tread, slowly and correctly, correctly and
slowly . . . (B:40)

Both Laforgue's brother Emile and his schoolfriend Jean Pérès agreed
that this was an exact description, not so much of Hamlet as of Jules
Laforgue: an affectionate self-caricature recalling others in the same
vein by Eliot. But Laforgue's most unusual and telling appearance
in the *Moralités* was as the dragon in 'Persée et Andromède', which
Pérès[50] considered to be 'the highest peak attained by Laforgue's
poetic inspiration'. It is a tale of great tenderness and irony,
written of course under the spell of Leah. In Laforgue's version
Andromeda declines to be rescued from the Dragon—an honourable gentleman whom she much prefers to the affected and self-
satisfied Perseus:

—Monster!
—Baby?
—Hi! Monster!
—Baby?
—What are you doing?

The Monster-Dragon, crouching at the entrance to the grotto,
his hind-quarters half in the water, turns round. And, as he does
so, his back shimmers with all the jewellery of submarine
Golcondas, and with pity he raises his great eyelids, set in multi-
coloured gristle, to reveal two sea-green pupils. And he explains,
in the voice of a distinguished gentleman who has known trouble:

—You can see, Baby. I'm polishing pebbles for your catapult. . .
—And what if I refuse them with harshness . . . an inexplicable
harshness?

For Andromède is as capricious as she is charming . . . as capricious,
perhaps, as Leah Lee, whom she resembles so exactly: she has red
hair, thick and silky, which, when it's put up, is inclined to be top-
heavy for her tiny face and long neck. Her slightly ravaged look,
'toute hagarde dans sa toison rousse' (B:183), reminds us of a

Laforguian fragment which says: 'She was very young, with the face of a baby, which on certain days could look very tired. On those days, if she told me a lie—smiling, with her eyes wide-open, looking at me directly—that tired face suddenly freshened as if kissed by a breeze from her native land.' (K:63) Androgynous Andromède fits well into the Laforgue canon (Motto: If only our little sisters would act like brothers). She has small breasts, slim straight hips, and legs that are 'strangely long and fine.' (B:183) Her eyes can be wan and dimmed, or clear as a sea-bird's. Laforgue refers specifically to her 'yeux noirs de mouette' (B:198) ('black seagull's-eyes').

As Mme Durry has said,[51] other heroines of the *Moralités* have had the Leah characteristics superimposed on them as an afterthought, but Andromède is Leah all through. Ruth's eyes, for instance, in 'Le Miracle des Roses', are 'sharp as a wild Atlantic bird's or lost in a fog black as tar.' (B:76) Elsa in 'Lohengrin' has

Extract from an early manuscript of 'Lohengrin'

the inevitable long neck, long legs and general flatness. Salome, too, has that merest suggestion of breasts, which so delighted Laforgue. Syrinx in 'Pan et la Syrinx' seems actually to speak like Leah ('Vraiment?' . . . 'Mais quoi?') but Andromède is the one who looks, moves, thinks, talks and *is* Leah.

These girls are perhaps his great literary creation. No one has understood the 'jeune fille' better, and it is fitting that they are the characters in his work who have never aged—like the delightful Salome who, in an unpublished note,[52] 'n'était plus une petite fille dont on coupe les nuits en tartines' ('was no longer a little girl whose nights were sliced and buttered for her'). One of her most renowned descendants is Helen of Troy in Jean Giraudoux' plays *La Guerre de Troie n'aura pas lieu* (*The Trojan War won't take place*).

'Hamlet' is without doubt the most famous of the *Moralités*, however. Its reputation may be due in part to the interest Jean-Louis Barrault took in it. Before tackling 'that great Annapurna of the theatre which is Shakespeare's *Hamlet*'[53] Barrault decided to approach it first by its Laforguian face, the humorous side. It was only his third production but no one who saw it (at the Atelier, Paris, in April 1939) can possibly imagine anyone else in the part. Directed by Charles Grandval, with music by Darius Milhaud, the text of the stage version had been cut fairly heavily—but not a word was added or changed. The impression one retains is of something very elegant but also wry, bitter, harsh and grimacing—a clown's mocking laughter issuing from a grinning skull. (Barrault was very lean and hungry—literally—in those days.) Since then Barrault has always regarded Laforgue's 'Hamlet' as an inspired synthesis of the Shakespeare play: 'A Hamletic version of *Hamlet*: variations on Hamlet by Hamlet himself.' He has also consistently praised Laforgue for his brilliant perception in seeing Hamlet as an artist and sad clown.

Barrault points out that Laforgue went back farther than Shakespeare to the original story of Belleforest and Saxo Grammaticus, notably in respect of the courtesan (Ophelia), who is sent to trap Hamlet and reveals herself as a childhood friend. This comes out in the scene where Laforgue affectionately calls Ophélie 'Lili', which Barrault chooses to spell 'Lee-Lee'. 'The great sad love of Laforgue,' he says, 'was for Miss Lee. When Hamlet so movingly weeps for his drowned love he says:

> Pauvre Ophélie!
> Pauv' Lee-Lee!
> C'était ma p'tite amie d'enfance,
> Je l'aimais, c'est évident,
> Ça tombait sous les sens!'   (B:49)

[Poor Ophélie! Poor Lee-Lee! She was my little childhood friend, I loved her, that's clear enough, surely it was obvious!] Barrault has amused himself in that quote by setting out the prose of 'Hamlet' as if it were *vers libre*, and it is a practice that has tempted others. Leonard Unger, for instance, in *The Man in the Name*

(1956), also quoted the following lines as verse:
> Elles furent aussi,
> Les petites gens de l'histoire,
> Apprenant à lire,
> Se faisant les ongles,
> Allumant chaque soir la sale lampe,
> Amoureux, gourmands, vaniteux, fous de compliments,
> De poignets de mains et de baisers,
> Vivant de cancans de clochers, disant:
> 'Quel temps fera-t-il demain?
> 'Voici l'hiver qui vient . . .
> 'Nous n'avons pas eu de prunes cette année.'   (B:46)

[They too existed, the little people of history, learning to read, manicuring their nails, lighting the dirty lamp each evening, loving, greedy and vain, longing for compliments, handshakes and kisses, living for local gossip, saying: 'What'll it be like tomorrow? Here's winter coming on. . . . There weren't any plums this year.]

Though this is an exercise that may not convince everyone, it contains one pleasant coincidence: lying hidden in this 'free-verse' passage is the title of his first *vers libre* poem, 'L'hiver qui vient'.

Once again Laforgue had a midsummer holiday. Did the Empress sense his growing restlessness? But though he spent twenty-three days in Paris during June and July—exactly as he had done the year before—almost nothing is known of his movements, beyond the fact that he had a suit made at Cossard's in the boulevard des Italiens, which Baedeker mentions as one of the best tailors in the capital.

He had certainly intended to see Vanier and arrange for the *Fleurs* to be published. He had told Kahn precisely that he wanted it out by October. But there is no evidence that Laforgue actually visited Vanier at the quai Saint-Michel. Did he spend the money on the suit instead? It seems a poor exchange, even if it was the best suit in Paris (inevitably black, made of diagonal twill and setting him back 100 francs—which was exactly what he had paid Vanier to print *Les Lunes*). Reboul has suggested[54] that he held up the book out of consideration for the feelings of Leah Lee—or, rather, because of the uncertainty in June and July of his own feelings towards her. This may well have been the case: he may have thought the poems too intimate to publish at a moment when the affair had not been resolved one way or the other. Whatever the reason, his decision not to publish was of vital importance. One could even say that his indecision was in this case inspired; for it enabled him to consider the whole matter afresh, and by the beginning of August he had other plans for the *Fleurs*.

The only other important thing that happened in Paris that year was that he deepened his friendship with Félix Fénéon, whom he had met at Henry's the previous autumn. Fénéon was another (and the last) of those god-sent friends whom Laforgue had a genius for meeting. This was the man who would look after his posthumous reputation. He began, though, by bailing him out over a little financial matter. Laforgue explained it in a card to Wyzewa (14 July) just before returning to Germany:

Many thanks for your concern about my situation. Luckily it was only a momentary embarrassment. Fénéon stepped forward, as cool as the Statue of the Commander (I like that image) and a money-lender—a young beginner—did the rest. I hope your own troubles melt away as easily. With all yesterday's business and then today (eve of departure) having to see my brother and so on, I haven't been able to meet you at the Vintimille or the Café. But there will be other times. (E:198)

Félix Fénéon was one of the grey eminences of French literature, filling a somewhat similar role to that of the by no means grey eminence Ezra Pound in our own literature. The resemblance can be taken further if one compares Pound's work on Eliot's *The Waste Land* with that performed by Fénéon, first on Rimbaud's *Illuminations* and later on Laforgue's *Derniers Vers*. Throughout his life one finds Fénéon effectively running magazines of which he was not the titular editor. It sometimes seems that he is running all the little magazines in France, even the bitterest rivals. If ever he collaborates with someone in editing a book he is inevitably the one who does the work and gets no publicity. Perhaps this unconcern

with publicity was not quite Pound's style, but when you consider
their political adventures they become again immediately comparable: Pound's fascism was as unreal as Fénéon's anarchism: both
went to prison for mental aberrations, while remaining in all
fundamental respects intelligent men. Physically, it must be conceded, they were entirely different: Pound's fiery manner matched
his red hair, while Fénéon was so restrained as to be immobile
(hence Laforgue's name for him, in allusion to the statue of the
Commander in Molière's *Don Juan*). If Rémy de Gourmont called
him 'an American Mephistopheles' it was solely because of his little
goatee beard. Jean Paulhan, an *éminence grise* himself, hailed him
as 'perhaps the only real critic we've had in a hundred years.' Painted
anonymously by everyone from Toulouse-Lautrec to Signac and
Van Dongen, he was eternally the man who made other people's
reputations. Certainly anyone who has examined his painstaking
work on the Laforgue manuscripts can only revere the memory of
this good and disinterested man.

At the particular moment that Laforgue arrived in Paris in 1886
—21 June—the eighth Impressionist exhibition had been closed a
week already, but the city was still buzzing with the excitement of
Seurat's 'La grande jatte', which had been drawing little groups of
perceptive people to 20 boulevard des Italiens (a step or two from
Laforgue's tailor). Fénéon had been the first to spread the news
and to tell Charles Henry, who later became Seurat's friend and
technical mentor. There is no doubt that Laforgue, too, was taken
to see the painting, although it was no longer on show publicly,
and that he instantly recognized its importance. A charming symbol
is that girl in the picture who wears the mid-eighties version of
the bustle (the *tournure*, which had evolved from the earlier *pouf*).

The mid-eighties silhouette as seen by Seurat.

Similarly the whole painting breathes the spirit of the times: the masterpiece of a painter who was to die hardly older than Laforgue himself.

The only other fact surviving from that high summer of 1886 is a note to Kahn asking for Verlaine poems which Théo was to set to music. As far as is known he never did so.

Laforgue returned to Coblenz for four days only; and then something unexpected happened. Instead of going to Homburg the Court broke completely new ground and went to a place in the Rheingau, to the west of Wiesbaden, called Schlangenbad. To quote the 1878 Baedeker, 'Schlangenbad is charmingly situated in a richly wooded valley, refreshed by a constant, invigorating current of air.' For whatever reason this unlikely place saw the birth of modern poetry as we know it today.

Laforgue wrote to Kahn about 23 July:

My address is The Lower Pump Room, Schlangenbad, Germany, a strange place indeed. More than ever I have the feeling that I won't return to this Empire. Best wishes to Valentine and the others. My respects to Fénéon, that deus ex machina, cold as the Statue of the Commander reconstructed from the residue of a soap factory. (C:197)

This last was a friendly dig at Fénéon's latest article in La Vogue— on saponaceous sculpture. Laforgue wrote to Kahn again on 29 July:

In this little place we know nothing about anything. A copy of La Vogue would be manna from heaven. . . . Drink your morning bowl of milk to my health (it goes with your poached eyes) and try not to wake the baker at four in the morning. When I shut my eyes and try to imagine you I always see the same picture: you are leaning slightly forward to choose ten-centime cigars in a tobacconist's, while the lady behind the counter regards you with suspicion. (C:199-201)

In early August he despatched another letter:

Does La Vogue still exist? I've had no news. The life you're leading must be quite fantastic: spiders' webs must be spreading visibly in the editorial office. As for me, I'm floundering about doing absolutely nothing. I haven't touched the book on Berlin. I'm not even doing my article for the Gazette. I haven't looked at my stories . . .

BUT . . . now came the news that must have agitated Kahn, delivered in the throwaway manner at which Laforgue excelled:

. . . to remove any temptation I might have to publish that book of poems I read to you in bed (red ink on yellow paper) I'm turning it into something completely different. Roughly what it will look like is that piece on Winter I sent you. I forget to rhyme,

I forget the number of syllables, I forget to set it in stanzas—the
lines themselves begin in the margin just like prose. The old
regular stanza only turns up when a popular quatrain is needed.
I'll have a book like this ready when I come to Paris. I'm working
on nothing else. This place is a dump: eating, smoking, twenty
minutes in the bath to digest—and the rest of the time: what
else can you do but write poetry? And I'll never write poetry
any different from what I'm writing now.

And so was casually announced the birth of *vers libre*.

I needn't repeat that I'm determined to come to Paris, Paris,
Paris. You know the belvedere on top of 5 quai d'Anjou, which
you saw at the time Henry moved in, is it still free? You might
ask him the price and the number of rooms and let me know....
Au revoir. The trouble here is mosquitoes.' (C:192-5)

Every letter now ends with greetings to Valentine, Kahn's new
girlfriend whom Laforgue must have met in Paris. Over the years
he had acquired a smooth technique for dealing with his friends'
friends, whether they were called Léonie, Régina, Valentine or
whatever. He tried to remember that, although they were precious
objects one week, they might not be there the next. His letter of
7 August ends: 'Do you want my "Persée et Andromède"? It's
about the same length as "Lohengrin" and absolutely ravishing.
I've surpassed myself and at such a young age! My civilities to
Valentine.' (C:204-5) But by the time of the next (and last)
letter from Schlangenbad, his 'civilities' were no longer required.
Valentine had departed and his concern was now entirely for
Gustave's morale.

This divorce is a terrible business because it's going to send you
off on a demoralizing search for new distractions, and then this
row you've had with Henry is absolutely idiotic: it's the sort of
little squabble that kids have when they're growing up. I think
you're intolerant, mean-spirited and short-sighted to take um-
brage just because Henry jokes about your poems. In the first
place Henry is extremely intelligent and has a right to his
opinions. . . . Besides which he has an attachment to you, a
deep and sincere friendship (no doubt because it's an old friendship; his first, and your first too—and those are things one
doesn't forget in a hurry). Then again, he's a marvellous person
to know and very loyal. So your attitude is clear: friendship for
ever, come what may. . . . So the belvedere of the quai d'Anjou
is out of the question. But do you think I'd find three rooms
under the roofs of Montmartre for the same price? Including
one with a top light where I can paint? And then the restaurants
are so expensive up there. (C:206-10)

Before the return to Berlin, the Court spent the customary August fortnight at Babelsberg. Laforgue wrote to Kahn from there on the 21st: 'Illustrious Gustave, I got your letter and *La Vogue*. Why do they put 'Specially printed at La Vogue Press, 4 rue Laugier'? Is this some new palace revolution? Or did your family bring you back a printing press from Vichy?' *La Vogue* of 16 August contained the first two poems of the *Derniers Vers*, and he sent off with his letter the next two, which duly appeared in the issue for 30 August. Nothing could better demonstrate the advantages of having an editor among one's friends. By the time he left Berlin the idea of the *vers libre* poem was fully formed, and he was to enter Paris riding high on his new reputation. Even so, he had at this time a few quibbles:

I won't point out the two misprints but I will complain that you didn't print me in italics. It's poetry, Monsieur! . . . My article for the *Gazette* prevented my copying out 'Persée et Andromède' but any moment now I'll bombard you with it. What else can I do for you? A piece about a pub? Or the Sedan fête on 2 September? Or a little study on how geysers work in New Zealand? Or a classified list of all your lovers? I'm shut up in a kind of Normandy-style château with nothing to do but eat, row and sleep. (C:214-15)

Ten days later he wrote again:

Here's 'Persée et Andromède'! . . . We return to Berlin on the first and I shall leave again before the tenth. I'm not too sure but I might stay with the Ysaÿes for a spell on the way to Paris. If I'm not mistaken you won't be going away at all this summer. Send me a nice long letter before I return to Paris for good. Once I'm there we shan't write again for ages—that is, unless I go back to Montevideo and you to Gomorrah. And how is Lillith? And what about that walk in the Garden round the fountain, you with yours and me with mine? And the Dowager of Sheba? Are your parents back? Don't you dine out any more? Tell me what's happening. From a distance Paris seems such a wonderful garden that I'll go mad with joy at the station and in the bus. But when I consult my memories I see only an exhausted gentleman waiting for his last bus at midnight and secretly hoping he'll miss it so that he can traipse around some more. Any idea where I can find a place on the rooftops with a belvedere—like at the quai d'Anjou—for 600 francs in the Batignolles, Montmartre? (C:211-13)

On 1 September another letter followed:

We're back in Berlin. A year ago on such a day, at this very hour in fact, I went to meet you at the station. Sic transit gloria mundi. Strange coincidence (almost Buddhistic): the Singhalese we saw at the Berlin Zoological Garden are now in Paris. I'll be free for ever on the fifth. But don't expect me at once, I'm coming via Namur, where Théophile will intercept me. I'll stay with him at Arlon probably till the 15th, which is an economy, a pleasure, a rest, and a unique opportunity to do my article for the *Gazette* (which I'm not doing here and would do even less in Paris). My address: chez M. Théophile Ysaÿe, Arlon. In heaven's name send me *La Vogue*. I shall have nothing to read: all my books, my overcoat, my tea-service are bound for Paris by the slow goods. It's the definitive proof that I'm leaving Berlin, but thanks all the same for your quavering advice. (C:217-8)

Kahn's quavering advice had been blunt and to the point. Years later he explained what it was: 'Laforgue wanted to come back to France and live by his pen. I wrote to him: "Be careful, Laforgue. Things are very tough here at the moment. There isn't much of a market for our sort of stuff." It was no good. He came back.'[55] Laforgue's letter continued:

If the Empress went to live somewhere else, say Coblenz, any-where but Berlin, I'd stay. But in five years, even a great bear like myself acquires enough social acquaintances to be their slave. That's one reason. The other is that, if I spent another winter in Berlin, I'd come back *inescapably* married to someone who is utterly forbidden me for my sake, her sake and every-body's sake. So I'm coming to Paris. I have enough to move in somewhere, pay a quarter's rent and eat for a month. I had a letter from *L'Illustration* asking me for articles on the Court and inviting me to name my terms. I'm going to say they must take the whole book for a good price, or nothing at all. (C:217-18)

And as our hero prepared to leave Germany for the last time, heading west, a symbolic event occurred—as if to suggest some of the true brilliance of the occasion: on the throw of a switch the Berlin Opera House was suddenly bathed from floor to roof in glorious electric light.

Part 3:
THE RETURN

CHAPTER 8
A Quiet Wedding
(London, 1886)

'MY Dear Marie'—the letter is postmarked 'Berlin, 8 September 1886':

I write to you with difficulty, dipping my pen into a dried-up inkwell which I haven't touched for three days. For it is three days since I was really at home. I don't know how to begin. I'd better tell it to you just as it comes.

Last winter, in my letters, did I mention a young English girl who was giving me pronunciation lessons? Well, to come straight to the point, in the evening of the day before yesterday, I proposed to her, she said yes, and we're engaged. Since the day before yesterday my life is no longer my own, and I feel all the grandeur of this idea. But also since the day before yesterday, whether near to her or alone, I'm in a state of nervous happiness that I would never have imagined. (I haven't kissed her yet. Yesterday evening I was sitting next to her in a cab and, as I looked at her, the idea came to me that I shall be able to caress her hair, and I felt dizzy, and I haven't done it yet, far from it.) But I must tell you everything, for I've only got you, and one of the first things she told me after I'd proposed was that I should write to you at once. She, for her part, is writing to her favourite brother.

I told you she was English. She has several sisters, married or otherwise, as well as brothers (one a barrister in Folkestone, another a priest in New Zealand and a third an officer in Zululand). Her mother died four years ago. Her father remarried, against the wishes of his children, who all left him. As for herself, she went to a boarding school in Switzerland, where she learnt excellent French, then here to Berlin, where she's been for two years. She lives partly on an allowance from her father, and partly on what she gets from her lessons.

It was in the second week of January that I first went to her for lessons. I'm the only male pupil she's ever had (I was recommended to her by a woman friend) and consequently the only man who's gone to her place for lessons. From the first moment, without knowing her character, I felt that either I'd ask her to spend the rest of her life with me, or else I'd have to leave there and then with the certainty of a long period of suffering and not being able to work. You understand me, don't you: Our lessons were limited to English readings, and Hello and Goodbye. But she was studying painting and, little by little, I began bringing her etchings and books and then my opera tickets. It all happened very easily, without even the handshake so natural to the English. Our first conversations—apart from the lesson—were about painting and, in particular, a local exhibition on which I brought her an article I'd written in the *Gazette*. And each evening I went home and I stayed there, feeling wretched and each time more wretched. I know that many women don't mind sudden declarations, but not for anything in the world would I have said a word to her or looked her straight in the eyes, before first having made myself known to her, patiently over the months, as someone good, loyal and scrupulous.

One day towards the end of April, I don't know how it was, we were talking painting and I suggested we visit the Museum together. She blushed, lowered her eyes and didn't reply. Rushing home like a madman, I wrote her a letter of apology, assuring her that I only meant something very simple; and at the next lesson it was she herself who suggested it, very simply. Well, that naturally gave us a chance to talk, and I escorted her home afterwards. After that museum, as you can imagine, it was another museum. Then often, when I'd given her my opera ticket, I'd reserve another one next to it, and we talked, and I saw her home and made myself known to her. Things went on like that, without any further developments, until the middle of May. I left for Baden-Baden, then Paris, Coblenz, Schlangenbad, Babelsberg. I came back to Berlin on the first of September, and today's the eighth. Our outings to museums and the opera and seeing her home afterwards began all over again. My plans had been to leave Berlin almost at once. We promised to write and remain friends. And each time, using various excuses, I put back the date of my departure. And the day before yesterday, seeing her home, I told her everything. I didn't say, 'I love you.' I stammered a whole lot of things that I've forgotten now. (It

was along by the park; imagine something like Passy or Neuilly).
I asked her if she really knew me and she said she did. I asked
her, in a very roundabout way, if she would like to spend her
life with me. (I remember my strangled voice and the tears in
my eyes.) And, not giving her time to reply, I launched into all
sorts of protestations. She said yes with an extraordinary look.
I didn't let her say she loved me, only that she had faith in my
devotion. I forget what else I said. I took her home and we
exchanged a solid handshake without quite looking into each
other's eyes.

I told you I was leaving the Empress. I had to in any case.
Either Miss Leah Lee (pronounced as if written 'Lia Li' in
French—that eternal letter 'L' as in our name, and Mama's name
and your husband's name), either she said no and I couldn't
stay on anyway; or she said yes and I'd still have to return to
Paris and quickly carve out a position for myself, so we could
get married as soon as possible. I can't leave her in Berlin, however. She's coughing a little and mustn't spend another winter
here. And then I'd be too jealous! And then it's impossible! So
this is what we've arranged: I'm leaving tomorrow evening for
Belgium. I'm going to stay with the Ysaÿes, as I told you, and
while there I'll work on my Berlin book, which is something I
can't do here any more. L'Illustration have already asked me for
certain chapters and if the book is published, what a dream that
will be! We'll get married at once and we'll be able to come and
see you, even if it's in the middle of January, provided I don't
die of happiness. So I'm going to Belgium, while she stays here
to tidy up her last lessons. That brings us to the first of October.

On the first of October I come back to Cologne and wait for
her at the station. She arrives there at eight in the morning. We
spend the day at Cologne and that same evening, on the ten
o'clock express, we leave for Paris together. As soon as we arrive
(at ten in the morning) I'll take her to a sort of *pension* run by
an old English lady, where she'll be with other girls, in the rue
Denfert-Rochereau (not far from the rue Berthollet!). She'll
stay there and have her meals there. Maybe she will give about
one lesson a day in the house itself, it will give her something to
do. For my part I'll find somewhere to live, and start working.
In the evening I'll go and call for her and we'll go out a bit.
During the day, too, if I have a moment, I'll take her to museums
etc. (She already spent a couple of weeks in Paris in 1878, with
two of her brothers who were at Asnières learning French.)
And then, as soon as possible, we'll get married.

What else can I tell you? I'm taking her photograph to Belgium

with me, so I can't send it to you yet. She's a little character
[*petit personnage*] impossible to describe. She's about the same
height as you and me, but very thin and very English—especially
very English. Her hair is chestnut with red lights in it, a shade
of red you can't imagine and which I never knew existed until
I saw her. A mat complexion, slender neck and eyes . . . oh her
eyes! you'll see them for yourself! For a long time I couldn't
hold her gaze, but you'll see: just imagine a baby face with a
mischievous smile and big eyes (the colour of tar) that are always
astonished, and a quiet voice, with a funny little accent when
she speaks French and such delicately distinguished manners, a
blend of natural shyness and attractive candour (just think that
she's lived alone and free for two years and has also travelled
alone, which is something natural to the English and of no consequence). As well as her own language she speaks German and
French. Her education's like that of other young girls, added to
what she's picked up on her travels and while learning two
foreign languages—and what she's retained from our interminable
conversations since last April. I told her all about our family. I
especially talked to her about you. She adores the career I've
chosen and has confidence in me.

I am writing to you from the eternal room in the Palace of
the Princesses, to which I'll never return. I have her photograph
before me as I write to you, and I'm looking at her. We were
together yesterday evening till eleven o'clock and I held her
hand; now, as I look at her portrait I can't believe it's a reality.
I'll call for her this evening at 5.30 after one of her lessons. And
tomorrow she'll come with me to the station. And on the first
of October I'll meet her in Cologne. Oh, if only we could get
married in January and come and surprise you! I forgot to mention, for your information, that she has no kind of dowry and
that all she has in future will depend on me. She's a protestant
but doesn't practise; it makes no difference to her whether she
goes to church or not. You know how English marriages often
happen: you go hand in hand, with four witnesses, to the clergy-
man across the way, where you sign something which lets you
off the civil ceremony. We, too, will get married very simply,
she in an ordinary dress. One fine morning we'll arrange to meet
our friends at the town hall. We'll sign, and we'll thank the witnesses. It'll be a Saturday and I'll take her home. The next day
(Sunday) we'll go and lose ourselves in some corner or other
during a High Mass with organ at the Madeleine or Notre-Dame.
And we'll imagine that the organ is just for us. This will give just
the emotion necessary to soften the dryness of the official

ceremony and make us feel we're really married for life. Then we'll leave and she'll be my own little Leah for ever.

I don't know exactly how old she is: the same as you, I think. How I long for you to see her! I don't call her by her first name yet. I call her Petit Personnage. She won't be bored with me, I promise you!

Talking of marriage, that's why I'm going to Belgium, for the marriage of Eugène Ysaÿe, the violinist I've often mentioned, not to be confused with my intimate friend, his younger brother, the pianist Théophile Ysaÿe.

My dear Marie, write me a good sisterly letter, and tell me you're pleased with me. I shall remain always your good brother and Mademoiselle's godfather. Write to me. I've given you my address: chez Ysaÿe, Arlon, Belgium. Did I tell you that Emile is doing his twenty-eight days. I've sent him something. Goodbye for now, tell your husband everything. Write and tell me you're pleased.

Even today, this letter is the chief source of information we have about Leah, and as such it is not entirely satisfactory. Gustave Kahn, who knew her as well as any of the friends, had a little more to add. He says unequivocally that she was the Andromède of 'Persée et Andromède' as well as the Syrinx of 'Pan et Syrinx'. Leah Lee's 'svelte allure', her 'grâce profonde et discrète' were immediately recognizable to him in both those stories. Particular passages, such as Andromède's fits of impatience and Syrinx's cool composure expressed clearly for Kahn different facets of Leah's temperament. Throughout the *Moralités Légendaires* he also discerned Laforgue's growing passion: beginning with a feeling of pity, then of astonishment at the character of a young girl at last understood; finally becoming enthusiasm for a physical ideal, and admiration for the cool firmness of a young soul, both complicated and determined. In the Syrinx especially Kahn recognized the ardent and pale face of that agile nymph, who was at once wilful, rebellious and proud, naively proud with a thousand susceptibilities. He knew well those sometimes sad cheeks beneath the big eyes that could be both surprised and determined. Twice he uses the word 'determined' ('décidé') in different articles written years after the event. He talks, too, of that harsh pink shadow on the cheeks, which was like a light but indelible sunburn beneath the pallor of her brow. Of all the friends Kahn describes Leah most sharply and pertinently.[56] That last observation, if read in the context of the time, is a clear indication that he knew she was consumptive: one thinks of the 'white face and pink cheeks' of Rollinat's 'Deux Poitrinaires'. Kahn's insistence on her being impatient, wilful, rebellious, proud, complicated, firm and determined is welcome in that it lifts her out of the sweet insipidity in which she often languishes, and which Laforgue's other friends always seemed to confirm out of a mistaken loyalty. The words most often used about her are 'frêle', 'irréelle', 'exquise'—all of which she may well have been, but we know too that she was a high-spirited and witty girl.

Until quite recently Leah's actual identity was unknown. The details of its discovery can be read elsewhere[57] but the culminating moment came when we cut back the overhanging branch of a cypress tree to reveal her name on a tombstone at Teignmouth, Devon. Descended from generations of sailors and farmers, Leah was the daughter of a rich draper. Laforgue got the family history

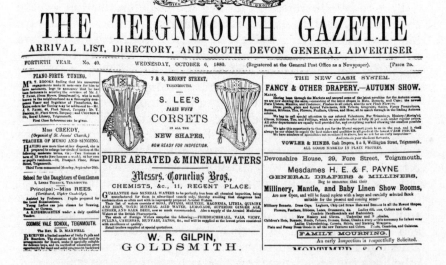

'S. Lee's Corsets', an advertisement from *The Teignmouth Gazette*, 1880

slightly muddled in his letter to Marie, and this—added to the fact that Leah took three years off her age when she signed the marriage register—confused scholars for years and made identification more difficult. When Laforgue named Leah's brothers as the barrister at Folkestone and the priest in New Zealand, he got his signals crossed: Edgar, the priest (and Leah's favourite) was at Folkestone; while Ernest, the barrister, was in New Zealand, where he eventually became Minister of Justice. Altogether it was a lively and original family: Edgar, for instance, was no ordinary priest but a powerful character who moved about in an aura of wild controversy. Leah herself was equally spirited and resourceful; the mere fact that she lived alone in Berlin for two years suggests that she belonged to that famous breed of Victorian woman travellers, so deceptively frail and yet so tough. Her reason for being there in the first place was also typical: her father had quite reasonably married the governess (for he was left with young children to bring up) but in Leah's eyes he did it too quickly and insensitively, and she simply walked out.

Laforgue left Berlin, as arranged, on 9 September. At Namur he was greeted by Théo and together they took the train south to Arlon, a Belgian town on the frontier with Luxembourg. Eugène was to marry a local girl on 28 September, and Laforgue was invited to stay there in the meantime. He wrote to Kahn on 21 September:

Just got your letter. Where did you hear that news about a vacancy in the museum of Versailles? What exactly does it involve? What qualifications do you have to have? The only one I've got is my five years on the *Gazette* and being able to write on art questions. But if a degree's needed it's not worth my wasting money on the stamped paper. Mind you, I wouldn't mind Versailles at all. At least it's near Paris. Look, would you do something for me: Henry understands these things better than we do, so could you go and see him and explain the whole thing. Ask him to find out if I'm entitled to stand as candidate. And if so, ask him to send them a demand for further information—

duly signed with my name since, not being in Paris, I can't do it myself. It should be a very simple demand without going into my qualifications, except, perhaps, my five years on the *Gazette* but definitely no mention of any 'protectors'. The latter will have to be sounded out face to face and delicately, and there'll be plenty of time for that. . . .

I'm still at Arlon. I attend the violinist's wedding on the twenty-eighth; then on the thirtieth I return to Paris, probably with the pianist (who's busy composing and sends best wishes). *L'Illustration* have sent me a series of engravings for a special number to mark the Emperor's death, and I'm preparing a text for them. They want me to name my own terms; could you find out from Wyzewa roughly how much I should ask? One thing I can guarantee is that my piece will be absolutely unique as to both general information and personal observations. In the meantime I'm working on the book itself. I've divided my notes into twelve exercise books and altogether they should make a good-sized Charpentier edition.

Thanks for the offer to stay at your place. I'll arrive in Paris with perhaps a louis. And if the pianist doesn't manage to get something out of his brother (who himself will have to borrow from his new father-in-law) he will be staying on at Arlon till his Bordeaux concert in November, and I'll have to take advantage of your place at least for my first week, while seeing what turns up.

You'll have seen the news about the old man. On the day of his death I shall obviously be taking articles round more or less everywhere, starting with the *Figaro* and the *République Française*, quite apart from *L'Illustration* special number. Any chance of my seeing you before you leave for your twenty-eight days? We lead a strange life here, two steps from the Luxembourg border. (C:219-22)

Laforgue was clearly worried about how Ephrussi and Bourget would take his flight from Berlin—especially as he would arrive in Paris, not with 2,000 francs but a mere twenty. It would seem that the plan for Leah to accompany him there was dropped almost as soon as it was made. Perhaps Leah had second thoughts about the convent in the rue Denfert-Rochereau, or perhaps she simply wanted to go home and inform her family, while her husband-to-be tried to get his career moving. And so, when Laforgue met her at the end of the month, it was only to escort her to Calais.

On the same day that he wrote to Kahn, he also wrote to Fénéon:

Are they still talking of a crisis in Paris? I hope to survive it!— but in the meantime I'm going to have to borrow Kahn's flat for

the first week, while he's on temporary call-up. I'm glad you are
charmed by my little friend Andromède. She's more modern
than the old one, and I was happy to be of service to her. The
pianist Ysaÿe sends his regards. He met you at Henry's the same
time as I did, and no doubt we'll all meet again in Paris. . . . It's
the older one who's getting married and who's going to live in
Brussels. I don't expect you know Arlon; we're living outside
the town, a few yards from the Luxembourg border. Last week,
as we strolled home, there were wonderful moonlight nights: we
saw people harvesting at one in the morning under a starry sky.
On Saturdays here you can see French soldiers who've come
over for the day from Longwy. For the first time in my sad
existence I had a ride on a roundabout, and performed amazing
feats in a shooting gallery. Apart from that I'm doing jobs on
Berlin, while thinking of the battering that may well await me
in Paris. Till we meet again, dear Fénéon of the famous profile,
and a good handshake. (E:160-1)

Two days later he wrote to Kahn:

Whatever I do I shall arrive in Paris without any money, for
reasons that I'll explain later. Here are the sixty francs you asked
for, it's the money for my return to Paris and it's all I've got.
The Ysaÿes haven't any either; one of them's getting married on
the twenty-eighth, and the other will be putting off his return to
Paris precisely for reasons of economy. And this stay of mine at
Arlon, which so surprises you, is also for economy. . . . I'll be in
Paris on 1 October—provided, of course, that you send me back
the money for the journey. I've completely uprooted myself. I
don't know what I'll do in Paris, where I'll stay or how I'll eat.
But that will only be a problem for the first week, for I've an
article coming in the *Gazette* and I'm in discussions with
L'Illustration for my book on Berlin. (C:223-5)

His letter of 25 September to Kahn was wryly urgent:

Without troubling you more than I absolutely must, I do hope
that you can repatriate me without too much bother. The famous
sixty francs are utterly essential for that. . . . It would be nice,
too, if you could send us *La Vogue*, as promised, to while away
the hours *en route*. All my luggage, including books etc., is
being sent on to Paris in advance. Can I count on the shelter
of your roof for the first week?—since I'm not allowed to stay
at the rue Papillon, and a hotel room would leave me no money
for food. *L'Illustration* job is still on but, since they only offer
forty centimes per line of forty-two letters (for the total 600
lines, which I've already done) I haven't yet accepted. Did
Henry send in that application on stamped paper? I can just see

you at this moment, on the eve of your departure for barracks, in a fantastic rush of errands and complications. But we're all more or less in that state. Better times will one day dawn? (C:226-8)

This is Laforgue's last surviving letter to Kahn, and probably the last letter they ever exchanged. Soon they were to see each other regularly and there was no need to write.

The wedding of Eugène Ysaÿe at Arlon on 28 September 1886 seems to have been a memorable experience for all, and for no one more than Laforgue. The high point was the reception in the Hôtel du Nord when Eugène Ysaÿe (violin) and Mme Bordes-Pène (piano) gave the first performance of César Franck's great (and only) Sonata, which the composer had sent to Eugène as a wedding present. Written that same year—a year after the *Symphonic Variations* and in the same lofty, lyrical spirit—it held the wedding party spellbound, and its effect on Laforgue especially must have been immense. The first theme of the first movement was later to become the model for Proust's 'little phrase' in the Vinteuil Sonata, described in *Swann's Way*: 'First the piano alone complains, like a bird abandoned by its mate; then the violin, hearing it, replies from a neighbouring tree. It was like the beginning of the world, with only those two alive . . .' In an interview with Jacques de Lacretelle (*Nouvelle Revue Française*, January 1923) Proust said: 'When the piano and violin weep together like two birds answering one another, I was thinking of Franck's Sonata.'

One can imagine that Laforgue left Arlon in a happy daze, with the allegretto of the last movement still ringing in his ears. He may already have been familiar with *Symphonic Variations*, which Théo, reputedly its finest executant, would have played for him in Paris the previous June. Certainly one feels that both the *Variations* and the Sonata were masterpieces essentially of the 1880s—and both were completely Laforguian in spirit.

From the Hôtel de Londres at Verviers Laforgue wrote a thank-you letter to Théo on 30 September:

O my dear Théo, Never have I lived a week (or even thought it

possible) like the one I've just spent at Arlon, in the atmosphere
of Eugène's wedding. As I left Arlon and breathed again the air
of Europe, it was like coming to one's senses after leaving an
enchanted house, not to say a madhouse. More than ever I feel
I'm the slave of fate. What others call their normal condition is
for me a miracle of utter intoxication that overwhelms everything else unchecked. It is at once awesome and divine.

As I pondered I asked myself: what does our fate depend on?
Nothing but poignant (and frightening) moments of chance! A
casual smile in a village, and we become Shakespearean, our
destiny is fixed. I sighed to think how sadly and desperately our
minds aspire to the Absolute, to the fullness of fate—ironically I
breathed in deeply the proud air of long voyages.

Then came twilight and an hour's wait at a little station: I
walked back and forth, gazing at the heavens and the multitude
of stars, and then I saw a lamp in the window of a heavy bourgeois home (it was a lamp with a pink shade) and I began to
dream. The Corinnas and Ophelias of our lives are lies; the
only ones who matter are the little Adriennes with a kind heart,
long eyelashes and young ephemeral smile, the little Adriennes
with an enchanting complexion that chance (and isn't everything
chance?) has put in our way. Yes, everything is chance because,
if Adrienne hadn't existed, there would have been a Leah; and
if there hadn't been a Leah, there'd have been a Nini and so on.
That's why we're enjoined to attach ourselves to the first that
chance presents to us and love her only (for she's the first) and
dream of no other. The old maxim of the wise man says: 'If
you love two women at the same time, don't choose either, or
you'll always regret the other.' But we surrender to the intoxication of joy in action, the intoxication of having obeyed the
Unconscious, the decree of fate.

It seems that at this point in the letter he fell asleep and completed
it next morning:

I'm going to put these lines in the post. They're full of literature,
but isn't literature, the truest thing humanity has, and the least
disappointing? I'm now off to the station. In half an hour I'll see
her. The thought of that moment makes my heart beat faster, and
in forty years I'll remember how long the waiting seemed. (E:162-4)

If this 'literary' letter seems also at times a little incoherent, it may
be because it has been translated more than was good for it: from
French into German, and then back into French. The original
French having disappeared, one cannot be absolutely certain what
Laforgue meant. One is fairly ignorant, too, of the next couple of
days in his life, but it seems that he met Leah's train at Verviers

at eleven in the morning, and that they then went on to Brussels together, where they spent the day and night of Friday 1 October. Next day they pushed on to Calais in the evening, and there is a piece he published[58] describing the 'blue and spring-like sea of the last fine days'. Later he put her on the Channel packet and stood there 'leaning on an old cannon at the end of the jetty, as the boat took thirty-five minutes to disappear into the horizon'. After which he turned on his heel and caught the train to Paris.

Kahn had an attractive flat at 4 rue Laugier, and it is not at once clear what went wrong with the plan to share it with Laforgue. Was he overwhelmed by the sheer quantity of Laforgue's artistic knick-knacks? Was he perhaps already sharing it with Valentine, or one of her successors? The back gave on to a courtyard with a fine tree and a cabinet-maker's workshop. Laforgue seems to have stayed there a few days only and then to have joined his brother and Théo at 8 rue Papillon (where the earlier objections seem to have been overcome). Whatever the arrangement, Laforgue now entered upon one of the most fruitful periods of his career: an Indian summer during which he was able to complete the work on which his reputation rests, *Moralités Légendaires* and *Derniers Vers*.

Teodor de Wyzewa always maintained that he was in excellent health when he returned from Arlon, and Gustave Kahn agreed: 'I never saw him in better form: his normal serenity had become a kind of serious and creative gaiety. All men have their moments of plenitude and I think Laforgue knew such a period at this time.' But Emile—who actually lived with him—expressed an opposite opinion in the unpublished notes: 'Though he assured me it was nothing but a cold, my brother already had a worrying cough.'

Immediately he got to Kahn's flat Laforgue began working on the last of the *Moralités* 'Pan et la Syrinx'. There is in existence an envelope addressed in Leah's handwriting to 4 rue Laugier and bearing the postmark 'London, 5 Oct 86' on which he has scrawled: 'Immortelle et jeune, Pan n'avait pas encore vraiment aimé comme je l'entends' ('Immortal and young, Pan had not yet truly loved, as I understand it').

Leah's own movements are unknown, but it is probable she would have spent time with her brother Edgar, the young priest, at Folkestone, and also with her sister Kate, who was about to become a nun in a Church of England convent at East Grinstead. She was probably too proud at this time to make it up with her father—though later on, when her situation became desperate, there is no doubt that she appealed to him for help and immediately received it.

On 4 October Laforgue wrote to Henry:
> I left Arlon on the thirtieth, spent a night at Verviers, a day at Brussels, then Calais—and from Calais back to Paris on Saturday night. Sunday (yesterday) I spent alone. I'm at Kahn's. I only saw him during the night and he could only give me the vaguest details—almost nothing, really—about that vacancy at Versailles. It was you, apparently, who told him about it, and you saw it in *Le Temps*. I was going to write you at Colmar, but then I had the good idea of calling at quai d'Anjou, where they gave me your real address. Can you send me a line saying where you saw the notice (the date of the journal if possible) and what sort of stamped paper I should write on. . . . My chief qualification—five years on the *Gazette*—will go down all right because I've got an article in the issue for 1 October, for which Gonse actually wrote and thanked me. But you know how it is: instead of going and saying to Ephrussi, 'There's a vacancy at Versailles, put me up for it', I'd rather just apply for the job, probably with a lot of others, and then start the wheels of influence turning later. . . .
>
> I sent my resignation to the Empress a fortnight ago, so on that side it's all over. Paris and my future in Paris—indeed my entire life—all that's changed drastically. Since 10 September an enormous and fateful influence hangs over me. It had to happen, since I am I, and my rights to existence are what I conceive them to be. To tell you the truth I feel as if the gifts of life have not only been offered me but heaped upon me. I'm no miserable faint-heart any more; I feel strong in myself, now and for a long time, perhaps for ever. But that's enough of me and I look forward, o wise and distinguished man, to our having a real talk. And what about you? How is your life going, by which I mean your work? We had so little chance to talk last June and July. Your concierge told me you will be back on the eighth. I'll come round immediately. (E:165-7)

One of his first acts was to seek out the friendly Teodor de Wyzewa, whom he found at the Nouvelle Athènes, the café on the corner of the rue Pigalle and the rue Duperré where George Moore claimed he had learned French. Dujardin and Wyzewa were at this moment planning to start yet another little magazine, the *Revue Indépendante*, which would be published from the nearby 79 rue Blanche. Partly on business, partly for pleasure, Laforgue (who was based not far away in the rue Papillon) spent considerable time in this part of Montmartre with Dujardin and Wyzewa. It was the *Revue Indépendante*, indeed, which published his one remaining *Moralité* and the two remaining *Derniers Vers*—as well as giving him bread-and-butter work.

One pictures Laforgue this autumn endlessly talking in these cafés just below the Montmartre boulevards. These were heady times. The word 'Symbolist' was beginning to be bandied about, and Rimbaud's *Une Saison en Enfer* (*A Season in Hell*) belatedly read. There was a great deal for young literary men to discuss together. Laforgue now had plenty of time to meet Wyzewa and his friends 'at the Vintimille and the Café', by which he meant respectively a small crémerie in the Place de Vintimille, and the famous Café de l'Orient at 84 rue de Clichy. Among others he met at the Café de l'Orient it is safe to include Seurat, for whom it was a regular port of call on the way home from his Montmartre studio.

Laforgue was not writing many letters at this period (except those to Leah, which have not survived) but in early December (Saturday the fourth) there is this isolated note to Dujardin:

About visiting J-E Blanche: let me just say I was there all yesterday and the day before, so I couldn't decently repeat the operation tomorrow. As for the Bal Bullier tomorrow evening, by all means—that's to say I've absolutely got to be at Hennequin's, rue Bara, at nine, so we could travel there or back together. Where should we meet? If it's Bullier, please send me a pass—I suppose you get them?—because otherwise. . . . I must say you know how to spend your Sundays!

The mention of the pass (Entry: 1 franc) is a reminder that cash was as scarce as ever. The Emile Hennequin he mentions was a journalist of Swiss origin then on *Le Temps*. Like Seurat and Laforgue himself he was one of the doomed young men of the period: to be drowned in the Seine aged thirty on a visit to the artist Odilon Redon.

With complete recognition of what was involved (and perhaps with some intuition of what was to come) Laforgue now began urgent negotiations with Vanier to get his life's work published: the *Moralités* and the *Derniers Vers*. The latter were not, of course, known to Laforgue as his *Last Poems*: in his mind they were *Des Fleurs de Bonne Volonté*—a phoenix risen from the ashes of his previous unpublished book of that name. That old book he now regarded merely as a collection of notes serving for the new one, which was to be written entirely in free verse. In the composition of the twelve *vers libre* poems already completed he had rifled a dozen or more of the old *Fleurs*. Now he planned to continue the process—but, as it happened, never did so. Michael Collie and Joanne L'Heureux have happily described the *Derniers Vers* as 'symphonic variations on a group of associated themes'.[59] There might have been many more variations, but we have to content ourselves with the dozen we have. They constitute a masterpiece.

In this final great work Laforgue found, as well as freedom of content, freedom of form. Here we have free association dictated by the Unconscious and expressed with great precision through the medium of *vers libre*. No longer naive and artificial, Laforgue has eliminated everything tentative and is in complete control.

Laforgue's *vers libre* had emerged in a way that was natural, gradual and inevitable. It came directly from his own previous poetry and from nowhere else. So desperate was he to burst out of his formal strait-jacket that certain pages of the *Complaintes* were already *vers libre* in all but name (for example, the last fifteen lines of the 'Complainte des formalités nuptiales'). Then again there are highly wrought passages of prose in the *Moralités* which, given a nudge, also break up into *vers libre* (as we have seen in parts of 'Hamlet'). But *vers libre*, as evolved by Laforgue, was something quite personal. It was to be followed very closely—in a spirit of homage—by T. S. Eliot. But none of Laforgue's contemporaries produced anything comparable. The two so-called *vers libre* poems by Rimbaud are irrelevant here, as is the entire output of Whitman, not to mention the Kahns and Krysinskas. Neither Whitman nor Rimbaud used rhyme in their free verse, whereas with Laforgue it remains an important element. The essence of Laforgue's *vers libre* is that it does not abandon the best of traditional poetry. With great skill it preserves all that is worth saving. Without ever rejecting exact rhymes, he adds the subtleties of internal rhymes and half-rhymes. He never spurns an old quatrain or couplet or rolling alexandrine if it can do something for the poem. Above all he includes wit and keeps out rhetoric. It was a form of *vers libre* that even Eliot in the end unfortunately rejected, though 'The Love Song of J. Alfred Prufrock' and 'Portrait of a Lady' were in a sense its apotheosis in English.

As in the *Fleurs*, Laforgue once again established his complete personal identity with Shakespeare's Hamlet: he did this immediately in a general epigraph to the whole sequence of poems by signing 'J. L.' to a passage from Hamlet's own letter to Ophelia (Act II, scene 2, lines 120-124)—a detail, incidentally, which remained unrecognized for eighty years until 12 May 1969 when I mentioned it in a letter to Pascal Pia, who printed it (correctly for the first time) in his *Poésies complètes* (1970):

> I have not art to reckon my groans . . .
> Thine evermore, most dear lady,
> Whilst this machine is to him.
>
> J. L.

It would be interesting to know exactly where and when and in what circumstances Laforgue wrote his first *vers libre* poem 'L'hiver qui vient'. Unlike most of the others, this opening poem of *Derniers Vers* owes nothing to the original book of *Fleurs*. It seems to have come right out of the air or, in Laforguian parlance, it was dictated by the Unconscious on a particularly good day. Alain-Fournier gratefully adopted two lines as epigraphs to his own poems: 'Crois-moi, c'est bien fini jusqu'à l'année prochaine' (A:279) ('Believe me, it's all over till next year') and 'Les fils télégraphiques des grandes routes où nul ne passe' (A:280) ('The roads with their telegraph wires but not a soul in sight').

The whole sequence of twelve poems maintains a consistently high standard—with the possible exception of the second poem, 'Le mystère des trois cors' ('The mystery of the three hunting horns') (A:282-3), a piece of inspiration from on high which Laforgue might have done well to reject. But the next two poems, both called 'Dimanches' and originally published as one poem in *La Vogue*, show Laforgue at the very top of his form. Number 5 continues the mood (in which familiar themes seem now to acquire a new resonance and one detects between the lines the groundswell of great poetry). But 'Simple agonie' (number 6) brings an abrupt change of pace. It is a poem of revolt and despair:

> Que nul n'intercède,
> Ce ne sera jamais assez,
> Il n'y a qu'un remède,
> C'est de tout casser.   (A:294)

> [Let no one intercede, to do so would be a waste of time, there's only one remedy, it's to smash everything.]

Not so much a call to revolution—more like the second movement of Walton's First Symphony: *Presto con malizia*.

Number 7 is the beautiful 'Solo de Lune', one of the most magical poems in the French language, and rightly celebrated in every anthology. The biographer might just add a footnote (or a foot-question): that night journey, lolling back on the top of a stagecoach with his feet up amid the luggage . . . was it the journey that took him to Schlangenbad in the Rheingau? The wit and light irony of the ending:

J'eusse été le modèle des époux!

Comme le frou-frou de ta robe est le modèle des frou-frou. (A:299)

[I would have been an unrivalled husband! Just as the rustle of
your dress is an unrivalled rustle.]
show a bold new sureness of touch, which is even surpassed in the
closing lines of Number 9:
Ainsi, elle viendrait, évadée, demi-morte,
Se rouler sur le paillasson que j'ai mis à cet effet devant ma
                                                             porte.
Ainsi, elle viendrait à Moi avec des yeux absolument fous,
Et elle me suivrait avec ces yeux-là partout, partout!   (A:304)
[And so would she come, scrambling away half-dead, to roll
on the mat, placed for that purpose outside my door. And so
would she come to me, crazy-eyed completely, and follow
me with those self-same eyes, everywhere, everywhere.]
Number 10 includes a favourite Laforgue quotation:
J'aurai passé ma vie le long des quais
A faillir m'embarquer
Dans de bien funestes histoires . . .
Oh, qu'ils sont pittoresques les trains manqués! . . .(A:306)
[I shall have spent my life on railway platforms almost but not
quite departing on fateful journeys . . . How picturesque they
are, the missed trains!]
But one would like to quote nearly all the eight hundred lines of
Derniers Vers, for Laforgue was writing with complete authority
in a medium he perfectly controlled. No trace remained of the
sobbing *Sanglot*. The last remnants of liturgical tedium from the
Complaintes had been swept aside, together with any lunar sterility
left over from *Les Lunes*. Laforgue had finally found himself.
One of the influences that smoothed his way was what he
himself had formerly called 'le goût allemand' ('the German
manner') or what might more accurately be called German Romanticism—or for that matter English Romanticism, since Keats is also
involved. Laforgue introduced only a breath of it and—to keep it
in hand—he introduced it through Heine. As the *Derniers Vers*
proceed it becomes evident that a feeling of deep compassion will
overwhelm everything in its path—and that, in the end, inexorably,
the marriage, rightly or wrongly, will take place. The first hint
comes in 'Solo de Lune':
Où est-elle à cette heure?
Peut-être qu'elle pleure . . .
Où est-elle à cette heure?
Oh! du moins, soigne-toi, je t'en conjure!   (A:296)
[Where is she at this moment? Perhaps she's crying. . . . Where is
she at this moment? Oh, at least look after yourself, I implore
you!]

In his prose translation of Heine's *Intermezzo*, poem number 57, Gérard de Nerval had written:

La pluie et le vent d'automne hurlent et mugissent dans la nuit; où peut se trouver à cette heure ma pauvre, ma timide enfant? Je la vois appuyée à sa fenêtre, dans sa chambrette solitaire; les yeux remplis de larmes, elle plonge ses regards dans la nuit profonde. [The autumn rain and wind scream and moan in the night; where can she be at this moment, my poor frightened child? I see her leaning on the windowsill of her lonely little room, her eyes full of tears as she stares into the night.]

In *Derniers Vers* Number 11 Laforgue took up this theme again, as one of those 'motifs which reappear from time to time':

> Je me dirai: oh! à cette heure,
> Elle est bien loin, elle pleure,
> Le grand vent se lamente aussi . . .   (A:309)

[I'll say to myself: oh! at this moment, she's far away, she's crying, the great wind, too, is complaining . . .]

T. S. Eliot remarked about the last two lines that Laforgue 'could write also simply'.[60] Indeed. After all his experiments Laforgue had learnt to write simply again, and it was 'mon ami Heine' who had shown him the way.

In the final poem, Number 12, after the solemn opening statement, reminiscent of César Franck at the organ, Laforgue returned to the theme of the girl lost in the black night:

> Oh, si elle est dehors par ce vilain temps,
> De quelles histoires trop humaines rentre-t-elle?
> Et si elle est dedans,
> A ne pas pouvoir dormir par ce grand vent,
> Pense-t-elle au Bonheur,
> Au bonheur à tout prix
> Disant: tout plutôt que mon coeur reste ainsi incompris?
>   (A:310)

[Oh, if she's out in this stormy weather, what tawdry affairs is she returning from? And if she's inside, unable to sleep in this great wind, is she thinking of Happiness, happiness at any price, saying: anything's better than a heart for ever unappreciated.]

And she appears one final time:

> La nuit est à jamais noire,
> Le vent est grandement triste,
> Tout dit la vieille histoire
> Qu'il faut être deux au coin du feu,
> Tout bâcle un hymne fataliste . . .
>
> Oh, qu'elle est là-bas, que la nuit est noire!   (A:311-12)

[The night is forever black, the wind is infinitely sad, everything tells us the same story: there must be two at the fireside, everything breathes a fatalistic song . . . Oh, how far off she is, how black the night!]

And all this time, an ominous leitmotif, have been the accompanying references to the girl's illness:

> Oh! soigne-toi je t'en conjure!
>
> Oh! je ne veux plus entendre cette toux!   (A:299)

[Oh, do look after yourself, I beg you! I don't want any more to hear you cough!]

Although the 'petite toux sèche maligne' ('small, dry, malignant cough') of 'Légende' (A:300) was in those days considered merely a precursor of tuberculosis (and not the classic sign that the disease had established itself), it is clear that the narrator of *Derniers Vers* himself had few illusions on the matter.

In the last lines of the poem, the situation is resolved, so to speak, in the nick of time, when Laforgue, in a final nod to his master Baudelaire, asks Nature (the Unconscious) to give him courage to go through with it all. But right up until the somewhat resigned ending *Derniers Vers* 12 has been one of the bitterest poems he ever wrote (and one of the best), living up well to its *Hamlet* epigraph: 'Get thee to a nunnery.' In fact the tone is such that one wonders if Laforgue was not thinking here of Keats's last letter to Fanny Brawne:

Shakespeare always sums up matters in the most sovereign manner. Hamlet's heart was full of such misery as mine is when he said to Ophelia: Go to a nunnery, go, go! Indeed I should like to give up the matter at once—I should like to die. I am sickened at the brute world which you are smiling with. I hate men and women more.

It was in this state of mind—which drew him to the lost girl on the one hand, but rejected her on the other—that he left for London to be married.

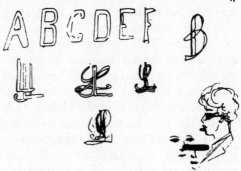

Although the *Derniers Vers* are (like the *Fleurs* before them) autobiographical, being concerned with a marriage that had not taken place—because the narrator, like Hamlet, had not acted in time, having doubts about himself and women and life generally— they are also far more than that. As Joanne L'Heureux points out in her 1974 Sorbonne thesis (unpublished): the missed marriage stands for all human relationships, and the poem is about solitude and the human predicament. In this sense it seems irrelevant to complain, as some critics have done, that Laforgue was immature. One might as well say that some critics are over-ripe. But, in fact, as Laforgue becomes better known, one hears less and less of his 'immaturity'. Indeed, Ezra Pound, who in his youth had praised Laforgue chiefly for his 'logopoeia' ('the dance of the intellect among words') came in his old age to a very different view, writing in one of the last *Canto* fragments:

> and Laforgue more than they thought in him . . .
> and I have learnt more from Jules since then
> deeps in him[61]

This is a side of Laforgue which Erica Ostrovsky understands well: 'It is characterized by a deep awareness of the terror, loneliness and abjectness of human existence, the grotesqueness of man's strivings, and the paradoxical dignity which he retains despite all this.' It is this particular aspect of Laforgue's poetic vision which 'seems to reach its culminating point in the work of Samuel Beckett. Fundamentally it is the view of man as both a ridiculous and a tragic figure, and of his life's quest as both a defeat and an ultim- ate affirmation.'[62]

In the final days before leaving Laforgue tackled once more the practical problem of getting his work published. In a letter to Vanier dated Christmas Day 1886 from 8 rue Papillon he wrote:

My dear editor, I live a long way from you, the journey in this weather isn't pleasant and there's not much chance of finding you free. My manuscript's ready and parcelled up. I leave for London on Tuesday and won't be back till the fifth. Let me have a note saying whether or not we can really do business. If so, I'll bring you my manuscript of the six short stories on Monday evening. You, for your part, will prepare an agreement in duplicate to include the following main clauses:

(1) The two books are not to be independent of one another.

(2) The one containing the six prose stories (*Petites moralités légendaires*), of which the manuscript will be handed over on signature of this agreement, shall be published without fail in

the first week of February 1887. The other—a volume of verse as yet untitled—shall be published not later than 1 May 1887.

On the delivery of the manuscripts you will pay advances of 200 francs for the first book and 125 francs for the second. (M:127-8)

The revolutionary thing about this contract is that the publisher will pay Laforgue, and not Laforgue the publisher. And it was for this reason, no doubt, that Vanier never signed it.

Immediately after Christmas, and with the help of Théo and Emile, Laforgue moved into his new flat at 8 rue de Commaille. It was just off the rue du Bac in the smart seventh arrondissement, a mere stone's throw from Bourget. And at six in the afternoon on Thursday 30 December he boarded the boat train at the Gare du Nord.

Afterwards his friends insisted that the trip to England killed him. Western Europe was having one of its worst winters for years. There was a gale in the Channel and when Laforgue arrived at Charing Cross early next morning he found London bitterly cold and foggy, with snow in the streets and ice on the lake in St James's Park. Indeed *The Times* carried the story of one unfortunate skater who had fallen the previous day and cracked his skull. Laforgue walked around for a while and then took a train to the address Leah had given him: a tiny terrace house on the west side of Warwick Road, W.14, near the junction with West Cromwell Road. According to her affidavit for a special marriage licence (discovered at the Guildhall) Leah had been in these Earls Court digs for fifteen days. It seems more likely, however, that they simply belonged to her brother's friend, the junior curate of St Barnabas, Addison Road, who had conveniently gone off for the weekend. Thanks to the curate, Leah was able to requisition the landlady Mrs Whitethorne as a witness for the wedding, the other witness being the church verger. The ceremony took place in the Addison Road church at one o'clock, and lasted exactly fifteen minutes. As Laforgue had promised his sister, it was a modest affair indeed, compared to the one he had lately attended at Arlon.

When she signed the church register Leah neatly clipped three years off her age, owning up to twenty-two years out of twenty-five. Laforgue himself was twenty-six and no doubt she had her reasons. This harmless act, however, had the effect of seriously disorienting scholars and researchers. Added to Laforgue's mix-up of her family history in the letter to Marie, it concealed her identity for eighty years.

Monsieur Jules Laforgue
a l'honneur de vous faire part
de son mariage avec Miss
Leah Lee.

Londres   31 Décembre 1886

Laforgue's wedding card

1886. Marriage solemnized at S. Barnabas

No.	When Married.	Name and Surname.	Age.
391	Decr 31st 1886	Jules Laforgue	26
		Leah Lee	22

Married in the Parish Church of S. Barnabas according to the

This Marriage was solemnized between us, { *Jules Laforgue* / *Leah Lee* }

The signed marriage register

As the Laforgues and Mrs Whitethorne came out of the church, they would have seen, two hundred yards away, the brand new Olympia, 'largest hall in the kingdom' according to an advertisement, which (like the Berlin Opera House) was 'brilliantly illuminated with electric light'. It was also being inaugurated by the Paris Hippodrome Circus, playing twice daily at two in the afternoon and 7.30 in the evening, and it is possible that the Laforgues paid it a sentimental visit: not only was he a circus addict but he had mentioned this particular circus in one of the *Fleurs* earlier that year. (A:240)

But what did Laforgue make of England in general? We know he was a keen Anglophile before he came, but how did the London of 1886 measure up to the Kate Greenaway land of his dreams? Let us hope that the bleak weekend gave him, as well as the fatal chill, some satisfaction. After all, in the eyes of most Frenchmen, what is London without a fog? And *The Times* did publish some most impressive *statistiques sanitaires*: 'Owing to the severity of the weather, the death-rate of London showed a considerable rise last week, nearly 600 persons dying from diseases of the respiratory organs.'

Perhaps it was not the most cheerful of omens.

CHAPTER 9
Death in Paris (1887)

AND so on Sunday night, 2 January 1887, Laforgue and Leah caught the 6.30 boat train at Charing Cross. Once again the crossing was in a gale and they must have felt half dead when, early next morning, they arrived in the top-floor flat at 8 rue de Commaille.

It was by no means the 'poor little flat' that has sometimes been described. In fact it was an excellent address, certainly beyond Laforgue's means at the time, in a house that (like his previous home at 5 rue Berthollet) had only just been built. But it was a cold flat in this cold winter—as it was to be a hot and stuffy flat in the ensuing summer—and it had the added disadvantage that all the rooms were *en enfilade*, each opening into the next without a corridor. On the first day they rested a little, and then Laforgue took his bride (who had only been to Paris once before) on a tour of the sights. His first disappointment on arriving home had been to find no letter from Vanier, so he hastily scribbled the following angry note on a visiting card, which he posted in a letter-box while they were walking down the Avenue de l'Opéra:

I'm back in Paris and would like to settle once and for all the fate of my *Moralités*—to get rid of this particular worry so that I can concentrate on other worries. You were to have sent me definite word last Wednesday 29 December. I beg you, candidly, let me have your final decision and let me have it this week. (M:130)

But 'Fabius Cunctator' was not so named for nothing. He still had the will to keep Laforgue guessing if it meant in the end saving a few francs. He seems to have begun by proposing that the 'advance' payable to the author of the *Moralités* should be divided in two, with the second half payable only six months after publication (a curious sort of advance). But this was only the beginning, and one suspects that his ultimate aim all along was publication at author's expense as before. Laforgue at last lost patience and Vanier drops ingloriously out of our story.

Laforgue's situation was as follows: the family at Tarbes had sold some shares but the money had all gone on furnishing the flat at 8 rue de Commaille. Gustave Kahn visited and admired the agreeable setting in which Laforgue and Leah hoped to live a civilized existence, working and entertaining their friends, but Laforgue was already anxious. He wrote to Dujardin on 21 January:

I wanted to see you yesterday evening. Wyzewa mentioned a column in the review. I've done it quickly, and it's probably heavy, dry and altogether unsuitable, but anyway here it is. Next time, if there is a next time, it will be better. But whether you like the column or not, I've a little service to ask of you. Next Saturday I shall have a three-hundred-line article in the [*Figaro* Literary] Supplement, for which I'll probably be paid on Monday. I would like to ask you quite simply (and you're the first one I've thought of) whether you could lend me a louis or two till the Monday in question . . . because something has cropped up suddenly. If you can manage it, the earlier the better—some time tomorrow, please. Don't imagine that all this is anything but an accident. If you're ever in these parts about 8.30 or nine, do come up and have tea with us. You'll realize it's not too easy for me to get about. (E:173-4)

It was typical of many of the letters which he would have to write in the coming months. The remark about the difficulties of travel referred probably to his state of health. Emile maintained in the Notes that when he went to London he was already ill, and Laforgue admits as much in a letter to his sister on 16 January. After explaining how he got married 'for 25 francs and no papers', he adds:

I still had my three-month cold. Back in Paris I had to see a doctor, who was a nuisance and took a week to get rid of—and even now I'm still coughing wretchedly. So much for the bad news. . . . As for the good news it's limitless. Our installation here is incomplete but very amusing, with sunny rooms and just enough money. I'm taking articles round here and there. (It takes 1,000 francs a month for a couple to live simply in Paris.) We're spending about fifteen francs a day. Luckily the *petit personnage* I married has a thin person's health, and is always full of fun and fantasy. It's nine o'clock. It's the time when friends who want to see me come and ring the bell. They know how difficult it is for me to get around at the moment. But we probably shan't have anyone. We've a good fire, a fine lamp, and excellent tea in the service the Empress gave me. And you, how are you and the little girl? And your husband's business? All going well, I hope. I hardly see Emile, who's too stupidly shy to call on us. Aunt's affairs are in a bad way; they've had to put their jewellery in pawn. As for me, I'm still too ill and exhausted by the fever I've had these last three months to be able to work properly and make all the calls I ought to. But I'll be better soon, much better. Let me have your news: you know that you and your family are the things in the world that most interest me. (E:170-2)

Laforgue thrashed about desperately, looking for a way out of his predicament, doing all the odd jobs that came up and at the same time trying to sell his Berlin book, which was now almost finished.

Chapters 4, 5, 6 and 7—first intended for *L'Illustration*—had now been taken over by *Le Figaro*, but payment was only on publication, and the paper was holding the pieces back in the hope that the German Emperor would make them suddenly more topical by dying. Moreover, as each one at length appeared, it caused fresh distress at the Berlin Court because the articles, being excellent journalism, were necessarily indiscreet. The earlier scandals of Catherine Radziwill and Amédée Pigeon were now being repeated —and who would have thought it of that nice M. Laforgue! For there were no doubts about who was the author (as Maxime du Camp has made clear in an unpublished letter). So all Laforgue's reluctance and (finally) refusal to use his own name—which in the end cost him the book's publication—was a waste of time. And meanwhile the pathetic begging letters had to continue. On 9 February he wrote to Dujardin:

Forgive my importunity but a setback this morning leads me to the following expedient: to ask you if my first column is to be paid for? Otherwise, as a friendly act, could you give me an advance on next month's, in which I promise to surpass myself. I hope you won't make me blush over all this but will continue to regard me as an honest artist. (E:177)

In fact, the *Revue Indépendante* made every effort to pay its contributors (at ten centimes a line)—except for the first article which was considered as a gift from the author and a gesture of goodwill. However, Dujardin responded loyally, as Laforgue's frequent letters show. So did Ephrussi who, like Bourget, had at first been annoyed by Laforgue's brusque departure from Berlin.

It was about this time that Fénéon recalls seeing Laforgue on the boulevards one afternoon, looking exhausted, his face yellow and bloated with fatigue. Fénéon was strangely shocked by the fact that Laforgue, usually so *soigné*, had forgotten to shave. In his usual impassive way 'the Statue of the Commander' offered immediate practical help.

Henri de Régnier remembers Laforgue on a visit to the Franco-American poet Vielé-Griffin. Laforgue had called, suggesting that Griffin might translate some of his work into English for a fee— but Griffin had replied rather grandly that he did not need to perform such chores. Laforgue, in a rocking chair, listened quietly, his head on one side, while the robust Griffin, standing in front of the fire, held forth at length. After Laforgue's death Griffin showed considerable devotion to his memory.

Bravely, Laforgue and Leah set off on expeditions to Montmartre (five miles there and back) for dinner with their friends at the *Revue Indépendante*—Dujardin, Wyzewa, Kahn—or coffee afterwards. Dujardin registered a clear picture of Leah at that time, already ill herself and almost immaterial in appearance. It is curious that Laforgue never mentions her worsening condition: was he too ill to notice, or did she (with her 'fun and fantasy') deceive him too well?

Another crisis arrived, and Laforgue—on 9 April—applied yet again to Ephrussi:

This is to ask you for a service, and a service concerning money. Not having been able to work, paralysed as I am by fever, and at the same time being fobbed off by a publisher—and with my big article in *Le Figaro* being put off till next Saturday—I find myself stupidly caught short by 15 April (the rent) and no way out. Would you have the kindness to save me? I need 300 francs. You know that I'm not a vulgar borrower; in fact, I'm not really a borrower at all. Believe me, if I permit myself to make this demand, it's only because I know I shall be able to repay you, half this month and half next. (E:184-5)

He acknowledged Ephrussi's asssistance on 11 April: 'Your kindness and simplicity are charming, and you know how I thank you. I wrote at a sad moment when I was ill in bed and feeling trapped. You have removed a great worry from me, and now I feel full of courage. Please let me thank you.' (E:186)

No doubt Ephrussi now had a word with Bourget, just as they had consulted once before. Perhaps it was instinctively that Laforgue had returned to the Bourget district with, only a few hundred yards away, that rue Monsieur, where the Sunday morning meetings of 1880 had taken place. And now, after a short period of coolness, 'Lord Buddha' was to assume again his role of protector and friend. He at once arranged for Dr Albert Robin—then considered France's leading tuberculosis specialist—to interest himself in Laforgue's case. As sometimes happens in France (or used to in those days) Dr Robin had a respect for literary people and was concerned enough about the fate of a young poet to give his services free. Even so, it meant that Laforgue, to see the great man, had to travel half way across the city to his consulting room at 4 rue Saint-Pétersbourg. And this he did every Tuesday afternoon, almost to the day of his death, stopping on the way home to have

a chat and a drink with Gustave Kahn at the newly-opened Café
Julien, 3 boulevard des Capucines, near the Opéra.

Robin gave him opium pills, which checked the terrible bouts of
coughing but left him numb and lifeless, unable to eat and work.
One supposes that Robin, within the limitations of contemporary
knowledge, was a good and honest doctor. In his books (which
were translated into English) he says that tuberculosis patients
should be sent to North Africa only in the earliest stages of the
disease—and since this is what he proposed for Laforgue, he may
have thought the latter's case less grave than it actually was. In
fact, Laforgue had only four months to live. But perhaps Robin
knew this all along and was offering the only thing he could: tea
and sympathy in the form of opium pills and kind illusions. On
24 April Laforgue wrote to Marie:

A sad Sunday, without strength, by the fireside. Two weeks
ago my illness suddenly grew worse. My friends got worried.
Bourget sent me with very special recommendations to a leading
light of the medical world, Dr Robin. I was sounded and tapped
as carefully as it's possible to be. It would be too long to recount:
anyway the result is I'm only allowed to remain in Paris until
the beginning of October. One of my lungs is threatened. For
four or five years I can't expect to spend a winter in Paris. So,
come what may, at the end of September I shall leave: my
friends are going to arrange everything. To find a suitable job at
Pau is fairly unlikely—but in Algiers it will be much easier. So it's
probable that by October we'll be in Algiers. My good Marie, I
have hardly enough strength in my hand to write to you. I overdid the opium pills which stop my coughing. My stomach was
affected by it and I've been a week without sleep or food . . .
hence my exhaustion. Now I'm beginning to get better, at least
I'm eating and drinking a little. Those three weeks of fever,
days in bed and fits of coughing, have stunned me like a poor
beast; I feel that for four months I haven't been properly awake. I
haven't got two penn'orth of ideas and yet I'm having articles
published and it's for my talent that my friends interest themselves in me. It's some time since you knew anything about my
literary affairs. It would take a long time to go into details; but
let me just say that I have the right to be proud: there isn't a
writer of my generation who's promised such a future as mine.
You can imagine that not many writers hear it said of them,
'You have genius.' Ah well, how I long to get cured and live in
a place where I can breathe without pain! (E:195-7)

A fortnight later he wrote again to Marie:

A letter from you and a good letter—you can't imagine the

pleasure it gave me. But first of all, really, you and your maternities, it's terrifying! It seems to me that if Leah was like that,
I'd be in a state of continual anguish. And with all your other
worries! Since your letter a week's gone by and I can only hope
that it was a decisively good week for Juliette.

My dear Marie, did I explain to you properly that I am ill?
Do you remember Papa's fits of coughing and his difficulty in
breathing? Well, it's the same with me now; I have those fits
regularly for half the night. But, as I told you, I'm in the hands
of one of the great Paris doctors (free care and medicine) who's
been treating me for a month (since when I've been improving
steadily) and it will go on until September. All this time I've
been housebound except for the consultations. Ah, if only
Papa, two months before going to Tarbes, had placed himself in
the hands of such a doctor, instead of doctoring himself from
books, it would have cost him 200 francs and he'd be alive today.

You tell me you were expecting our visit. It's sweet of you,
but didn't I tell you that I had to stay here for treatment with
the doctor till September, and then leave Paris? Didn't I tell
you that I have to leave Paris definitely by the end of September
and that I shan't be able to spend the winter here for three or
four years? This move, as you can imagine, is a big problem:
when I arrive at the place, wherever it is, there's got to be a
job waiting for me.

I can't go out, of course, and get on with my career, but you
have no idea what friendship and devotion are brought to me by
the little things I publish. The slightest page is a success and I
haven't a single enemy (and if you knew what a rare thing that
is!) That's why a journalist—with, I must say, an excessive
admiration for me!—is spreading the good word and trying to
get me something in Algiers. But most likely we'll go to Egypt, to
Cairo—thanks to Bourget, who hopes to get me a job as translator
at the Consulate. You can't imagine what Bourget has done for
me; it's because of him that Dr Robin gives me this special (free)
treatment, as well as supplying me from the pharmacy of his hospital. And it's half due to Bourget that I've been able to stay
alive this past month, that and the back pay from my articles.

I've a book which, if I can publish it soon enough, will allow
us to come and see you on the way from Paris. Leah would love
to see you. And you would like her; she still astonishes me. She's
such a funny little character. Needless to say, I'm terribly spoilt
—I'm looked after with a happy smile and big eyes. . . . My dear
Marie, I kiss you and wish for you a gentle delivery and a boy.
(E:205-7)

Laforgue's wish was granted: on 14 May Marie had her second child, a boy named Paul.

In a feverish torpor Laforgue spent the hot summer months sitting permanently upright in a chair. He was afraid of lying down and not being able to breathe. As he sat there he watched the poplar tree in the gardens of the little square below and marvelled that, however breathless the day, it was never quite still. That poplar tree—or a descendant?—is there today.

Laforgue's mood at this time is caught in a passage spoken by the dying hero of Teodor de Wyzewa's novel *Valbert* (1893). Since Valbert must be at least partly based on Laforgue, these words from the book's epilogue may have been taken from life:

Oh, it's nothing. Just a stupid cold I got last autumn, which won't go away. But it's nothing. I'm really fine. A miracle changed me: I've discovered love. No, don't alarm yourself about my cough. They told me the spring or the summer would see the last of it. But why worry? It will be autumn then, a charming season that I've always liked. You see, I'm twenty-seven, I have the right to live, and I need to live. No really, I promise you, this cough's only a cold. . . .

The summer sweltered on—and the Laforgues sold, one by one, the albums, prints, books and bibelots which he had so proudly listed in his letter to Kahn. Bourget was now in Venice, where he had rented the Palazzo Dario for the season, complete with gondola. Dujardin, too was on holiday. Laforgue wrote to him on 26 May: 'Could you send me the thirty francs for my column, I shall be a bit short between now and the first.' (E:188) He wrote again on 2 June: 'Quickly, quickly, my "salary" please! Hoping to God you haven't left town . . .' (E:189)

To Ephrussi, who once more came to the rescue, he wrote on 13 June: 'Every day I look forward to a tolerable tomorrow, when I shall be able to call on you in a calm state, instead of replying to all you say with uncontrollable fits of coughing—which are a bit sad and not always very pretty.' (E:192)

The faithful Wyzewa, who himself spent eight hours a day giving private lessons all over Paris, discovered (or invented?) a Pole named Rzewuski (or Jevousky?), an apparent admirer of Laforgue who sent him hundred-franc money-orders. Laforgue saw through the game but was too weak to resist, especially as his last chance to publish *Berlin* had just fallen through. Laforgue wrote to him on 26 July:

I'm just back from Dr Robin and I write to you with the sort of half-breath that isn't to be found even in Dante. First things first, though: I got a hundred francs from Aix-les-Bains, and this morning another hundred francs! I've paid a half quarter's rent. I also had another hundred francs with which I paid some local tradesmen who were getting particularly interested in my state of health. Finally I got a letter from Malherbe, on behalf of May, who only wants the book under certain grotesque conditions. (E:208-9)

Gustave de Malherbe was well disposed towards *Berlin* but he had only just joined the publishing firm of Quantin and was instructed by C. H. May, managing director, to say that the part dealing with social life in the city was already too familiar. 'On the contrary,' commented Laforgue bitterly, 'I only gave what was essentially new: I happen, moreover, to have lived there steadily for five years and not just spent a fortnight in some hotel.' Furthermore, said M. May, the section on the Court must be enlarged. ('Impossible,' said Laforgue. 'I know everything there is to know, and there isn't any more.') Finally, said M. May, Laforgue must put his own name on the title page, with the mention, Former Reader to the Empress Augusta. (Laforgue said: 'I shall go and collect the manuscript at once.') In another letter about this time (E:201) he pointed out wistfully to Wyzewa: 'Did you read about that young man I know at the *République Française* being decorated? Now, there's someone who's got his health back! He cured his stomach with six visits to Vichy!' It was Delcassé.

Paris was emptying for the month of August. Wyzewa was off to Poland and Bourget to England. On 29 July Dujardin had given Laforgue his last good news: the *Moralités Légendaires* would finally be published in the autumn by the *Revue Indépendante* itself. He announced it in a letter (E:210-12) which raised various questions relating to the book. Laforgue returned the letter with a simple Yes or No scrawled at intervals in the margin: it was all he could manage. Soon his pen would not move at all. And the book would be dedicated to Teodor de Wyzewa, his last good friend.

Bourget had gone to Dover, where he wrote to a friend (from 7 Marine Place): 'The town is quite delightful.' He had refused an invitation from the Jules Ephrussis to stay at Meggen because he wished to accompany his brother Félix, who had been recommended sea-bathing for a nervous complaint. He was putting the finishing touches to his novel *Mensonges* (*Lies*), a serialization of which began in the *Nouvelle Revue* on 15 August.

Was anyone left in Paris? Was Dr Robin there?—supposing that Laforgue could still make the effort to reach him. Even the five flights at 8 rue de Commaille were now beyond him. Early in August he made a supreme effort and wrote to Wyzewa in Poland: 'What do you do with yourself in Cracow? . . . Tell me about a day in Cracow, I'll look on the map. . . . Truly you're the only one I'd lift my pen for in my present torpor. Devotedly and for ever. My wife shakes you warmly by the hand.'

On Friday 19 August—three days after his twenty-seventh birthday—Laforgue took a simple piece of paper and, in a spidery and shaky hand, wrote a letter to the Minister for Public Instruction:

Monsieur le Ministre, I have the honour to solicit, if I may, a grant from the fund set aside for men of letters momentarily in need. After five years' residence abroad, and during my first year back in Paris, I find myself incapacitated by an illness, of which the end is barely in sight after eight long months. My claims on your kindness are based especially upon my contributions to the *Gazette des Beaux-Arts*. I could, indeed, were it not for their absence, have sought support for my appeal from MM Gonse and Charles Ephrussi. Of your Excellency, Monsieur le Ministre, I remain the devoted servant JULES LAFORGUE. (M:256)

It was the last begging letter he ever had to write, for things were now moving fast. Of the final hours all that is known is contained in Emile's (previously unpublished) Notes:

Up until the last day my brother thought he would get over his illness. He refused to go to bed, preferring to spend his days in a chair, in the desperate hope that he could do some work. He also made plans to go to Algiers, and even fixed a date for the departure.

One morning, the day before his death, I arrived at the flat and surprised him in the act of trying on his wedding ring, which had become too big for his wasted fingers and which he had removed long before.

At the same time he was looking with great curiosity and wide-open eyes at each of the objects that surrounded him.

Before that moment I had listened to his plans and believed

them, just as his poor wife did. I had never once thought, during all those months, that my brother would leave us.

But now I understood.

A few minutes later he wrote, resting the paper on his knees, an appeal for help to the Minister for Public Instruction.

Then he said to us:

'I am not seeing things as I used to. I am not thinking the same way, either. Oh, you'll see . . . you'll see the things I shall write now!'

From then I never left his side. The following morning at six o'clock he said to us:

'I think I'm hallucinating . . .'

His poor wife gave me a quick questioning glance.

I hadn't wanted to share my anxieties with her. I was afraid that a moment's weakness on her part might reveal to my brother that his agony was near.

So I looked away.

She understood.

Five minutes later it was all over.

On the day of Laforgue's death (Saturday 20 August 1887) two telegrams were sent to England: one to Bourget at Dover, the other to Kate Lee at East Grinstead. Both Kate and Bourget responded immediately and were in Paris next day.

It was Leah, of course, who had sent the wire to Kate in the convent—and the nuns' records are so exact that we even know the trains Kate had to catch: the 4:06 p.m. to Victoria and the 8.00 p.m. boat-train arriving Paris 5.05 Sunday morning. She had leave only till Wednesday.

Hasty preparations were meanwhile made in Paris, and someone had the time and application to make a remarkably complete *faire-part* listing most of the ramifications of those two huge families, the Lees and the Laforgues. (M:241)

The funeral on Monday morning was a simple affair, which moved off from the house at eight sharp without waiting for late-comers. It was a sultry, slightly misty morning. In a cab rode Leah and Kate with a couple of Tenaillons (aunt and cousin) from the Batignolles. And, walking behind the coffin, were: Emile, Bourget, Kahn, Théo Ysaÿe, Fénéon, Seurat, Paul Adam and Jean Moréas (the poet, to whom Laforgue had once said, 'You and I, Moréas, can't co-exist'). Seurat, who had probably been brought along by Fénéon, had to leave directly after the ceremony for his twenty-eight days' military service.

Slowly the little procession moved through southern Paris. Gustave Kahn has described[63] the transition from smart convent gardens to depressing shop-fronts painted *sang-de-boeuf* (the dreary bull's blood colour then favoured by tradesmen). Down the sad rue des Plantes to the fortifications which Laforgue had loved, and the recently opened Bagneux cemetery with its bare plots and stripling trees—and Leah's despairing little laugh as the municipal workman held up the wooden cross shouting, 'Hey there, are you for Laforgue?' Nobody that day felt like making graveside orations, and Leah was quickly taken off by Kate and the Tenaillons. The dozen mourners quickly dispersed.

Bourget later gave Leah 500 francs—a large sum—for the funeral expenses and to tide her over. In his diary he quoted *King Lear* (Act V, Scene 3, line 306): 'And my poor fool is hanged!' In the days at rue Monsieur he used to call Laforgue 'Mon petit pessimiste'. After the quotation he wrote: 'J'ai pleuré sur sa tombe comme un enfant' ('I wept on his grave like a child').

On 16 September the Minister of Public Instruction awarded Leah 200 francs in response to Laforgue's last letter; and next day *Le Figaro*, sensing a topical angle at last, published his long-delayed article on the Empress Augusta (Chapter 5 of the doomed book) for which one hopes that Leah at least received payment. But her whereabouts during the next three months are unknown. Did she move in for a time with Emile and Théo at 142 boulevard Raspail, near the rue Stanislas? And then go back to England to make peace with her father?

The *Moralités Légendaires* were duly published on 5 November by the *Revue Indépendante*, who had now left the rue Blanche for 11 rue de la Chaussée d'Antin, where a bureau de tabac had been converted into a bright little office-cum-art-gallery, with a second entrance on the Opéra side.

A month later, on Monday 5 December, Leah turned up in a small hotel just off the rue Saint-Honoré called the Hôtel de Londres et Milan. From there she sent word to Teodor de Wyzewa at the new offices of the *Revue Indépendante*, asking him to call on her. Written in English, it is a *pneu* or *petit bleu* (one of the first, since the express letter service was only introduced that year)

and it was despatched from the rue Littré post office, near the
Gare Montparnasse, to the office in the Grand Hôtel:

Should I be troubling you very much if I were to ask you to call
on me sometime tomorrow. I am leaving for Mentone, on the
evening of Tuesday and have, before I go, a kindness to beg of
you relative to my husband's papers. If you send a line to my
hotel I will be in at any time you mention.[64]

Next day Leah handed over to Wyzewa a case crammed with
Laforgue's manuscripts—an action for which Laforguians have
been eternally grateful. 'She destroyed nothing,' says Pascal Pia.
'Not even the palest pencil scrawl on the smallest scrap of paper.'

That night she caught the seven o'clock train to Menton, arriving
about six next morning. She had six months to live. A few miles
along the coast, at San Remo, Crown Prince Frederick was also
struggling for his life.

Three weeks later Laforgue's old friend Teodor de Wyzewa was
sacked from the *Revue Indépendante* and replaced by his older
friend Gustave Kahn.

On 9 March 1888 the old Emperor William I of Germany died
at last—but he was soon followed to the grave by his son Frederick,
who had had to wait too long and reigned only a matter of weeks.
The way was open for Kaiser Wilhelm II, the brash young man
who had slapped Laforgue on the back in the Unter den Linden.

Menton did nothing for Leah (how could it?) and in the spring—perhaps on 10 April, the day after her twenty-seventh birthday—she was brought back to London. As she left Menton the April issue of Gustave's *Revue Indépendante* was on sale in Paris with thirty-three of Laforgue's unpublished *Fleurs*.

Leah entered St Paul's Convent, Kilburn, London, where Kate visited her on 22 May. She died a fortnight later on 6 June.

By train her body was taken back to the Teignmouth she had known as a child: it had been a good setting for little Andromède, though Laforgue never knew Teignmouth—any more than Leah knew Tarbes.

The faithful Edgar, by now priest in charge of St Columba's Mission on the Isle of Skye, made the long journey from the north of Scotland to the south of Devon to take his favourite sister's funeral service on Monday 11 June. From St James's Church, with its squat thirteenth-century tower of red sandstone, one can imagine the procession struggling painfully up the Exeter Road, a one-in-ten climb between red walls, to the little *cimetière marin* on the hill.

Here lies Leah, buried beside her parents at the foot of a cypress tree, where in spring the ground is covered with primroses and violets. At the base of the white marble cross an inscription reads:

LEAH LAFORGUE
daughter of Samuel and Leah Lee
died June 6th 1888
aged 27 years
'Jesu, Mercy'

Happily her name is spelt correctly—for which one must no doubt thank Edgar. The death certificate, issued in London, had described her quaintly as the 'widow of Jules Laforge [*sic*], a French Reader'.

Jules Laforgue himself might have appreciated that last irony—and he would certainly have enjoyed some others that followed.

The Empress Augusta, for instance, died in January 1890, which was just two months too soon. It meant that she did not see the downfall of her old enemy Bismarck.

Later that year Laforgue would have been somewhat baffled to see himself and Leah described as 'little people whose lives were essentially little and who lived in a little apartment' by the odd Irishman who was Dujardin's friend, George Moore.[65]

In 1891 he would have blushed to learn that, in Huret's inquiry on the state of literature for the *Echo de Paris*, young Paul Adam went completely overboard and placed him in the following line-up: Moses, Aeschylus, Virgil, Dante, Rabelais, Shakespeare, Goethe, Flaubert, Laforgue.

In 1894 he would have been amused to hear that the first collected edition of his works had been slightly delayed because the editor, that po-faced M Fénéon, was spending four months in prison as an anarchist.

In 1896 he might possibly have been alarmed to hear that the readers of the *Mercure de France* had clubbed together to place a granite slab on his tomb—and that the organizer was that same M Griffin who had seemed less concerned during his lifetime.

He would have been charmed to find himself admired by Alain-Fournier; and he would have admired in his turn the skill of T. S. Eliot in adapting his poetic methods into English; indeed he would have recognized much of himself in the tousle-haired Eliot of 1910—and when the ageing eagle elected to get married in the same church[66] as he and Leah had, he might have exclaimed: 'That's a symbol, if ever there was one!'

Over the years he could have watched, with mixed feelings, as his young friends and acquaintances grew into venerable old gentlemen: Dujardin (88), Bourget and Fénéon (83), the Kaiser (82), Jacques-Emile Blanche (81), Gustave Kahn (77), Lindenlaub (75), Eugène Ysaÿe (73), Delcassé (71).

But he would have been delighted to greet all his children and grand-children: Alain-Fournier, Apollinaire, Supervielle, Pound, Eliot, Giraudoux, Anouilh, Cocteau, Crane, Queneau, Beckett, Eluard, Prévert, Ogden Nash and Lorenz Hart.

And he would have accepted as epitaph for his granite slab the considered judgement of an English critic:[67]

JULES LAFORGUE (1860-1887)
Buffoon and Ironist
Romantic Dreamer
and
Desperate Metaphysician
R. I. P.

REFERENCES

Translations in this book are based on texts specially revised and prepared for the new *Oeuvres Complètes de Jules Laforgue* edited by Pierre-Olivier Walzer, Daniel Grojnowski, Pascal Pia and Jean-Louis Debauve. References, too, should normally have been made to this edition, which is clearly destined to become the standard work for Laforgue studies. Unfortunately, as we go to press, it has still not been published. We therefore give, where possible, the roughly corresponding references to earlier editions, though these editions are in many cases out of print and only to be found in certain libraries. Furthermore it should be noted that, since the new texts may differ substantially from the old, reference can only be approximate; and where quite significant changes occur (for example, in the order of letters) it should be accepted that any disparity is more likely to be deliberate than accidental. Where the material is completely new we say: Unpublished. Otherwise code letters in the text refer to the following publications:—

A	*Poésies complètes*	ed Pascal Pia	Livre de Poche	1970
B	*Moralités legendaires*	ed Pascal Pia	Folio	1977
C	*Lettres à un ami*	ed G. Jean-Aubry	Mercure de France	1941
D	*O. C.*, Vol. IV	ed G. Jean-Aubry	Mercure de France	1925
E	*O. C.*, Vol. V	ed G. Jean-Aubry	Mercure de France	1925
F	*O. C.*, Vol. VI	ed G. Jean-Aubry	Mercure de France	1930
G	*Berlin*	ed G. Jean-Aubry	La Sirène	1922
H	*Stéphane Vassiliew*	ed François Ruchon	Pierre Cailler	1946
J	*Dragées*	ed André Malraux	La Connaissance	1920
K	*Mélanges posthumes*	ed Camille Mauclair	Mercure de France	1903
L	*Les pages de La Guêpe*	ed J.-L. Debauve	Nizet	1970
M	*Laforgue en son temps*	ed J.-L. Debauve	La Baconnière	1972

As we go to press Gallimard announce a new two-volume edition of the *Poésies complètes* in their pocket *Poésie* series.

NOTES

1. (p. 13) Acknowledgements to Mme de Mazières and J.-L. Debauve.
2. (p. 18) Acknowledgements to Mme de Mazières and J.-L. Debauve.
3. (p. 25) *Jules Laforgue and the Ironic Inheritance* (1953) by Warren Ramsey, p. 23.
4. (p. 29) Written about 1879, *Amours* appeared in *La Vie Moderne* on 27 August 1887. Having presumably been submitted much earlier, it seems to have been opportunely disinterred at the time of the author's death, and there is no record of his ever having been paid for it. The story was subsequently published in Vol. I of André Malraux' *Textes inédits de Jules Laforgue* (La Connaissance, 1920).

The manuscript of *Stéphane*, which is now in the Houghton Library, Harvard, is dated April 1881. Laforgue apparently left it with Paul Bourget, among whose possessions it was found during the Second World War. After a limited edition by Constant Bourquin in 1943 it was published in 1946 by Pierre Cailler.

5.   (p. 30) Acknowledgements to Mme van Rysselberghe and J.-L. Debauve.

6.   (p. 35) The 'incoherent jottings' are in the collection of J.-L. Debauve, who is not responsible for my rash attempt to make sense of them.

7.   (p. 36) Discovered by J.-L. Debauve in the archives of the Bibliothèque Nationale, Paris.

8.   (p. 38) Also discovered by J.-L. Debauve at the Bibliothèque Nationale.

9.   (p. 39) cf Warren Ramsey, op cit, p. 42.

10.   (p. 45) In presenting the letters we have made use of the three-dot device to discard extraneous matter, but without enclosing the dots in square brackets.

11.   (p. 49) *En ménage*, Chapter V.

12.   (p. 54) cf 'The Love Song of J. Alfred Prufrock', lines 45-6. Eliot read Laforgue closely in the 1903 edition—letters and fragments as well as poems.

13.   (p. 67) *La joyeuse enfance de la 3ème République* (1931) by Gyp, pp. 128-39.

14.   (p. 69) Typical of these summaries is a pencilled note in my collection, which compares the lighting and cleaning costs of various cities and reveals Paris to be the cleanest and brightest capital in Europe. This obviously would have gone down well with the Queen.

15.   (p. 74) The Empress's will was published in the *Deutscher Reichsanzeiger*, number 234 (1890).

16.   (p. 74) 'Les mémoires de Joseph Corbeil, valet de chambre de la Reine Augusta, 1858-90' are in the *Oeuvres Libres*, January 1935.

17.   (p. 85) 'L'Horloge', Baudelaire.

18.   (p. 94) 'Das verurteilte haus' ('The condemned house') in Reinhold Schneider's *Der Balkon* (1959).

19.   (p. 96) *Mercure de France*, April 1964, p. 622.

20.   (p. 97) Acknowledgements to Mme van Rysselberghe and J.-L. Debauve.

21.   (p. 97) Acknowledgements to Librairie Robert D. Valette and J.-L. Debauve.

22.   (p. 101) Introduction by Jacques Rivière to Alain-Fournier's *Miracles*, pp. 20-21.

23.   (p. 103) Some of Laforgue's Rhine drawings are contained in a remarkable Notebook owned by that most Laforguian of Paris booksellers Marc Loliée of 40 rue des Saints-Pères, 7ème.

24.   (p. 103) *Mercure de France*, November 1953, p. 436.

25.   (p. 103) *Moralités légendaires* (Mercure de France edition, 1964), pp. 230-33, 236.

26.   (p. 103) *Mercure de France*, November 1953, pp. 436, 440.

27.   (p. 103) *Mercure de France*, November 1953, pp. 436-7.

28.   (p. 104) Acknowledgements to Librairie Robert D. Vallette and J.-L. Debauve.

29.   (p. 104) 'The Poetic Development of Jules Laforgue' (Cambridge, 1956), doctoral dissertation by Dr Anne Holmes, pp. 442-3.

30.   (p. 105) Collection of J.-L. Debauve; published in *Revue d'Histoire Littéraire de la France*, September-October 1964, p. 667.

31. (p. 114) Communicated by J.-L. Debauve.

32. (p. 116) *Gazette des Beaux-Arts*, 1 July 1884.

33. (p. 128) 'Myosotis' had then just been published. It remained in print till a year or two ago at Cramer's, St Martin's Lane, London.

34. (p. 133) For a description of a *tingeltangel, cf Les mystères de Berlin* (1879) by Victor Tissot and Constant Améro, Chapter VII, pp. 45-52.

35. (p. 140) *Jules Laforgue et ses poésies* (1977), pp. 51-2.

36. (p. 142) Useful references in connection with the Bernstein Impressionists and the Gurlitt show include: *Erinnerungen an C. und F. Bernstein* (Dresden, 1914); *History of Impressionism* (1973) by John Rewald, pp. 496-8, 519; *Gesammelte Schriften* (1922) by Max Liebermann, pp. 121-31; *Staatliche Museen zu Berlin: Forschungen und Berichte*, Vol. 15 (1973); 'The Liebermann Collection' by K.-H. and A. Janda, pp. 110 *et seq*; *Berlin* (Copenhagen, 1885) by Georg Brandes, pp. 535-9; *Zeitschrift für bildende kunst: Kunst-Chronik* (Leipzig), 18 October 1883; and *Die Gegenwart* (Berlin), 22 December 1883, pp. 400-1.

37. (p. 142) *Jules Laforgue* (1952 edition) by Marie-Jeanne Durry, p. 234.

38. (p. 153) Presented to the Library of Congress, Washington, by William Jay Smith when he was Poetry Consultant there in 1968-70.

39. (p. 155) *Mercure de France*, October 1953, pp. 206-8.

40. (p. 166) *Nouvelles Littéraires*, 12 January 1929.

41. (p. 168) *Mercure de France,* 1 December 1922.

42. (p. 170) Communicated by J.-L. Debauve.

43. (p. 176) Collection of J.-L. Debauve.

44. (p. 179) In an unpublished interview with G. Jean-Aubry.

45. (p. 179) *Les premiers poètes du vers libre* (1922) by Edouard Dujardin.

46. (p. 181) *Jules Laforgue* (1952) by M.-J. Durry, pp. 235-41.

47. (p. 183) Acknowledgements to Mme de Mazières and J.-L. Debauve.

48. (p. 185) Edouard Dujardin in an unpublished interview with G. Jean-Aubry.

49. (p. 186) *The streaks of the tulip* (1972) by William Jay Smith, p. 340. cf the same author's *Selected writings of Jules Laforgue* (1956) p. 227.

50. (p. 189) *Journal de Psychologie*, December 1922, p. 922

51. (p. 190) *Jules Laforgue* (1952) by M.-J. Durry, p. 157.

52. (p. 191) Acknowledgements to Marvyn Carton and William Jay Smith.

53. (p. 191) For the Barrault quotes *cf Réflexions sur le théâtre* (1949), p. 88; *Nouvelles Réflexions sur le théâtre* (1959), p. 36; and *Cahiers Renaud-Barrault*, April 1962, pp. 90-2.

54. (p. 193) *Laforgue* (1960) by Pierre Reboul, p. 155.

55. (p. 199) *Nouvelles Littéraires*, 20 June 1936.

56. (p. 208) *Mercure de France*, 1 December 1922; and *Le Figaro*, 25 August 1923.

57. (p. 208) cf 'Leah Laforgue' by David Arkell, *Times Literary Supplement*, 10 June 1965, p. 480.

58. (p. 214) 'Bobo', published in Paul Adam's *Le Symboliste*, 15 October 1886 and re-published in Vol. I of André Malraux' *Textes inédits de Jules Laforgue* (1920).

59. (p. 217) *Derniers Vers*, edited with an introduction by Michel Collie

and Joanne L'Heureux, 1965, p. 10.

60. (p. 220) 'The metaphysical poets', *Times Literary Supplement*, 20 October 1921, p. 670.

61. (p. 222) *Drafts and Fragments of Cantos CX to CXVII* (Faber and Faber, 1970).

62. (p. 222) *Jules Laforgue: Essays on a poet's life and work* (1969) edited by Warren Ramsey, pp. 130-1.

63. (p. 236) *Revue Blanche*, 1 November 1901; and *Nouvelles Littéraires*, 26 January 1929.

64. (p. 237) Collection of David Arkell.

65. (p. 238) *The Hawk*, 23 September 1890.

66. (p. 239) As Mrs Valerie Eliot explained in a letter to the *Times Literary Supplement* (1 July 1965), her wedding on 10 January 1957 had been the occasion of a double coincidence: 'St Barnabas was chosen because the vicar was a friend of [Eliot's] solicitor and we wanted privacy. Shortly before the wedding, while glancing through a book on his desk, my husband discovered to his pleasure that Laforgue had been married at this church. After our ceremony (at 6.15 a.m.) the Rev C. P. Wright gave us breakfast at his home, 10 Kensington Church Walk, where Ezra Pound had lived.'

67. (p. 239) The description I have borrowed for Laforgue's tombstone is from Michael Hamburger's *The truth of poetry* (Pelican, 1972), p. 64.

INDEX